UMPQUA VALLEY, OREGON
AND
ITS PIONEERS

To Reginald R. Stuart
With Sincere Regards
Harold Avery Minter
Sept. 16, 1968

UMPQUA VALLEY, OREGON
AND
ITS PIONEERS

By
Harold Avery Minter

BINFORDS & MORT, *PUBLISHERS*
Portland, Oregon
1967

Umpqua Valley, Oregon, and Its Pioneers

COPYRIGHT © 1967 BY HAROLD AVERY MINTER
PRINTED IN THE UNITED STATES OF
AMERICA. ALL RIGHTS RESERVED.

Library of Congress Catalog Number: 67-19752

First Edition

Dedication

TO MARY ANN MINTER
My Beloved Pioneer Mother

*Correction for page 76, Umpqua Valley, Oregon and It's Pioneers, (October 1967) Wilbur A. Burdick is reported to have been Gardiner's first pharmacist, registered on June 12, 1912. He took charge of the Gardiner Drug Company, owned by Dr. R. H. Fields, September 5, 1912, and operated it until the spring of 1919, when he moved the stock to the Umpqua Drug Company store that he had opened in the fall of 1918 He sold his store in Reedsport on October 20, 1965, and retired from business.

Preface

This volume covers a period of time approximately from 1850 to 1950; and it deals with that area of the Umpqua Valley in Oregon comprising old Umpqua County, which was created in September 1850 and established in June 1851. This area was roughly bounded on the north by the Calapooia Mountains; on the east by Calapooia Creek, or River; on the south by the Umpqua Mountains, and on the west by the Pacific Ocean. This territory forms a natural historical and geographical unit.

It is the purpose of this book to bring to mind the pioneers who took part in the settling of old Umpqua County, and in founding the commonwealth of Douglas County, after the merger of the two counties in 1862; and to preserve for posterity a record of life as it was lived by these pioneers of the Umpqua Valley . . .

In my early life I knew and associated with the first generation of descendants of these pioneers, and was sometimes eyewitness to occasions related, which I think gives me the advantage of being able to speak with authority about happenings of that time. Some families may seem to take precedence; however, some men and women were leaders and their accomplishments helped make history in their area. Memories have been dulled by time, and exact dates have become uncertain, but the incidents recorded really happened. They remained vividly in the minds of the persons interviewed, though it has been necessary at times to fix the nearest date by association with known and recorded incidents. This accounts for any discrepancy of time.

My parents, Charles McClellan Minter and his wife, the former Mary Ann, "Polly Ann" Powell, were emigrants from Jackson County, Kentucky. They arrived in Oregon in March 1884, with their only child, Anna Belle, then one year old. They made their first stop at Elkton, in Douglas County, where William Rader and his wife, the former Arminta Powell, Polly Ann's sister, were located. The latter had come to Oregon two years earlier, and—according to accounts coming down through the years—they were living in one of the Fort Umpqua buildings.

I was born on April 9, 1892, near the mouth of Yellow Creek where it joins the Umpqua River, ten miles northwest of Oakland. I was five years old when the family moved to the Ziba Dimmick donation claim on the Umpqua River, six miles south of Elkton. The old military road opened by Colonel Joseph Hooker in 1858 ran through the northwest corner of the claim.

My father operated the old "Crescent Ferry" at this location
——then called the "Dimmick Ferry." He was drowned on January 19, 1900, while assisting Theodore Dimmick, Wallace Fryer,
Louis Rapp, Louis Smith, and Robert "Bob" Hutchinson replace
the ferry cable, which had been broken during a December
freshet. This left my mother with a family of five boys and two
girls, the oldest a girl sixteen, the youngest a girl aged three and
one-half years.

Mother bought eighty-eight acres of unimproved land adjoining the Ziba Dimmick claim on the north, where she built a
house and reared her family and made it her home until her
death in 1944. It was here that I spent my adolescent years, during which time I became familiar with the geography of the
lower Umpqua Valley. Because of many years of continued
association, I can, at seventy-five years, and without boasting,
say that if I were blindfolded and taken to any spot on the
Umpqua between Scottsburg and the Umpqua postoffice in Coles
Valley, and the blindfold then removed, I could immediately
identify my surroundings. I have been up and down the Umpqua River many times since early childhood, some portions in a
rowboat.

I have been privileged to know even a few of the original
settlers. One such was Cyrus Hedden. I was nineteen years old
when he died. Others were Jacob A. Sawyers, the pilot on the
Swan, the sternwheel steamer that navigated the Umpqua River
from Scottsburg to Roseburg in 1870; John A. Fryer, Sr., who
owned the first threshing rig in the lower valley; James T. Cooper, who came to the Umpqua aboard the *Kate Heath* in 1850;
and Uncle "Alf" and Aunt "Jane" Dougherty Walker. Mr. Walker
came to the Yoncalla Valley in 1850, and Mrs. Walker, ten years
later. She arrived over the southern route, by way of California,
and settled with her parents in the west end of Yoncalla Valley.

I have listened to these oldsters reminisce about their early
experiences, and have attended school with their grandchildren.
There was a pervading historical consciousness among these eld-
ers and their descendants, and it was through them that I obtained much of the background for this volume.

Harold Avery Minter

Contents

Part One

IN THE BEGINNING

CHAPTER I

The River and Its People

The river of our story is the Umpqua in southwestern Oregon. Word of the region roundabout reaches back into ancient records of Spanish navigators who sought the world's prize in the Northwest Passage, the "Mystic Straits of Anian," which would pass from one great ocean to another and shorten the route to the wealth of the Indies.

On January 19, 1603, Martin Aguilar, of the Viscaino expedition of Acapulco, reported that he reached the 43rd parallel and found a westerly headland which he called Cape Blanco. North of the cape he reported a great river. Both "discoveries" were made on a then-uncharted west coast, and both are clouded by time and conjecture. Nevertheless, after 1603, Spanish charts long included mention of Aguilar's River, with various spellings.

More than two centuries had elapsed, when on a rainy Sunday in October 1826, exploring English botanist David Douglas recorded in his Journal: "The last two days' march we descended the banks of Red Deer river (Elk Creek) which empties itself into the River Aguilar, forty-miles from the sea. . . Shortly after midday (Monday) we had the pleasure to arrive on the River Aguilar and camped close to the junction of Red Deer River. Aguilar River is here ninety yards broad, clear and rapid, on a bed of soft white sandstone cut and divided into separate channels." Deer were plentiful and the natives treated him kindly, bringing gifts of salmon trout, roasted hazelnuts, and "water from the river to drink."

That same year of 1826, Hudson's Bay fur trader, Peter Skene Ogden, recorded sight of the "Umpqua Mountains," when he viewed the Cascade Range from the Deschutes River. To the Astorians (1811) the river was the "Imp-qua." Though the Umpqua is not the "great river" proclaimed by Aguilar, some say that it has a kind of sorcery. Affection for it is like a virus in one's blood; once to drink of its waters is to be forever under its spell. And this seems to be the experience with those who come to the beautiful valley of the Umpqua.

River Route

The river and its tributaries flow entirely within the present boundaries of Douglas County. Its watershed and also the county's boundaries are determined by the dividing ridges of five mountain chains. To the north and east are the Calapooia and Cascade ranges; to the south and southwest are the Canyon and Rogue River mountains; to the west and southwest is the Umpqua or Coast Range. The relationship of these ranges resembles the contour of a huge pear with the small end meeting the Pacific Ocean on the west.

The area makes up about one-twentieth of the state of Oregon, but were it spread out flat it would probably be larger than Texas. The river's grandeur lies in its scenic route to the ocean—nearly 120 miles through the mountains and overlapping secondary ranges. Flowing in a general westerly direction, it zigzags through rugged terrain, where succeeding bends and turns compete in color and splendor.

The North Fork originates in Diamond Lake, which is supplied by melting snow from the high elevations of the Cascade Range. The South Fork heads in the secondary ranges of the Cascades, the Rogue, and Umpqua mountains—which area constitutes the Umpqua National Forest Reserve. The South Fork is not so picturesque as its sister stream to the north, but its tributaries and mountains are a fertile field for the prospector, as well as the source of timber supply for the many wood-working industries in southern Douglas County.

Because of the peculiar pattern of the Umpqua basin, both branches have hundreds of bends, straightaways, and deep, narrow channels worn through the sandstone bedrock. The streams unite at Melrose, twelve miles northwest of Roseburg, but continue to wind and twist through hills that seem far away, then come close together from either side as if to block further progress. At these places the river appears to come awake as though it were preparing to wrestle its way down the narrow gorges with sharp, quick turns from one rocky ledge to another.

Boulders weighing many tons are piled and scattered along the river's course, like the steps of a great, broken staircase; and the water rushes and pushes and roars along its course. There is something joyous and exultant in its sound; perhaps that is what makes one love a river such as the Umpqua.

When the branches unite after leaving the higher elevations, the stream becomes more peaceful and rapids appear less often. From here to tidewater, average fall is 3.5 feet a mile, a total of 316 feet. The river twists and turns past farms and small ranches tucked among the hills, past others lying on slopes and benches above, and still others back on low, rolling ridges. Some of these are old donation claims settled between 1850-55, a few of which are still operated by descendants of the original claimants.

Growth of evergreen trees, mostly Douglas fir, are scattered over the hillsides, their trunks tall and straight among the steep slopes and their different shades of green enhanced by stands of madrona, chinkapin, and many deciduous trees common to the Umpqua Basin. Downriver, the valley alternately narrows and widens with bottom land and benches on one side and mountains on the other. At Scottsburg, the head of tidewater, the mountains close in, seemingly in a final effort to halt the river's progress. Then suddenly a corridor opens up through bluffs from 500 to 1,000 feet high, and the Umpqua can flow unfettered to the sea. Winchester Bay at the river's mouth is a sheltered estuary of approximately 1,500 acres and is girdled landward by spruce-clad hills.

The Name "Umpqua"

How the Umpqua River received its name has had many explanations. One is that an Indian chief, in his search for new hunting grounds, inspected the area and spoke a single word, "umpqua," meaning "This is the place." Another is that natives had long referred to it as "unca" or "this stream." Mrs. Violet Johnson, of Reedsport, when interviewed in 1960, recalled hearing her father, a full-blooded Umpqua Indian, say that when living with his people at Winchester Bay, some white men appeared across the river from their village and by signs and shouting indicated that they wished to cross over. "Umpqua," she explained, meant "yelling," "calling," or a "loud noise." Her belief is that from then on the river was referred to as the Umpqua. However it was named, its origin is undoubtedly native.

The Umpqua Basin was populated by native tribes of Indians centuries before the white man came. Natives occupying the area at the time of the white conquest were identified as the Lower Umpqua, Yoncalla, and southern Molallas, who were related to the Navaho and other Athabascan tribes. Their ancestors are believed to have been Mongolians, who reached the American continent through the Bering Straits. Their resemblance to the Asiatic's swarthy complexion, coarse black hair, scant beards, broad flat faces, and prominent cheek bones seems to bear out this assumption.

The Lower Umpqua Indians claimed and occupied most of the territory west of the Calapooia River to the Pacific Ocean. The Upper Umpqua Indians occupied the upper reaches of the Umpqua River and extended south into the Rogue River Basin. The latter tribe spoke the Athabascan language, while the Lower Umpqua spoke the Alsea, Coos, and Siuslaw dialects, as did other coast tribes.

Many artifacts relative to early Indian culture have been

found in southwestern Oregon and preserved by private citizens residing in that area. Among those found by Fred Lee of Yoncalla is a stone last over which moccasins were shaped; it was so constructed that it could serve for either the right or left foot. This was found near Yoncalla, the ancestral home of a distinguished Indian Chief named Halo, who lived in that area in the early 1800s.

The Halo Trail

Along the ancient Indian highway known as the "Halo Trail," about four miles northeast of Yoncalla and three fourths of a mile west of Scott Valley turnoff on Interstate Highway No. 5, there is a large boulder bearing an inscription which still awaits scholarly deciphering. According to popular lore, it contains the tribal history of the Calapooias, a branch of the Umpqua, of which Chief Halo was a member. Halo and others of his tribe revered this stone which was thought to be a deity's seat serving as a gate to the underworld. The Indians believed that the wicked spirits confined beneath the stone would be set free if the stone were moved. Theresa Warner, in the *Drain Enterprise*, gave the following account of the origin of the Halo Trail:

"Lying east and north of Yoncalla . . . is an area where the mighty Umpqua and their old enemies from the north met in what was the last battle of the Indians in this part of Oregon. Neither being able to subdue the other, each tribe retired to his territory, decimated and shattered.

"One tribe was the Calapooias . . . they chose one of their number as chief. In due time the small band of Calapooias called the new chief "Halo," which meant poor and no-account . . . for they had no ponies, dogs, weapons, or squaws. But fortune smiled on Halo; when the first white settlers came to their valley, they then numbered about sixty adults, and a chief who had two squaws. The Halos were peaceable, friendly Indians and graciously adopted the white men in their village and shared their wares with them.

"Many moons have waxed and waned since then. The Indians, one by one, have left the valley for happy hunting grounds—Halo, the old squaws, their two daughters, Moliet, La Louise the wolf-faced girl, Paul called Be-el, blind John, and Jake—the last of the Halos. The village and the bark houses have returned to the earth, and the burial ground is nearly obliterated. Only the old Indian Rock in the western gap remains, its carved story still unrevealed. . .

"In the summer of 1948, when a group of women met at the Hugh Warner home to decide a name for their little valley—one of the few remaining unnamed areas in the wide Applegate country—they spoke again of the old names and recalled the olden times and decided on Halo as the name of the valley. Again the old pony path has become the "Halo Trail."

Campsites Uncovered

An early Umpqua Indian campsite was located on the historic Ziba Dimmick property at Kellogg, on the north bank of the Umpqua just east of the present bridge. An Indian burial ground was located on the same side of the river one-half mile above the bridge, but it has been obliterated by a secondary highway. Around the turn of the century, the site was well defined by charred cedar slabs set upright, separating individual graves.

Another historic campsite and burial ground is located on the Thomas Levins donation land claim near the mouth of Elk Creek. This ancient campground was uncovered by Francis Mode, a resident of Elkton, when excavating for a basement in the late 1950s. The fire pit and cooking stones were about four feet below the present ground level. The burial ground is located just west of the Elkton cemetery; its site was known and respected by the early settlers.

John, the Last Great Chief

The rapid expansion of white settlement crowded the Indians off their hunting grounds and overran their villages. This they

vigorously resented, and their opposition led to a general uprising in 1855-56, during which many acts of violence were committed on both sides. But even by the white man's standards of
justice, the Indians were defending their homes and protecting
their families.

In 1856, most tribes agreed to a truce, and a council was
called on May 21, by Joel Palmer, United States government
agent for Indian affairs in southern Oregon. This council convened at Oak Flat on the right bank of the Illinois River where
it joins the Rogue River near the present postoffice of Agness.
Chief John, a leader of the Ech-ka-tw-a clan or tribal group
residing on Deer Creek in Josephine County, and leaders from
other bands from the Rogue River country represented the natives. Lieutenant Colonel Robert C. Buchanan acted as chairman.

Agent Palmer read the conditions of the truce from a document that the Indians called the white man's "talking paper." It
stipulated that the Indians would be taken to the 6,000-acre
Grande Ronde Reservation in Yamhill County, and that each
Indian would be given as much land as he had occupied in the
Umpqua Valley, with a house as good or better than the one he
had left, and he would receive pay for the property he had
abandoned. Clothing was to be supplied for himself and family
until they were settled in their new homes. None of these bene-
fits was to be deducted from the annual annuities promised them.

All except Chief John agreed to reassemble on May 26 and
surrender their arms. Delivering his "declaration of independence," Chief John addressed Buchanan: "You are a great chief,
so am I. This is my country; I was here when these trees were
very small, not higher than my head. My heart is sick with fighting but I want to live in my country. If the white men are willing
I will go back to Deer Creek and live among them as I used to;
they can visit my camp and I will visit theirs but I will not lay
down my arms and go to the reservation, I will fight." With these
words the old chief strode from the council unmolested.

Because of Indian unrest, Captain Andrew J. Smith, with a company of soldiers, was stationed at Oak Flat, May 26, the day set for the Indians to surrender. The day passed without their putting in an appearance, but toward evening two Indian women arrived to tell Smith that Chief John planned to attack immediately. Smith hurriedly moved his platoon of infantry to higher ground and fortified his position. His detachment was armed with rifles and supported by one howitzer.

At 11 a.m. on May 27, the Indians attacked, and fighting continued until five in the afternoon when Captain C. C. Augur arrived with a company of soldiers. The Indians also received reinforcements, estimated at 200 to 400. The Indians withdrew at nightfall. Had Chief John pressed his advantage, he might have won the engagement; Smith had lost about one third of his men; nine were killed and twelve wounded.

In the days that followed, Chief John vigorously opposed his white aggressors, but his career as a liberator was doomed to fail. After one month his resources were exhausted and his supporters were weary of fighting. However, he did not surrender unconditionally. He exacted a promise that neither he nor his warriors would be held accountable for their acts or be required to surrender any property taken from their enemies.

An appraisal of the great chief was written by Dennis H. Stovall, staff writer of the *Evening Telegram*, Portland, Oregon, on September 19, 1903: "Chief John was a man of strong physique, brave and sagacious; his strategy was unsurpassed. From the summer of 1855 to the fall of 1856, he and his braves were a continual terror to the whites. He vigorously opposed the encroachment of the settlers upon the land that he honestly believed to be the rightful property of his people. His hate for the palefaces were deepseated and savage. For all his courage, sagacity, and terror tactics, the mounting tide of white settlement could not be stemmed."

Chief John acknowledged military defeat but his spirit was not broken. On July 19, he and the remnants of his bands were taken to Yaquina Reservation. There he led a revolt in 1858 that resulted in his being taken, along with his son, to Vancouver as a prisoner of war. Eventually both he and his son were transferred to the Federal Prison at Alcatraz in San Francisco Bay. It was on his trip to California that the proud old warrior made his last bid for freedom. Circumstances attending the event were told in a letter to the Oregon Historical Society, June 1858, by Mrs. M. L. Lockwood of La Center, Washington, an eye witness:

"I was a passenger on the steamer *Columbia*; co-passengers were Chief John and his son. Sergeant Davis from Vancouver was in charge. The two Indians were in irons until after crossing the Columbia River bar when they were given the liberty of the deck. Because of the rough weather the vessel anchored off Humboldt Bay at Port Orford, where it was to deliver mail the next day. The Chief and his son seemed to know where they were and talked together for some time.

"During the night I was awakened by a heavy blow on the head that split some of my teeth, which had to be extracted the next day. The weapon used proved later to be a piece of ashwood. My husband also received blows on the head. It being dark, we could not see what was going on. The watch on deck heard the noise and shouted fire and all who heard him rushed on deck. When I became fully awake I took stock of my surroundings and saw Chief John striking at everyone within reach, using an iron wrenched from one of the tables. I was clad only in my night clothes. I tried to carry my fourteen-months-old baby up the stairway. John tried to strike the baby's head, and one blow broke my arm. Upon my reaching the deck, the steward took me and my husband, who had joined us, gave us a pair of blankets, and took us to a small room and locked us in.

"All this time John's son was trying to kill the sergeant. The ship's officers tried to capture the Indians but the old chief would break their lanterns as soon as they came within reach. Finally the young Indian was shot in the leg and John through the face, the ball entering his right cheek and

going out on the opposite side. Officers pounded him with a
gun until the stock was broken; finally they overpowered
him and both Indians were taken below and well guarded
until they reached San Francisco."

John and his son were held at Alcatraz as prisoners of war for
several years, before they were pardoned and returned to Oregon.
It was reported that the son later became chief on the Klamath
Reservation, but John was lost in obscurity. There seems to be
no record as to when he died or where he was buried.

CHAPTER II

Pathfinders

Captain Robert Gray's discovery of the Columbia River was the first of a series of explorations by which the United States government established the right of colonization for its citizens in that vast region west of the Rocky Mountains comprising the states of Washington, Oregon, Idaho, parts of Wyoming, Montana, and British Columbia. This area was then a disputed territory. Britain, the United States, and Russia were all probing for a foothold, with Great Britain leading the race. When the United States finally won the region it was largely due to the scores of Americans who had infiltrated the disputed area. It was this three-cornered contest for control of the lucrative fur trade that led to the settlement of the Pacific Northwest.

Jedediah Strong Smith

During the thirty-three years of Jedediah Strong Smith's life, he succeeded in building up a personal legend excelling that of most pioneer heroes of the Great West. His exploits have been described in many versions and by as many writers, but his activities in southwestern Oregon as recounted by Dr. John McLoughlin in his private papers are the most reliable.

Jedediah Smith, fur trader-adventurer, was born in Jericho, New York, in 1799, the son of Jedediah and Sarah Strong Smith. With a smattering of grade school education, he went to work at the age of thirteen, and in 1822 joined General William Ashley's exploring expedition into the Yellowstone country.

Smith's ability to establish directions and traverse uncharted territory was invaluable in his explorations, and this ability was supplemented by instructions from such famous scouts and trappers as Hugh Glass, Tom Fitzpatrick, and Jim Bridger, whom he

23

met while exploring east of the Rocky Mountains. His advent
into Oregon in 1828 was by way of California. He and his party
of eighteen men traveled north from the American River to the
vicinity of the Russian River, crossed over to the coast in the
region of the Trinity and Klamath Rivers, then traveled north to
the Umpqua River to where it joins the present Smith River,
which bears his name. It was at this location that the historic
Umpqua Massacre occurred.

On Monday morning, July 14, 1828, Smith and two companions went on a scouting trip. They had not gone far when they
heard a commotion at the camp. Perceiving that it was an Indian
attack and unable to render assistance, they fled to the woods for
safety. Fourteen of Smith's men were massacred on the spot.
Smith, John Turner (one of Smith's companions), and Arthur
Black—one of the men in camp at the time of the attack—made
their way to the Hudson's Bay Fort on the Columbia River.
Black was reported to have traveled up the coast, where he was
assisted by some friendly Tillamook Indians and guided to the
fort. Smith and Turner seem to have followed the Umpqua to
Elk Creek, where they turned east to the old Indian trail leading
through the Willamette Valley to Portland.

Dr. John McLoughlin Reports Their Arrival

"One night in August, 1828, I was surprised by the
Indians making a great noise at the gate of the fort (Vancouver), saying that they had an American. The gate was
opened and a man came in, (Arthur Black) but was so
affected he could not speak. After sitting down some minutes he told me he was, as he thought, the only survivor of
Smith's party. However, he was inclined to believe that
Smith and one companion might have escaped. He made a
plea for us to search for them. At daybreak next morning I
sent Indian runners with tobacco to the Willamette chiefs
to tell them to bring Smith and his companion to the fort
and I would pay them. As the Indian runners were embark-
ing, to our great joy, Smith and his companion arrived.

"I then arranged as strong a party as I could to recover all that we could of Smith's property. I divulged the plans to no one, but gave officer Thomas McKay written instructions which were to be opened early when he reached the Umpqua, because if they had known before they got there the officers would have talked among themselves. The men would have heard of it from them and it would go to their Indian wives who were spies on us and my plan would have been defeated.

"The plan was that the officers were as usual to invite the Indians to bring their furs to trade as if nothing had happened. They were to count the furs, but as the Americans marked all their skins, they were to keep these separate and give them to Mr. Smith and not pay the Indians for them. The officers were to tell them that the skins belonged to Smith, and they got them by murdering his people. The Willamette chiefs denied having murdered Smith's party, but they admitted they had bought the furs from the murderers. The officers told them to look to the murderers for payment. Consequently a war was kindled among them, and the murders were more severely punished than we could have done. Mr. Smith admitted himself that this was much more preferable than going to war with the Indians as we could not distinguish between the guilty and the innocent. In this way we recovered to the amount of $3,000 without expense to him. This was done as a principle of Christian duty, and a lesson to show them they could not wrong the whites with impunity."

The lone companion to arrive at the fort with Smith was John Turner. Smith, Black, and Turner were the only known survivors of the party of eighteen. The Lower Umpqua Historical Society has placed an historical marker near the scene of the massacre; it is situated on the right side of Highway 101 south bound, about midway between Gardiner and Reedsport.

According to Dr. McLoughlin, Thomas McKay had been sent out to police the scene of the incident and to help recover Smith's furs, but the main responsibility of retrieving them had been given to Alexander Roderick McLeod, with McKay and Michelle La Framboise assisting. While McLoughlin states that Smith's property was recovered to the "amount of $3,000," Hiram M. Chittenden, in his *American Fur Trade of the Far West*, says: "The total value of the furs was $3,200, Dr. McLoughlin deducted from this wages for the men employed on the expedition at the rate of $60.00 per year, and $4.00 for every horse lost on the trip."

Philip Parrish, in his *Before the Covered Wagon*, gives a somewhat different version of the incident, stating that Arthur Black was "a member of a party of 78 Americans under the command of Captain Jedediah Smith, who had been attacked by Indians in southern Oregon." He also reports that McLoughlin purchased the recovered furs from Smith at the market price, giving him a draft for $20,000, and charging him only wages for the men who went to the Umpqua and a nominal price for horses lost on the trip. As to the actual price paid Smith for the furs, readers can form their own conclusions.

Smith, who had escaped two massacres, was ambushed and killed by the Commanche Indians on July 4, 1831, on the Cimarron River, between the Arkansas River and Santa Fe. His estate of nearly $100,000 was administered by William L. Sublette and was divided among his brothers and sisters.

McLeod and Turner

The explorations of Jedediah Smith and other fur traders into the Northwest prompted the Hudson's Bay Company to expand their fur trade to the southwestern Oregon territory. Alexander Roderick McLeod, an employe of the fur company, spent the better part of 1828-30 exploring up and down the coast from the Umpqua River, and at the same time reclaiming much of Smith's property that had found its way to various Indian tribes in that area. In the spring of 1831, McLeod organized an exploring expedition into southwestern Oregon and northern California as far

south as the headwaters of the Sacramento River. For a guide
he procured the services of John Turner who had been with
Smith. Other members of his party of forty men included Joseph
Gervais, after whom the town of Gervais in Willamette Valley
is named; and Etienne Lucier, who later played an important
role in helping establish the provisional government of Oregon.

McLeod traveled south to the upper end of the Willamette
Valley and crossed the Calapooia Divide into the Umpqua watershed near the present community of Divide, which marks the
boundary between Lane and Douglas counties. He journeyed
south to what is now Oakland on the Calapooia River, where he
camped a few days before continuing on to its junction with the
Umpqua River. Six miles downstream he selected a site for the
establishment of a trading post.

Thomas McKay supervised the construction of the necessary
buildings and the post was called "Umpqua." It was staffed by
two French-Canadians, Francois Campoiga and one Depatty,
with Indians from the expedition. After establishing the fort in
1832, McLeod explored the Rogue River country. On his way
through the valley, he encountered a trapping party led by
Ewing Young, whom he informed of the erection of a Hudson's
Bay Company post on the Umpqua.

On their way south, McLeod's party bestowed several place
names. The Siskiyou Range received its name from an incident
which occurred along the trail. While the men were camped on
the north slope of these mountains, the Indians stole an old bob-
tail white horse belonging to the explorers; so the camp was called
"Siskiyou," which means a bob-tail horse. Present Mount Shasta,
in northern California, McLeod named Mount McLoughlin. Fur
trader Peter Skene Ogden was responsible for the renaming of
Mount McLoughlin to Mount Shasta. McLeod wintered on the
Sacramento River near the base of Mount Shasta and in the
spring returned with his men to Fort Vancouver, their home
base, traveling north to American Falls on the Snake River and
down the Columbia.

Umpqua "old fort"

John Work, another employe of the Hudson's Bay Company, came to the Pacific coast from the York Factory on Hudson Bay in 1823, with Peter Skene Ogden, who was in charge of the annual fur express that year. Work succeeded Ogden in 1830 as head of the Snake River brigade, and in the summer of 1834 made a tour of the lower Umpqua Valley and visited the trading post established by A. R. McLeod in 1832, which he called Umpqua, "old fort."

He put its location about six miles below the confluence of Umpqua River and Calapooia Creek (or river). Dr. Hubert L. Priestly, one-time librarian of the Bancroft Library in the University of California at Berkeley, who claimed to have examined Work's original Journal (now in the Provincial Library at Victoria, British Columbia) gave the following as Work's description of the location of the "old fort."

"Umpqua 'old fort' is about six miles below where the Calapooia River joins the Umpqua, and a little below the station. The mountains are rugged and steep and strike close to the river. Where we are camped, a little above, there are a few open places and the rock on the higher ground are of a free sandstone. The Umpqua here is about 150 yards wide and a horse can ford it at this time." (June 16, 1834.)

Work's description, if Dr. Priestly is correct, coincides with the physical appearance of the old William Lawrence place, opposite the mouth of Hubbard Creek, six miles below the mouth of the Calapooia. E. H. Branton is the present owner. Mt. Tyee, just north of the Umpqua postoffice, near the confluence of the Calapooia and Umpqua Rivers, strikes close to the river at the Branton place and the stream can be forded here during the summer months. If Work didn't see this place, he surely did a good job of describing it.

John Turner

Our story thus far has kept the spotlight on such well-known

frontier characters as Jedediah Smith, Alexander Roderick Mc-
Leod, Michelle La Framboise, Thomas McKay, and John Work,
who were beyond a doubt the forerunners of the colonization of
the Umpqua River basin. They were men of great capabilities
and were outstanding in their professions; they capitalized on the
fur trade. Among these professional traders and trappers who
traveled the wilderness trails were other remarkable but less
well-known men who seemed to welcome the myriad dangers
that awaited them along the way. One such individual was John
Turner, the scout who escaped to Fort Vancouver with Smith;
"Honest John," as he was called by those who knew him well.

Turner was of pioneer stock, born in 1807 on the headwaters
of the Cumberland River in the hills of Clay County, Kentucky,
near the border of Virginia. He could neither read nor write, but
illiteracy was not unusual in the mountains of Kentucky prior to
the war with England in 1812. Turner's exploits ranged from
eastern Kentucky, west to the Pacific Ocean, and south from the
Canadian border to the Rio Grande. He was only nineteen years
old when he made his debut into early southwestern history as
guide to the McLeod party into the Umpqua basin in 1826. One
of his most spectacular encounters was with the Rogue River
Indians in southwestern Oregon in June 1835. Turner and a party
of eight were trapping along the Rogue River when the fight
took place. Members of his group were: Dan Miller, Edward
Barnes, Dr. W. J. Bailey, George Gay, and four others not so
exactly identified: Saunders, Woodworth, an Irishman called "Big
Tom," and Turner's squaw.

Circumstances attending the incident were described by William M. Colvig, writing for the *Oregon Historical Quarterly,*
(Volume 4, page 230):

"The fight took place at a point below Rock Creek on the
south side of the Rogue River, near the barn of W. L.
Colvig.* Without warning the Indians attacked the camp of
the trappers, and three of the party were killed outright.

* Bailey later visited the scene of the battle and pointed out the exact spot.

(These must have been Miller, Barnes, and Turner's squaw.) Turner, Bailey, Gay, Woodworth, Saunders, and Big Tom, all of whom were wounded, escaped. . . . Saunders and Big Tom died along the trail, Saunders on the South Umpqua, and Big Tom at (what is now) Winchester. Bailey was also wounded . . . he received a tomahawk wound which split his lower jaw from the point of the chin to his throat . . . the parts never united correctly, causing an unsightly scar which distorted his face for life.

". . . After the party had made its way to the head of the Willamette Valley, they mistook the [Willamette] river for the Columbia; Turner, Bailey, and Woodworth followed the stream to the Methodist Mission at Salem. Woodworth was drowned while attempting to swim the river at the settlement. Gay kept along the foothills on the west side of the river and crossed the Rickreal River about where the town of Dallas now stands. He crossed the Yamhill River near the falls at Lafayette, where he passed along the west side of Wapatoo Lake and over the Tualatin Plains to Wyeth's trading post on Sauvies Island.

"Gay had cut up his buckskin breeches to make moccasins for the party, thereby making the journey in a semi-naked condition, clad only in the remnants of an old shirt. The mosquitoes nearly devoured him as he passed over the Columbia River bottoms."

Two years later, Turner, Bailey and Gay, were members of the Willamette Cattle Company with Ewing Young on his historic cattle drive from California to the Willamette Valley. As the herd passed through the Rogue River country, the company had an altercation with the Indians at the same location. It stemmed from the previous encounter. The three had vowed revenge, and while passing through the area a young Indian was shot and a fight ensued. No one was killed but Gay was wounded and carried a stone arrowhead in his body for several years.

For an uneducated mountain boy, Turner certainly knew his way around. Following the Umpqua massacre (1828), he took a leisurely trip back to Hendrix County, Indiana, and this time married a white wife. He got back to California in time to go on a trapping expedition in the San Joaquin Valley with Ewing Young. It appears that after the cattle drive with Young he settled down. In November 1853, he located a donation land claim of 320 acres, Township 14, Range 5 West, in Linn County. Samuel Swift and Horace Lane attested his application. Turner was evidently a good citizen as his "mark" appears on several petitions to the Territorial Legislature. Information received from the Linn County Historical Society indicated that so far as known to the society he left no descendants.

Jesse Applegate

Jesse Applegate could claim the title of Pathfinder by right of inheritance, training, and life-long habit. The trails that he traveled to reach the Oregon country were long and wearisome. His appearance in the territory portended the end of the autocratic rule of the Hudson's Bay Company and the introduction of a democratic form of government by the colonists. This was his avowed intention when he joined the first sizable immigration of Americans to the Pacific Northwest.

He was born in Kentucky on July 5, 1811, the youngest son of Daniel and Rachel Lindsay Applegate. Daniel was of English extraction, a native of New Jersey. He had enlisted in the Continental Army of the Revolution as a fifer when he was fifteen. At the close of the war he emigrated to Kentucky, where he married Rachel Lindsay, also of pioneer stock. Forty years later they moved to Missouri where Jesse, their youngest son, began his basic training as a pioneer.

Preparation for his place in the pioneer history of Oregon—specifically the Umpqua Basin—was acquired early in life with a zeal and determination of one having foreknowledge of his predestined calling. Jesse had acquired a good elementary education and had taught the village school. Later he was employed as a deputy in the Surveyor-General's office in St. Louis. While in that city he boarded at the "Old Green Tree Tavern," where he met Jedediah Smith, David E. Jackson, and William L. Sublette.

Jesse wrote later: "I was handy with the pen, and still handier with figures, and volunteered my services to those mountain heroes. Hearing them recount their experiences was my sole reward."

From Smith he learned about the potentials of the Umpqua basin, as well as about Smith's personal experiences on the Umpqua River in 1828. From all three men he acquired knowledge of how to follow wilderness trails; also the best routes west. In the surveyor's office he mastered the rudiments of surveying and the use of a Burts Solar compass. Applegate also developed a close friendship with several leading men of that day, one being William Price Hunt, the postmaster of St. Louis who had been John Jacob Astor's agent in expanding the fur trade in the West. Another such friend was Edward D. Baker, a distinguished lawyer and a close friend of Abraham Lincoln. It was from him that young Applegate received training in legislative procedure. He also had access to good libraries; whatever he found in print about the West he read. The single most important item was the Journal of Lewis and Clark, published in 1814. It was Applegate's privilege to meet Captain Clark, then a white-haired veteran of the western trails.

Answering a Call

Jesse remained in St. Louis from 1823 to 1831. In the spring of the latter year he married Cynthia Ann Parker and settled in Osage Valley, St. Clair County, Missouri, one of the western border states. By 1843 the people in these states were dissatisfied with their role as producers without a market. New Orleans was the only outlet for states bordering the Mississippi and Missouri rivers, and this market was glutted. Reports brought in by explorers and fur traders concerning the vast undeveloped natural resources of the Oregon territory reacted on these free-born Americans the same as the migrating instinct in birds and other wild creatures. Jesse Applegate and his two older brothers, Charles and Lindsay, were part of the first sizable group to respond to this call, in the spring of 1843. Daniel Waldo — a neighbor of Jesse in Missouri and a fellow traveler — said that when Applegate came west, he sold a steamboat load of bacon and lard for $100; the bacon was used for fuel on the Mississippi river boats. When Applegate left for Oregon he did not attempt to sell his land, he simply abandoned it, according to Waldo.

When various groups assembled at Fitzhugh's mill, twelve miles west of Independence, Missouri, on the 20th of May, a meeting was held and the assembly adopted the usual road rules. Peter H. Burnett was chosen captain and J. W. Nesmith, orderly sergeant. John Gnatt, a former army officer, was engaged to conduct them to Fort Hall. After eight days of travel, Burnett resigned and William Martin was selected to replace him.

On the Trail

Martin's first official act was to separate the company into two divisions; one wing consisted of those who had no stock to drive, and the other column was made up of men with herds of extra cattle and horses. This latter was called the "Cow Column," with Jesse Applegate in command. During the first five days in July, the South Fork of the Platte River was crossed on ferries made from wagon boxes over which green buffalo hides had been stretched.

The company arrived at Fort Laramie on July 14, forty days and 667 miles on their journey. They spent a few days here repairing equipment and restocking supplies, for which they paid exorbitant prices. On August 3, they reached the Sweetwater River, where they had their first view of the Rocky Mountains. The first casualty on the trip was Claybourne Payne, who died of fever on August 14. The Reverend Parrison, a Methodist minister, conducted the funeral. Another death occurred on August 29, at the Big Sandy, a tributary of the Green River.

At Fort Hall the usual discussion of changing from wagons to pack horses took place. The chief objection to wagons was the lateness of the season. Dr. Marcus Whitman, who had been east on mission business, joined the caravan at the Platte River. Both Whitman and Richard Grant, the Hudson's Bay factor at Fort Hall, were consulted as to the feasibility of changing to pack animals. Grant admitted that wagons "might" be taken down the Columbia, but seriously doubted it. Whitman, who claimed considerable knowledge of the territory, advised in favor of continuing with wagons. After careful consideration it was decided to proceed to the Columbia with the wagons, in spite of approaching winter.

After ten days' rest, and wagons repaired, they resumed their march. Their captain, William Martin, continued to conduct the train as far as American Falls. From there on Dr. Whitman acted as guide, piloting the emigrants down the Snake River to Salmon Falls. The route from here lay across an expanse of sagebrush plains to Fort Boise, which was reached on September 20. There the party was kindly received by Francois Payette, the Hudson's Bay agent. The fording of the Snake River was made without delay, but not without incident; Myles Eyres, who was riding a mule, missed the shallow water of the ford and was drowned.

After crossing the Snake at Payette, they took a northwesterly course and entered Burnt River Canyon on September 24. Burned and fallen timber prohibited traveling along the banks of the stream, so their only alternative was to follow the river bed for twenty miles. At the head of the canyon the first grading of the road from the Platte to the Columbia was necessary—this was the first occasion where they had to use double teams.

By October 1, the main body of the party had arrived at the Grande Ronde Valley, and on the morning of the 2nd, the first ridge had been crossed; beyond lay the Blue Mountains, covered with timber. With axes, picks, and shovels, forty men in five days cleared a road over the dreaded pass.

A severe snowstorm caught the emigrants as they came through the Blue Mountains—which made the Umatilla Valley appreci-

Oregon Historical Society

Left: Indian Rock, located along the "Halo Trail" about four miles northeast of Yoncalla. A popular legend is that the tribal history of a Callapooia tribe, a segment of the once powerful Umpqua, is inscribed upon the huge boulder. A grandson and namesake of Charles Applegate recalled that when one of Chief Halo's sons died, one of the few remaining tribal members inscribed some characters on the rock.

Right: Chief John, the last of the great chiefs of the Umpqua. From the summer of 1855 to the fall of 1856, he and his bands were a constant terror to the whites in southwestern Oregon.

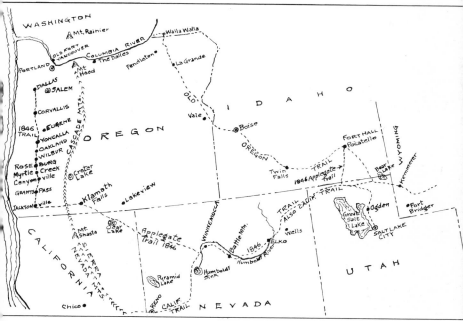

Floyd C. Frear

Routes of the Applegate Trail (1846), the Old Oregon Trail, and the California Trail. This map was prepared in 1961 by the late Floyd C. Frear, retired surveyor and roadmaster of Douglas County, from 1920 until his retirement in the late 1950s.

Left: The likeness of Jesse Applegate, the leading figure in the organization of old Umpqua County. The drawing was made from memory by a relative after his death. Applegate was reluctant to have his picture taken. It is said that he requested that his private papers be withheld from public inspection.

Right: Levi Scott, the founder of the historic town of Scottsburg, named in his honor. Among his contributions to southern Oregon history was the establishment of *The Umpqua Weekly Gazette*, in 1854, the first newspaper south of Salem.

A birds-eye view of the property once claimed by the Hudson's Bay Fur Company, 1836-1858, as it appears from a promontory near the family burial ground on the Ira Wells donation land claim, one mile south of the old Fort site.

ated. At Grande Ronde, Whitman received word that two of his helpers, Henry Spalding and his wife, were seriously ill. Whitman immediately left the party and struck off for the Spalding station at Lapwai. The responsibility of guiding the emigrants was placed on Sticcas, a Cayuse Indian Chief. Sticcas led the travelers safely to the mission at Walla Walla. J. W. Nesmith remarked that Sticcas was the only Indian he ever knew who had any conception of, or practiced, Christianity.

Difficulties Arise

October was well advanced when Whitman arrived at Lapwai and found the Spaldings convalescing. He immediately returned to his station at Walla Walla to meet the emigrants and furnish them supplies as he had promised. Privations of the trail had begun to have their effect on the weary travelers. Tempers were short over misunderstandings involving the purchase of supplies; the emigrants thought they were being charged exorbitant prices —which they were not, when the cost of having goods packed in to the mission was considered. Some refused to buy wheat at $1 per bushel, which caused those who had purchased to divide with those who had not.

The emigrants were further indignant over a proposition made by the mission leaders to exchange Spanish stock for American cattle—one fat Spanish critter for two lean oxen. This would give the mission two work oxen which would have regained flesh in the spring. A few accepted the offer and immediately butchered the fat cattle.

Another offer made by the mission was to winter the cattle at $1 per head, with the animals to be claimed in the spring—or Spanish cattle to be taken in exchange in the Willamette Valley. To Daniel Waldo, this seemed like a scheme to get American cattle at Spanish cattle values. In Missouri, American cattle brought $48 per head, but in the Willamette Valley, $100, whereas Spanish cattle sold for $9. Among those who accepted the trade offer for Spanish cattle was Jesse Applegate, who with

Waldo, had more stock than any two men in the migration. (When Applegate finally arrived at Vancouver, McLoughlin protested against his making such a bad bargain. The doctor not only ordered Applegate's American cattle restored, but refused compensation for the care they had received.)

The Columbia Gorge

After this delay at the Lapwai Mission, the company moved toward the Columbia River with their stock and wagons. Waldo led the main body to The Dalles by land, but seventy-one decided to descend the Columbia in boats. Among these latter were Peter H. Burnett, William Beagle, and the three Applegate brothers, Charles, Lindsay, and Jesse, with their families. Dr. Whitman decided to accompany them in order to bring home his wife, who had taken refuge at The Dalles from the violence of the Cayuse Indians.

Burnett bought, or hired, a boat from the Hudson's Bay Company and secured an Indian pilot. Beagle, who accompanied Burnett, was a good boatman, but his experience had been on the Ohio River, which compared with the Columbia, was insignificant. Nevertheless the Indian guide delivered Burnett's party safely at The Dalles.

The Applegate party was less fortunate. They constructed their own canoes, which proved unwieldy and hard to manage, and it was on this lap of their journey that a tragic accident occurred. One of the canoes swamped, taking five lives, one of them Jesse's son. Another was William Bates, who, along with three others, was drowned. A son of Lindsay Applegate narrowly escaped, and a son of Charles Applegate was crippled for life.

Hampered and delayed by misfortune, the Applegate party ran short of provisions and were on the verge of starvation before reaching The Dalles. James Waters, who was among the first to arrive at the settlements, was sure of this shortage; he presented the situation to McLoughlin, who supplied a boat with provisions and sent it to The Dalles under Waters' supervision.

The only condition imposed upon Waters was that the food be dispensed at Vancouver prices. He reached The Dalles just as the Applegate party arrived. Jesse is reported as saying that this food provided the first full meal his party had enjoyed for three weeks. This incident radically changed Jesse Applegate's attitude toward the Hudson's Bay Company, or at least toward its agent McLoughlin. The timely relief saved many of the immigrants from death by starvation. A member of the immigration who had gone on to Vancouver returned to the Cascades (Bonneville) to assist some friends but ran out of food on the way back. Remembering that he had had breakfast at a certain spot on his trip upriver, now on his way down, he searched in the snow for crumbs that might have fallen; finding none, he wept bitterly.

Journey's End

They still had a most difficult portion of the trail ahead. There was no road from The Dalles to Fort Vancouver over the rugged mountains separating them from the Willamette Valley. Those who came down the river from Walla Walla in boats continued on past The Dalles to the Cascades, but the others had to devise some plan to continue their journey past the high bluffs which came down to the river's edge. Their solution was to build rafts. They went to the foothills near The Dalles and cut trees from one foot to eighteen inches in diameter and twenty feet long and lashed them together to form the rafts. Then they took the wagons apart and placed them with their loads on these make-shift boats. A few covered wagons were reserved, however, as cabins for the women and children; and a child was born in one of these cabins on the way, between The Dalles and the Cascades.

Some left their wagons and stock at The Dalles, but others swam their cattle and horses across to the north side and drove them to Vancouver, where they were ferried back to the south side.

The terrain adjacent to the Cascades on the south side broadened out enough to allow the emigrants to construct a road; this took two weeks and further depleted their food supply. Late in November 1843, the main part of the group reached Vancouver. The last lap of their journey between The Dalles and Vancouver proved the most trying but, considering their hardships, the death toll was light—there were only nine deaths.

At Vancouver it was difficult to find shelter for so many. McLoughlin, very accurate in all his reports, put the 1843 immigration at 875 men, women, and children. The lateness of the season made it impractical for the majority to select land and build houses before spring. Those who had means bought the necessities of life from the Hudson's Bay Company, and those who were less fortunate went to work at whatever they could find to do. Quite a number wintered in Oregon City. Waldo drove his cattle into the hills southeast of Salem, and these hills still bear his name. The Ford family and Nesmith remained a short time in Oregon City but eventually settled in the Yamhill district, which constitutes present Polk County. The Applegates wintered in the old mission ten miles north of Salem. Jesse found employment surveying at Salem and Oregon City. In the spring the three brothers opened farms in the Yamhill country near the present town of Dallas.

CHAPTER III

The South Road Company

Members of the 1843 immigration were a body of freedom-loving Americans. They were confident that with perseverance they could make homes for themselves and their posterity in the raw and undeveloped land which they had endured so much suffering to possess. Each felt an individual responsibility for the welfare of his neighbors.

Being neighbors in Oregon in its early years was a way of life, now almost forgotten. Neighborliness was incorporated in the Preamble of the Constitution of the United States, and as loyal American citizens, they felt it their duty to obey it. The poorest of the immigrants were rich in this respect. It meant that they were allies in the fight for survival in this new land; without it the hard, often cruel, life could not have been endured.

As yet the provisional government was in its infancy. Lively interest centered around the framing of laws that would improve conditions and protect the rights and property of the settlers. One of the foremost needs discussed was the opening of a route to Fort Hall by way of southern Oregon and northern California. Such a route would bypass the dreaded Snake and Columbia rivers.

Representing the colonists in the Provisional Legislative Assembly of 1844-45 were five members of the 1843 immigration: Jesse Applegate, M. M. McCarver, T. D. Kaiser, Daniel Waldo, and A. J. Lovejoy. With the hardships of the trail still fresh in their memory, they were concerned about future immigrations.

Concerted action was taken in the spring of 1846. With the support of their representation in the Assembly, the settlers promoted plans for a road-viewing expedition into southern Oregon and the establishment of a route to the Willamette Valley from

that direction, if such were possible. Under the leadership of
Daniel Waldo, $8,000 was raised by popular subscription, the
same to be used to pay expenses and equip an exploring party to
further the scheme. It was in this connection that Levi Scott
made his initial debut into Oregon history.

Levi Scott

Levi Scott, road builder and founder of Scottsburg in Douglas
County, was born in New York State in 1798, which date happens
to coincide with the birth years of two other men associated with
the settlement of the lower Umpqua: John Jacob Sawyers and
the Reverend J. A. Cornwall. Scott's father served in the Continental Army. After the Revolutionary War, he moved his family
to Illinois, where Levi spent his early life. Young Scott served
with Lincoln in the Blackhawk War and was advanced to the
rank of captain. Later on he married a Miss Ennis, and thirteen
children were born to their union. Scott lost his wife and several
of his children in 1842. He said that the blow so unsettled him
that he sought relief in pioneer life.

He started west from Burlington, Iowa, in 1844, accompanied
by several of his sons, two of whom were William J. J. and
John M. They crossed the plains by ox team, following the same
route as the 1843 immigration. Arriving in the Willamette Valley,
Levi became acquainted with the Applegate brothers. Thus began a friendship which was to endure the rest of their lives.

The South Road Company

The South Road Company was organized in the spring of
1846 at what was then Dallas, in Polk County, the home of Jesse
Applegate and Levi Scott—who were to lead the enterprise. The
first attempt to carry out the expedition was undertaken by Scott.
His party left Dallas early in May and traveled seventy-five miles
south over an old Indian trail which will later be identified under
various titles: The Territorial Road, Willamette Road, or the
California Trail. They arrived in the vicinity of what is now

Lorane, at the foot of Elk Mountain on the Calapooia Range. Here four of Scott's men deserted just when they were nearing hostile Indian territory. Scott wisely returned to Dallas for reorganization.

Reorganization

The reorganized company consisted of fifteen men including Levi Scott and his son John M., Jesse and Lindsay Applegate, and Moses Harris. Harris was referred to as "Black Squire, Major Harris," and sometimes just plain "Black Harris" by the mountain men. This famous scout had arrived in the Willamette Valley in 1844 as scout and guide for the immigration that year. His knowledge of the Shoshone dialect was of great service to the expedition. In physical appearance he was described by the noted artist, Alfred Jacob Miller, as "of wiry form, made up of bone and muscle, with a face apparently composed of tan leather and whipcord, finished off in a peculiar tint as if gunpowder had burned into his face."

Others of the party numbered Henry Bogus, who left the road company at Thousand Springs with the intention of returning to St. Louis and was not heard from again; John Jones, Samuel Goodhue, Bennet Orsborne, William Sportsman, William Parker, David Goff, Benjamin Burch, John Owens, and Robert Smith. William Parker was a brother of Mrs. Jesse Applegate. David Goff was an 1844 immigrant and father-in-law of J. W. Nesmith. Robert Smith married a daughter of Charles Applegate and was a brother of Mrs. Stephen Chadwick. These were the men who set out to explore an easier route to Oregon; the nucleus of the pioneers who settled the Yoncalla Valley, the Home of the Eagles.

Each member of the road company was equipped with a saddle horse and a pack animal, a rifle, a side arm, a share of the camp equipment, and a few personal belongings known to the mountain men as their "possibles." Of course Jesse Applegate's most necessary "possible" was his Burts Solar Compass. (This old compass is now the property of Jesse Applegate's grandson, the son of Milton B. Germond, former County Surveyor of Douglas County, who married Applegate's daughter.) It was reported that the company vowed not to return until they had found a feasible route through southern Oregon, if such existed.

On the March

The company assembled at the La Creole settlement near Dallas, on June 22, 1846, under the leadership of Jesse Applegate. The first night was spent at the mouth of Mary's River, now the town of Corvallis. From here they passed through the upper reaches of the Siuslaw watershed, through what are now the sites of Veneta, Elmira, Crow, and Lorane. They crossed the Calapooia Divide, at Elk Mountain, to Pass Creek (now Curtin), and proceeded to the Yoncalla Valley over the same route as present Interstate Highway 5 to Scott's Valley turnout. Their course from this point was the "Halo Trail" to "Mount Yoncalla," where they skirted the foothills through the valley. The country so fascinated the Applegates and Scott that they moved their families there in the summer of 1849. Jesse Applegate chose a claim at the foot of Mount Yoncalla; and Scott and his sons went to the valley that still bears their name.

Their progress from Deer Creek, now Roseburg, lost momentum as they entered the South Umpqua Canyon. In cattle drives, Ewing Young and others had kept to the high, wooded hills, but the road company found this route impractical and explored the bottom of the canyon. The road they marked through this defile was virtually the same as the military road located by Major Benjamin Alvord and Jesse Applegate seven years later. Later, Highway 99 followed the same route most of the way to the California line.

Six miles north of the border the party left the old trail marked by McLeod and La Framboise and turned eastward near the 42nd parallel toward the Cascade Divide, following up Skene Creek to Round Prairie. They spent three days exploring for a pass over the summit and, on July 4, crossed the divide and got their first view of the Klamath Basin.

Blazing New Trails

No clearly defined trail existed after they crossed the Cascade Divide. From this point the land formations changed from rugged, timbered hills to a semi-arid volcanic wasteland pock-marked with lakes—some of which were alkaline—and rocky buttes without vegetation other than sagebrush; these were evidently old volcanic cones. From here on the route had to be determined by trial and error. They reached the Klamath River and followed it for six miles to where it left the lower Klamath Lake, then crossed over to the east side and followed the shore of the lake for two miles. They made camp near the shore at Hot Springs, where John C. Fremont's party had stopped a short time before. This they learned from fragments of newspapers lying about which indicated recent use. (A later change in the route at this location brought the road past the east end of the lake to Link River, a little below Linkville.)

After reaching Hot Creek they traveled east along a high rocky ridge, and at its eastern base they discovered Tule and Modoc lakes. On approaching Lost River they crossed over to the north side, taking an easterly course until they found a good spring where a camp was made at the base of the same rocky ridge to the north.

Keeping Scorpion Point in view as a landmark at Modoc Lake, the party passed toward the east between Langell Valley and Clear Lake and on to Goose Lake. Ascending a mountain spur bordering Goose Lake they could see Surprise Valley into which a good pass led to plenty of water and grass. The men pitched camp beside a small stream later called Lassen after Peter Lassen who, two years after its discovery by the road company, led a group of immigrants into the Pitt and Sacramento River valleys. It was found that this stream originated in Mud Lake, a name it still bears.

On the eastern side of Mud Lake they were confronted with a sheer wall of granite several hundred feet high. The party separated and explored the country from north to south until a gap was located, ranging from 200 feet in width to barely room for a wagon to pass. Along the base of the ridge they found grass and water; at the extreme end was a large spring, but the water was too alkaline to use except for coffee, although their horses drank freely of it.

On the morning of July 8, the company reached the Humboldt River near the present site of Winnemucca, Nevada. After two days of travel they arrived at a dry branch of the river coming in from the north, where they found plenty of pasture for their horses. A camp was established while they explored the country to the north, working up the dry bed of the stream. A high table land was discovered with plenty of grass; from this point Black Rock mountain to the west was plainly visible. They called the place Humboldt Meadows.

The explorers were now positive that they had discovered a direct route from the Humboldt River to Black Rock. Knowing that Fort Hall was in the vicinity of the source of the Humboldt, they continued northeast. It was first proposed to locate the road along Bear River, which would bring them to the Oregon Trail fifty or sixty miles southeast of Fort Hall; but as their provisions were running low, it was thought best that part of the company should proceed directly to the fort while the rest, led by Levi Scott, explored the Bear River route and reassembled again at Fort Hall. Jesse Applegate, Moses Harris, John Owens, David Goff, and Henry Bogus went to the fort.

Arrival at Fort Hall

When Applegate's party reached Fort Hall, they found the 1846 immigrants resting, stocking supplies, and repairing equipment. Applegate discussed the Columbia River route in comparison with the one that his party had just been over and declared the southern route superior to that of the Snake and Columbia rivers. He also thought it was nearer. In this he was incorrect, but he was right in stating that it provided better forage for the stock. One segment of the present immigration was led by William Kirquendall, (later spelled Kirkendall), who persuaded his company to take Applegate's advice.

After Scott and his party arrived at the fort, a caravan of some 100 wagons and 1,700 persons was organized to take the new southern route.

Road Builders Point the Way

The road company did not engage in actual road construction along the way; they only marked the route. Before the caravan started out, Applegate, with all of his South Road Company except Levi Scott and David Goff (Henry Bogus had left the company after his arrival at Fort Hall), went ahead to open the road. They were accompanied by a volunteer group from the caravan taking the southern route. These included Thomas Powers, Alfred Stewart, Charles Putnam (who later married Roselle Applegate, Jesse's daughter), William Kirkendall, who retired from leadership in favor of Harrison Linville, J. W. Wair; and Burgess, Shaw, and Cranahan, whose given names were not recorded.

Those of the emigration who elected to take the southern route organized into two companies, one under Harrison Linville, the other under Meadows Vanderpool. The entire caravan left Fort Hall, August 9, and rendezvoused at Thousand Springs on August 12. There they were met by Levi Scott and David Goff, who were assigned to guide the two groups to the Willamette Valley.

The first company to take to the road was Harrison Linville's, with Levi Scott as guide. The second, under Meadows Vanderpool, was guided by David Goff. From the start, the latter company was plagued with quarreling among its members. The collective characteristic of this group was that they were unwilling to accept their captain as the final authority.

Especially troublesome was J. Quinn Thornton, a native of West Virginia. He had studied law for three years in England

and finished his legal training under John Howe Payton, an eminent lawyer at Staunton, Virginia. In 1845 he opened a law office in Palmyra, Missouri, but the following year decided to move to Oregon. He joined a group of emigrants from Illinois, who merged with other companies along the way. It was reported that Thornton quarreled with a man named Good, who had loaned him a wagon at the Platte River. Good demanded his property back but Thornton needed it to take care of his dependents. The immigrants settled the dispute by dividing the oxen and cutting the wagon in half to make carts. In this manner they continued their journey.*

Hardships on the Trail

By October 10, the rear company was in the open country on the west side of the Cascade Divide, sixty miles from the upper end of the Umpqua Canyon; yet they did not arrive at the pass until November 4. The fall rains began on the 21st and caught them in the upper reaches of the canyon. By this time they had consumed most of their reserve rations and their stock had become weakened by lack of forage and could not pull the loaded wagons. To speed up their progress, they began discarding household goods and even extra clothing. Finally they had to abandon their wagons when their cattle became too weak to pull them. Women and children rode the starving animals until the creatures could no longer carry them. The unfortunate travelers then continued doggedly on foot, carrying a few cherished possessions.

The lead company, guided by Levi Scott, reached the Willamette Valley in late October without serious difficulty other than could be expected while traveling a wilderness trail. When word was received in the settlements of the predicament of Goff's company, help was immediately sent.

Relief Expeditions

Jesse Applegate, who had arrived home ahead of the first

---

* Antonio Rabbison, *Growth of Towns in Oregon.*

company, took steps to get meat and flour to the starving immigrants. A relief expedition with cattle and flour was sent out from Dallas on December 1, led by "Black Harris." Shortly afterward, another rescue party was organized under the leadership of Thomas Holt of French Prairie, accompanied by a French-Canadian and five half-breeds. Holt left the St. Paul Mission in the Willamette Valley on December 2, with horses and all the provisions he could gather. Father Boldoc of the Catholic Mission contributed food from his limited supply.

On December 5, Holt met David Goff with a remnant of his charges who had managed to bring their wagons through. With him was Mrs. Newton, whose husband had been killed by the Umpqua Indians. On the 8th of December, Holt overtook Harris and they traveled together. That same day they met three families on horseback, also a single wagon, and supplied them all with flour. The next day they met eight wagons, which they also supplied with provisions.

On the 10th they came on three families whose teams were exhausted and whose food supply was gone. At this point the Canadian and half-breeds turned back, fearful that if they crossed Elk Mountain they would be unable to return that winter. Holt and Harris, with four others, continued on their way, distributing food to the starving travelers.

Near the head of the Willamette Valley they met five families who were unable to go farther. Assisted by the rescue party, they were able to resume their journey. On the north side of Elk Mountain the rescuers found three families without food and their oxen too weak to travel; these were given flour and left to the mercy of other immigrants who might follow with horses.

On the summit of Elk Mountain they encountered a family riding horses, and they saw many dead cattle along the way. On the south side of the divide were two families and their wagons, with oxen too weak to travel; these families were furnished flour. On December 14, at Pass Creek on the North Fork of Elk River, were five families without flour, meat, or salt. One of the half-breeds killed a deer for them, and they were given salt and flour.

These were the families of Ezekiel Kennedy, Croizen, R. B. Hall, Lovelin, and a man whose name was not recorded.

Five days later the rescue party crossed Elk River at Thief Creek by swimming their stock and ferrying their packs on rafts. At the junction of the Calapooia River and a creek now known as Cabin Creek, they came to the camp of James Campbell, Rice Dunbar, and the Reverend Josephus Adamson Cornwall. These had wisely decided to spend the winter on the Calapooia and had built a cabin. The Reverend Cornwall's nephew, Israel Stoley, was a good hunter and had kept them well supplied with meat. Black Harris remained with the Cornwalls and later helped them move to a donation land claim three miles from McMinnville in Yamhill County. The Reverend Cornwall lived there with his family until 1866, when he removed to Ventura County, California, remaining until his death on January 2, 1879. During Cornwall's nineteen years in Oregon, his life and influence as a gospel minister were a credit to his adopted state. He was the first ordained Presbyterian minister in Oregon before 1851 and was privileged to meet Dr. Marcus Whitman, whose friendship he valued highly.

Holt Completes His Mission

Holt and his party, who had gone on, now consisted of the two French-Canadian half-breeds, Baptiste Gardapie and Q. Delore; also Duskins, Patton, and Owens of the Harris' party. They met the last of the travelers on the South Umpqua, December 17. The persons rescued were Crump, Butterfield, and the latter's sister-in-law, a widow whose husband was killed by the Rogue River Indians; also J. Baker, and David and James Townsend. There had been no flour among them for eight weeks. They had been fashioning pack saddles, preparing to pack out their goods when their few remaining horses were stolen by the Indians. (According to the late Kearney Emmitt, son of John Emmitt, an early settler of Coles Valley, the J. Baker rescued in the last group on the South Umpqua later settled in the valley. A Jonathan D. Baker was postmaster of the Coles Valley postoffice in 1877, which lends credence to his statement.)

On December 20, all—both rescued and rescuers—started for the Willamette Valley. The natives, at what is now Winchester on the North Umpqua, refused to lend their canoes to ferry the women and children across until they were paid with a gun belonging to DeLore. Andrew Riggs, a full-blooded Umpqua Indian residing near Willamina in Yamhill County, told V. O. Huddleston, a gunsmith at Willamina, an incident which seems to relate to the 1846 emigration. Mr. Riggs related (1959):

"My father was a chief of an Upper Umpqua tribe. He lived with his people on the North Umpqua above Winchester. Late one fall there appeared on the opposite bank of the river from their camp a group of white men, the first he had ever seen. They indicated by signs that they wanted to cross the river. These men had wagons and oxen, and the river was too high to ford. The white men explained that delay would deplete their food supply, both for them and their stock.

"The Indians were friendly and cooperative, and agreed to help the party across. These white men had long hair and beards and were fierce looking in their ragged clothing. The only discernible feature of their faces was their eyes which peered out through the hair like those of a wild animal. My father said that the whites called us savages, but to us these people looked like wild beasts.

"The Indians made a ferry by lashing two large canoes together. Wheels were removed from the wagons, and the running gears were lowered onto the makeshift boats. When all equipment was ferried over, the immigrants offered the Indians gold in payment. They had never seen coined money and had no idea of its value but they accepted it and used the pieces as ornaments.

"My father told me many things concerning the coming of the white man and urged me to learn to write in order to record the history of my people but I did not take his advice, much to my regret. In the fall of 1856, my father was taken to the reservation in Yamhill County where I was born, one of fourteen children, and given the name "Riggs."

Andrew Riggs looked to be past eighty years old when interviewed, but he did not know the exact date of his birth.

It began snowing on December 22 while Holt and his charges traveled toward the Yoncalla Valley over the old California Trail, and was snowing hard when they arrived at Elk River. They found the river overflowing its banks and lost two oxen while swimming their animals across. On Christmas Day the snow was a foot deep and no progress was made. On the 26th they reached the camp of Ezekiel Kennedy whom they had helped earlier that month. The camp had now been without food for four days, except for a little tallow boiled in water without salt. The situation was so serious that Holt persuaded Baker (rescued on the South Umpqua) to butcher one of the oxen he had bought from the relief party and divide it among them.

Journey's End

That same day, December 26, the first clear day since the 3rd of the month, these weary stragglers of the 1846 immigration joined the rescue party for the last lap of their journey. So many of their cattle and horses had died, or been stolen, that the lean oxen in Holt's company had to be used as pack animals. By January 1, 1847, the snow was three feet deep on the Calapooia Mountains and the weather had turned cold. It was so cold that their clothing—wet from crossing swollen streams—was stiff with ice.

On January 5, they arrived at the home of Eugene Skinner, the last settler south in the Willamette Valley (now the site of Eugene in Lane County). On the 12th they reached the house of a Mr. Williams on the Luckiamute River in Polk County. It was the 21st of January before the storm-beaten travelers all reached friends in the Willamette Valley.

Balancing Accounts

Holt and those who went with him to the rescue of the beleaguered immigrants were absent from their homes for fifty days —and had asked no special reward for their services. They had expended $400 over and above assistance rendered by others of the company. Jesse Applegate himself was perniciously attacked by J. Quinn Thornton, who accused him of purposely starving the immigrants to make a market for his beef and flour. Yet, despite the tragedy and hardship, the opening of the southern route by the 1846 immigration was a prelude to the eventual settlement of the Umpqua Basin and Umpqua County. Historian Hubert Howe Bancroft states that about a dozen families sought refuge for the winter of 1846-7 at Fort Umpqua, at the mouth of Elk Creek, and some of them found homes in the Umpqua Basin. These included Elijah Bunton, who settled at "Bunton's Gap" (now Wilbur); and Charles Putnam, who made a home in "Tin Pot Valley," four miles west of Drain. John Long, the father of John H. Long, left his wagons in the Umpqua Canyon and returned in the spring of '47 to retrieve them. He then went on to Polk County but returned to the Yoncalla Valley in 1849.

Merits of the Applegate Trail

In May 1847, Levi Scott led a party of men bound for the states over the southern route to Fort Hall, and on his return to the Willamette Valley guided a portion of the 1847 immigration over this road. Among the company were the three Wells brothers, Ira, Dr. Daniel, and William W. The caravan arrived in the valley in good time and in good condition. In fact, their record established the southern route, or the historical "Applegate Trail." The Territorial Legislature of that year passed an act authorizing its improvement and making Scott commissioner, allowing him to collect a small toll for his services.

During the winter of that same year, 1847, trouble with the Cayuse Indians broke out, and had it not been for the Oregon Volunteers, the Indians would have closed the Snake River route.

This confirmed the wisdom of the settlers in opening other means of approach. *Overland Monthly*, appendix 19, v. 581, quoted Applegate as saying: "It is a well-known fact that when it was necessary to meet the Oregon Rifle Regiment, then on the march to Oregon, beef cattle could not be driven to Fort Hall by the Snake River route with any beef on their bones; yet the regiment slaughtered fat bullocks at Fort Hall from the Willamette Valley, kept fat by the abundant pasture along the southern route." The route opened by Applegate and Scott, in 1846, was basically the same now followed by Interstate Highway 5, which runs the full length of Oregon. The Federal Government re-surveyed the route in 1853-54; a result of this was the opening of a military road from Camp Stuart in southern Oregon in the summer of 1858.

Settlement of Yoncalla Valley

In 1849, the Applegate brothers, with Levi Scott and his two sons, moved from Polk County to the "Halo" country—the Applegates to the Yoncalla Valley, and the Scotts to what is now Scotts Valley. And it was not long before they were joined by pioneer neighbors. To quote from Anne Applegate Kruse's *Yoncalla, Home of the Eagles*: "While this 1850 settlement is significant and worthy of commemoration, full occupancy of the valley did not take place in any one year. . ."

Jesse took a donation claim in the northern portion of Yoncalla Valley at the base of Mount Yoncalla. If we interpret history correctly, he left most of the management of the farm to his sons. His later activities bear out this assumption. The following is from the records of the Donation Land Claims in Oregon:

"Re: Applegate, Jesse. Application number 103, 642 acres in Township 22 South, Range 5 West, Sections 21, 22, 27, 28. Arrived in Oregon in the Autumn of 1843; settled on claim June/Aug. 7, 1849. Married Cynthia Ann (Parker) 12/13 of March, 1831, in Cole County, Missouri. On 9 July, Applegate gave affidavit that he had eight children; Rozzelle, wife of Charles F. Putnam; Alexander M.; Robert S.; Gertrude; Henry H.; Daniel W.; Sally and Peter Skene Ogden Applegate. Patt., delivered, Feb. 27, 1866."

Jesse Applegate and Levi Scott did not retire to private life, but worked diligently, with the cooperation of their neighbors, to establish a commonwealth that has endured for over a century. Their faithful comrade and friend, "Black Harris," returned to Independence, Missouri, where he died of the cholera in 1847. A contemporary carved the following epitaph on Harris's grave marker:

"Here lie the bones of old Black Harris
Who often traveled far beyond the West,
And for freedom of equal rights
Crossed the snowy mountain heights,
He was a free and easy kind of soul
Especially when he had a belly full."

CHAPTER IV

A New Era

It was said of the 1843 immigration that as soon as the grass began to grow in the spring, promptly and without preconcert, but as if by appointment, they assembled at Fitzhugh's Mill, east of Independence, Missouri, with the words "For Oregon" painted on their wagons. So it seemed with the parties destined to usher in the "New Era"; they were moved by the same unseen force to assemble at the mouth of the Umpqua in June 1850.

Job Hatfield

First to arrive was Captain Job Hatfield and a party of twenty-nine companions. Hatfield was a seafaring man, born near Yarmouth, Nova Scotia, on August 31, 1813. He chose a seafaring life, making his first voyage at the age of fourteen years. He spent sixteen years of his life as pilot, working the *Mary Taylor* over the Sandy Hook bar, off the coast of New Jersey. In the winter of 1849-50, he came to Oregon where he worked as pilot over the Columbia River bar till June, when he, with twenty-nine others, went on an exploring trip to the Rogue River country. The company traveled as far as present Drain, where they camped for several days.

Hatfield, who wished to examine the Umpqua and the depth of its bar, along with five companions, left the main party camped at the trail leading to the lower Umpqua Valley, and made a side trip to the mouth of Elk Creek where it joins the Umpqua. They followed the Umpqua River to the head of tidewater, obtained a canoe from some friendly Indians, and navigated the stream twenty-six miles to its mouth. Satisfied with his findings, Hatfield returned with his company to the main party and all resumed the journey to the Rogue River. Not finding anything to their liking, they returned to the lower Umpqua Valley.

54

Applegate and Scott's Party

Upon their arrival back at the head of tidewater on the Umpqua River, the Hatfield party found Jesse Applegate and Levi Scott, with three companions, surveying a claim which Scott had selected. Applegate explained their presence by saying that he and Scott and their three companions had moved to the Yoncalla Valley the previous year and were interested in getting better mail service in the interior and southern Oregon, and were on their way to the mouth of the river to meet the United States surveying schooner, *Ewing*, which was to chart the harbor.

When the Hatfield party learned this, they made plans to accompany Applegate and his group to their rendezvous with the *Ewing*. The party now consisted of Job Hatfield, Rufus Butler, William Golden, James McGuire, Dave Johnson, Jesse Applegate, Levi Scott; and the three Wells brothers, Ira, Dr. Daniel, and William W., with William Sloan making eleven in all.

Rendezvous with Destiny

After finishing surveying Scott's claim, the party continued on to the mouth of the river, locating en route a claim for William Sloan on the north side of the river, a mile or so below Scott's claim. When they reached the mouth of the river, the *Ewing* had not yet made its appearance. While waiting for it, Applegate briefed the Hatfield group on the details which had prompted their mission.

He explained that in the spring of 1849, A. D. Bache, superintendent of coastal surveys, had ordered Lieutenant Washington Bartlett of the United States Navy to proceed to the Umpqua River with the surveying schooner *Ewing*, which had been cruising off the coast of California, with instructions to survey and chart the Umpqua harbor. It seems the steamship company, headed by G. G. Howland and William H. Aspinwall, who had the mail contract, refused to enter the Umpqua after one of its steamers had been damaged in making an attempt. In order to compel them to carry out the terms of their agreement it was necessary to survey and chart the harbor.

The Ewing Delayed

The reason for the *Ewing*'s delay in keeping her appointment was that when Lieutenant Bartlett put in at San Francisco for supplies, the 1849 gold fever was at its height and he lost five of his men in an attempted mutiny in which Midshipman Gibson was nearly drowned. The leaders of the rebellion were court-martialed and sentenced to hang. Because of this and other delays it was April 3 before he put to sea and then with barely enough men to operate the vessel.

While the Hatfield-Applegate party was waiting for the *Ewing*, an unscheduled vessel put in at the mouth of the river. This craft was the *Samuel Roberts* from San Francisco, with Captain A. Lyman in command.

Little did the Oregon group realize that the company aboard this vessel were the ones they had been waiting for, that they had arrived promptly on schedule, and that the "new era" for the Umpqua basin was well under way.

Captain Lyman's Journal

Captain Lyman's Journal, "Voyage to the Umpqua," tells the nature and purpose of his presence in the Umpqua estuary on Sunday, August 4, 1850, and introduces the personnel who were to play an important role in bringing in the new epoch. From the leaves of Captain A. Lyman's Journal:

> "On the 27th of June, 1850, I was chartered to take a party for the purpose of making explorations on the coast of Oregon for the rivers, Klamath and Umpqua. The Company was styled the *Klamath Exploring Expedition,* and was set on foot by five persons under the name of Winchester, Paine and Company. We sailed from San Francisco on the 6th of July. The following are the persons comprising the expedi-

tion: C. T. Engbrodt, R. W. Larritt, W. C. Evans, P. Flana-
gan, Dr. H. Beals, F. Fletcher, T. T. Tiernney, E. E. Broad-
bent, A. W. Pierce, Rufus Coffin, W. Stevens, N. Schofield,
Chas. McDowell, Chas. Steinfield, Dr. E. R. Fiske, Alex
Davis, R. S. Philpot, J. E. Farrell, Dr. (Joseph W.) Drew,
C. T. Hopkins, H. Winchester, H. J. Paine; Captain A.
Lyman, master; Peter Mackie, mate; S. E. Smith, 2nd mate;
C. Moore, cook; Chas. Brown, J. Anderson, J. M. Dodge,
J. Magranery, and James Cook, seamen; thirty-four souls all
told. All the persons who went were share holders in the
expedition."

Umpqua Land Company

The men aboard the *Samuel Roberts* intended to take up land
at strategic points along the trails to the gold fields and to establish towns. Most members of the company were successful professional and business men; the persons named by Captain Lyman
were later to become leaders in the communities they helped to
establish. This chance meeting of the Oregon group and the
California party at the mouth of the Umpqua completed the
course of events that brought together the founding fathers of
old Umpqua and Douglas counties.

When the Applegate-Hatfield party learned that the members
of the Klamath Expedition were land speculators and interested
in founding towns, they offered their cooperation, which was
accepted by the Californians. A joint-stock company was formed
under the title of The Umpqua Townsite and Colonization Land
Company, hereafter referred to as the Umpqua Land Company.
A written agreement provided that all lands claimed by the company were to be divided into shares and drawn by lot among the
original members. Three days were spent in surveying the harbor
and planning further moves. The mail program was tabled for
the time being.

On the morning of the 7th of August, the *Samuel Roberts*
proceeded up the river with a small boat going ahead to sound

the channel. Hatfield's and Butler's previous examination of the channel came in good stead. The men found an average depth of twelve feet for the first twenty miles; then the vessel grounded in eight feet of water. The company spent the night waiting for the next high tide. Captain Lyman noted: "The night was celebrated by an extra indulgence on board, the bounds of sobriety were exceeded by not a few. That place we named Brandy Bar." The location still bears that name.

The next day the vessel was taken six miles farther up river to a point where the men observed sunken rocks in the channel. On the way down, the schooner was anchored opposite William Sloan's claim. There the company divided into three groups; one, headed by Jesse Applegate, was to explore the main valley; another, led by Herman Winchester, was to proceed to the North Umpqua, and the third group was to stay with the ship. To show his appreciation for the Klamath Expedition's opening the river to navigation, Levi Scott donated sixty acres of his claim to Winchester, Paine and Company.

Herman Winchester and his group made their way immediately to the North Fork of the Umpqua River. There they found the land already claimed. After exploring the surrounding territory they returned to where the California Trail crossed the river and bought the ferry and the land which is now the present site of Winchester. The terms of the sale are recorded in Umpqua County's deeds record book:

> "John Aiken and Thos. Smith sold to Herman Winchester, C. Thomas Hopkins, Horace J. Paine, Eldridge B. Hall, and Galen Burdel, also under the name Winchester, Paine and Company, title and interest and claim in and to said land continuous and adjoining, water crafts and all improvements thereto, the ferry across the Umpqua at the road leading to the United States and California. Consideration for $5,000 dollars gold or lawful money of the United States. Received payment from Winchester, Paine & Company, Oct. 26, 1850, $1,600 in hand, $3,000 in drafts due in two, four and six months from date, Total $5,500."

Ships That Pass in the Night

By October 1850, the Umpqua Land Company had sold a number of lots and the *Samuel Roberts* had returned to San Francisco. The California Company had meanwhile dispatched their schooner, or brig, *Kate Heath* with a cargo of merchandise and industrial machinery for the new country. These ships passed each other en route and neither group knew of the passage of the Donation Land Act by the Territorial Legislature in September of that year. This act doomed the success of the Umpqua Land Company; it prohibited companies and non-residents from holding lands for speculation.

The *Kate Heath* arrived at the Umpqua River and crossed the bar without difficulty on October 11, with Captain Woods in command and Addison Crandall Gibbs in charge of the company's goods. Besides her cargo of merchandise she had aboard seventy-five immigrants, many of them stockholders in the now defunct land company.

On the way upriver, the *Kate Heath*'s company observed the wreckage of the schooner *Bostonian*, which had foundered crossing the bar on October 1. The vessel was a total loss; her captain, George L. Snelling, with her crew of nine, had salvaged most of the cargo and gone into camp nine miles up the estuary near what is now Gardiner. A Boston merchant named Gardiner had outfitted the vessel for trading along the Oregon coast, with his nephew, Captain Snelling, in command. *The Bostonian*'s crew called their camp "Gardiner" in honor of the ship's owner.

The *Kate Heath* picked up the cargo and stranded crew and carried them to Scottsburg. Members of the land company now had the cargo of two ships on their hands, but this proved to be a minor problem. Although the land company had failed in its original plan, its members went ahead with the colonization program. They had seventy-five immigrants and the cargo of merchandise from two ships dumped in their laps; the result was the early development of the Umpqua Valley.

Rufus Butler

After the Umpqua Land Company disbanded, Rufus Butler, like others of the Hatfield party, took a donation land claim in the Scottsburg area and later became a prominent citizen in the lower valley. He was a native of New Bedford, Massachusetts, born on May 29, 1812, and, like Hatfield, he was a seafaring man. He followed the sea until 1850, when he came to Oregon and settled on a claim at Long Prairie, eight miles east of Scottsburg. There he engaged in lumbering and freighting.

Butler is credited with shipping the first cargo of piling from the new town of Scottsburg; for this cargo he received 22½¢ per running foot. He is also credited with driving the first freight wagon out of Scottsburg to Roseburg. He was chosen the first justice of the peace of the Scottsburg precinct, and the first civil case was tried in his court.

Butler's wife died before she had the opportunity of joining her husband on his claim, leaving two small children, a boy, Joseph, and a daughter Etta. In 1854 Butler married Sarah Wells, a native of Kentucky who had crossed the plains that year. They reared a large family, including the children by Butler's first marriage, and resided on the Long Prairie farm until their deaths; Rufus in 1884, and his wife in 1897. They are both interred in the Scottsburg Cemetery.

The author interviewed the late Aurilla J. Butler, widow of A. L. Butler, a son of Rufus Butler, at her home on the Butler homestead in January 1962. Mrs. Butler was then ninety years old, and during the conversation she revealed that the farm had been in the Butler family for 112 years; also that when the property was transferred to her daughter, Mrs. Muriel Monson, it was the first time that any name other than Butler had appeared on the deed.

Saga of James T. Cooper

A document by James T. Cooper—who was a passenger on the schooner *Kate Heath* when it arrived in the Umpqua River in October 1850—gives eyewitness account of many important historical occasions and also furnishes dependable data on the four townsites selected by the Umpqua Land Company.

This author was personally acquainted with Mr. Cooper and used to listen to him reminisce of the early life—and was fortunate enough to get a copy of what he had heard Mr. Cooper recite.

The original manuscript is in the possession of Mrs. Cynthia Rust of Blachley, near Triangle Lake, Lane County, Oregon. Mrs. Rust, a grandniece of Mr. Cooper, made the paper available in November of 1964. Mrs. Rust's father, George W. "Little George" Dimmick, a nephew of James T. Cooper, had prevailed upon his uncle to record his memoirs concerning his coming to Oregon. The pages of the manuscript are undated; however, the context reveals that it was written after 1864. The signature of Mr. Cooper proves its authenticity. He wrote:

"J. T. Cooper was born at New Pitstigo, Aberdeen Shire, Scotland, August 10, 1821. Married Harriet Dimmick, April 13, 1854. (Daughter of Ziba Dimmick and Cynthis Delight Hall Dimmick.) Ziba Dimmick crossed the plains in 1853 from the state of Ill. I started to cross the plains from Rockford, Ill., in 1850 with a 2 horse team, crossed the Mo., [Missouri] river at Council Bluffs, where I got my supplies for the long journey across the plains.

"I arrived at Salt Lake in the first week in July. I stopped to recruit my horses. I left my wagon and came on on horse back. I worked in the harvest 2 weeks and bought provisions from the Mormons to last me to Sacramento, Cal. I did not remain in California. Started to Oregon some time in September 1850 by water. I took passage on board the brig *Kate Heath*. The Captain's name was Woods. Sailed into the mouth of the Umpqua about the 10th of Oct. 1850, had a very rough passage up the coast, but passed over the bar without any trouble. The vessel anchored opposite to where Old Umpqua City or Military Fort was established in 1856.

"There was quite a company of young men that came when I did. We all got on shore in caravans as there was a large camp of Indians at the mouth of the Umpqua. We hired the Indians to bring us to Scottsburg. There were 2 cabins there, Scott's, who the place was named for, and Dr. E. R. Fiske. An Indian brought me as far as Sawyers Rapids, there we camped for the night. The Indian speared a salmon on the rapids and cooked it on sticks before the fire. I thought it the sweetest meat I ever ate. We had neither bread or salt.

"I came on to the Hudson's Bay Fort which was across the Umpqua above the mouth of Elk Creek. There was an old Frenchman by the name of Gardiner, [Gagnier] who had been there 25 years. At that time he had an Indian wife. I did not tarry long in that vicinity. I took the Indian trail up Elk Creek to Yoncalla Valley, the noted homes of the Applegates, where I went to work to make rails for Robert Cowan, John Long and Uncle Billy Wilson.

"I took my first claim where Mr. Fen Sutherlin now lives, in November 1850. It was in what was then called Benton County. Marysville was called the county seat. I sold my claim to Sutherlin in November 1852 and took a place now owned by John Fryer [this would date the document in the 1870s] and helped establish the ferry long known as the Dimmick ferry. The Indians called it "Chinnagouche," meaning "Crescent," and Crescent Ferry was the name given the first license, which was obtained at Elkton, the county seat of Umpqua County in 1852.

"I cast my first vote for Joe Lane [first territorial governor of Oregon] as delegate to congress in June 1851. Joe Drew was sent from this section in 1851 to confer with the Benton County delegation in reference to having a county organized on this side of the Calapooia Mountains to be called Umpqua. . .

"I enlisted in Co. F. of Oregon Volunteers under Colonel W. W. Chapman at the outbreak of the Rogue River war in

1855-56. I entertained Indian Agent Joel Palmer and his interpreter Mr. [John] Flett, George M. Brown's grandfather on his mother's side, at my cabin where he treatied with the Indians in 1856.

"I was elected the first constable of the first Elkton precinct. I was elected as one of the representatives to the (state) legislature in 1872 and got up the bill for $10,000 to build the bridge at Winchester and $15,000 for the wagon road from Wilbur to Green Station. (Two miles south of Roseburg.)

"Fendal Sutherlin took up the Bushby place in 1850 where Roseburg now is and I went from my place in the Swale [present Sutherlin] on foot to help him build a cabin. I had on a pair of buckskin pants and it rained and my pants began to stretch and I commenced to roll them up and when they dried I could hardly get into them. Fen did not put in his appearance and I had had my tramp (ten miles) without any dinner. I made my way back to Aiken's (at Winchester) and found them all in bed.

"There was quite a large camp of Indians on Deer Creek at that time, nearly a mile above where Roseburg now stands. Scottsburg became quite a trading post and pack trains came from Yreka, Cal., to get supplies there. Flour, beans, coffee, and dried peaches came from Chile by way of San Francisco. Flour was 15¢ to 20¢ per lb., and from that up to 50 cts., and sometimes we had to do without. Wild game was plentiful. We occasionally killed a beef of the Hudson's Bay Co., when we could not buy from them. They charged 25 cts. per lb. for beef. Flour was $14.00 per hundred and kept high until 1854, and everything else. Then they commenced to raise grain in the Willamette Valley and the large emigrations coming every year, bringing stock of all kinds, soon made things cheaper and plentiful."

[signed]   J. T. Cooper

Part Two

FOUNDING OF TOWNS

CHAPTER V

Umpqua City

Members of the Klamath Exploring Expedition were land speculators, but their well-laid plans to control the best locations in the new country backfired when the Territorial Legislature passed the Donation Land Act in September 1850, prohibiting companies and non-residents from holding public lands for speculation. The joint-stock company, the Umpqua Land Company, had committed itself to the point of no return, and in order to protect their investments, had made the best of the situation and the economy of the Umpqua Basin was established.

Socrates Schofield notes in his diary that when the *Samuel Roberts* entered the Umpqua harbor, their company made an immediate survey of two townsites, one called East Umpqua and one called West Umpqua; this was before the land act was passed (by one month). Later, Amos E. Rogers took a donation claim of 320 acres near the mouth of the river, which embraced the whole of East Umpqua, later "Umpqua City." Nathan Schofield took 640 acres, which included all of West Umpqua. Schofield's holdings bordered on the west river front for three miles to a point opposite Gardiner.

Later, Samuel S. Mann and Henry J. Paine obtained property in both locations. They believed that a town in this location was essential to commerce, and endeavored to influence business firms to invest. Edward P. and Dr. Joseph Drew invested in the Umpqua City site. The first buildings erected were the pre-fabricated zinc houses brought in on the *Kate Heath* in 1850. The only commercial business there at that time was a hotel opened by Joseph Clark. A postoffice was established on September 26, 1851. Amos E. Rogers was the first postmaster appointee but never qualified as he had moved to Empire City to engage in coal mining with Patrick Flanagan. On February 2, 1852, Mann was named to the position.

BULLY WASHINGTON *Comes to the Umpqua*

The real estate firm of Paine & Mann immediately began promoting their town. Apparently their first customers were Stephen F. Chadwick, Adolphus Germond, Lloyd Minturn, and Barkley J. Burns. Old Umpqua County record books reveal the nature of this transaction:

"We, Henry J. Paine and Samuel S. Mann of the first part, and Lloyd Minturn, Adolphus Germond, Barkley J. Burns, and Stephen F. Chadwick of the other part do hereby agree as follows: that said Paine and Mann do hereby convey and assure to said Minturn, Burns, Germond and Chadwick, an unclaimed half . . . of townsites known as East and West Umpqua for the following consideration; that wharves and storehouse shall be built on said West Umpqua by parties of the second part, and a steam boat be placed on said river, (extraordinaries expected) and said Paine and Mann further convey and agree to give further agreement for securing of the above upon the request of Chadwick, and it is further agreed that Scottsburg, or that portion claimed by Dr. Fiske is to be considered a part and parcel of the following conveyance provided that Dr. Fiske is willing. In witness whereof we have set our hand this 2nd day of October, A. D., 1851.

J. W. PERIT HUNTINGTON, C. C.

In compliance with the above indenture, steam navigation on the Umpqua River began in August 1853, with the advent of the steamer *Washington*, so called by E. W. Wright in his *Marine History of the Pacific Northwest*. After being placed on the Umpqua, it operated under the name *Bully Washington*. Hubert Howe Bancroft in his *History of Oregon*, Volume II, page 256, records. "In the autumn of 1851, a small steamer, called the *Bully Washington*, was placed on the lower [Willamette] river. This boat was subsequently taken to the Umpqua where it ran until a better one, the *Hinsdale*, owned by Hinsdale and Lane was built."

Neither the *Bully Washington*'s dimensions, date, and place of construction nor its builders are recorded. It was purchased in San Francisco by Captain Alexander Sinclair Murray who shipped it to the Columbia River aboard the bark *Success*. The vessel was then dismantled and transported in sections to the lower Willamette River where it was reassembled upon arrival.

It was first placed in service above the Willamette Falls at Oregon City, and operated between Canemah (a small town laid out above the falls by A. F. Hedges, a member of the last session of the Provisional Legislature) and the mouth of the Yamhill River in Yamhill County. The *Bully Washington* made its first run on the Willamette River on June 6, 1851. After it had been in service for some time, Captain Murray sold the vessel to the firm of Allan, McKinlay & Company for $3,000. It was taken below the falls where it operated between Oregon City and Portland until July 1853. In the spring of that year it was again taken above the falls and ran the upper Willamette for a few months, when it was once again transferred to the lower river and sold to Captain Sylvester Hinsdale. Captain Hinsdale brought the *Bully Washington* to the Umpqua River to operate between Gardiner and Scottsburg.

The *Bully Washington* made her last run on December 12, 1857, when her boilers blew up just after she had left the dock at Scottsburg on her way to Winchester Bay. Five persons were aboard when the incident occurred but no one was seriously injured. George Bauer, an early pioneer on the lower Umpqua,

Left: The Darius B. Cartwright house on the west side of the old Territorial Road near Lorane. The large tree standing in front of the historic building came across the plains in 1852, in the form of a walnut in the pocket of Mr. Cartwright.

Right: One of the few wooden bridges remaining in the confines of old Umpqua County, located at the junction of Thief and Elk creeks. It was at this location that a group of storm-buffeted immigrants were camped on Christmas Eve 1846. Their Christmas dinner was a little tallow boiled in water without salt.

Plaque placed in front of the Darius B. Cartwright house. Its inscription tells its story.

Early navigation on the Umpqua River. The tug *Hunter* has an unidentified schooner in tow. From the way the tow rides in the water, it is on its way to Gardiner for a cargo of Lumber.

The sternwheel *Eva* on its run between Gardiner and Scottsburg. The tiller from this historic boat was preserved when the hull was dismantled and is now on display in the "History" room of the Reedsport bank.

was acting as engineer at the time. The hull of the historic old steamer was maneuvered into position at the dock at Scottsburg and filled with ballast left there by schooners loading cargoes of piling for San Francisco.

The remains of the *Bully Washington,* her iron hull buried with silt from many a freshet, lies on the north side of the Umpqua River just below the highway bridge at Scottsburg. The outlines of her deck could be seen until recent years. It is fitting that her last resting place is on that parcel of ground stipulated in the agreement that placed her on the river.

Umpqua City's Place in History

The Paine & Mann Realty Company had little success in their efforts to establish Umpqua City as the hub of commerce; it was destined for other roles in history. Thomas Smith of Winchester, in a letter to George H. Himes, then curator of the Oregon Historical Society, June 1908, had this to say: "I was down there (Umpqua City) in February 1851 and found quite a little village composed entirely of galvanized houses. I should think there were at least 300 men there at that time, but not a white woman in probably fifty miles. They were all seafaring men and men cutting timber for piles."

The wreck of the *Bostonian* in the fall of 1850 alerted the colonists to the dangers of the unpredictable Umpqua bar; it was apparent that certain aids to navigation were an absolute necessity. The first step in that direction was the establishment of a pilotage at the mouth of the Umpqua in 1853, and creation of the office of wreck master for the several counties along the coast. Samuel Mann was appointed for Umpqua and Jackson.

In July 1856, the United States government established a military post on the site of Umpqua City. Edward P. and Dr. Joseph W. Drew at that time owned the ground used for the buildings, which were rented to the War Department for $2,500 per year. A Lieutenant Hardin made the lease, witnessed by Dr. Vollum (U. S. medic) and Lieutenant Lotian.

The post at Umpqua City was called "Fort Umpqua," and the first commanding officer was Captain Stewart with a complement of two companies of 3rd United States Artillery. Stationed at the post at different times were Lieutenants Lotian, Pieper and Hardin. An interesting article appeared in an eastern newspaper, *Frank Leslie's Illustrated News*, New York, N. Y., dated April 24, 1858:

United States Fort

"Established in July 1856, two and one-half miles from the river mouth on the north side, it occupies a sandy situation, and is well protected from all the coast winds by a thick growth of pines and encircling timbered sand hills. It is garrisoned by two companies of United States 3rd Artillery. Situated as it is, at the southern extremity of the great coast reservation, and at the junction of the north and south trails with the river, its position is regarded strong and important as a barrier between the Indians on the reservation and the settlements south and east of it. Practically, the post is situated on an island, for all the communication with it from the lines of travel and the post routes must be made by water. Facilities for communication with the interior and San Francisco are quite abundant. Two small steamers ply between Scottsburg and the river's mouth. Ocean steamers and sailing craft (travel) direct to and from San Francisco."

Soldiers stationed at the garrison at Umpqua City never had actual combat with the Indians. On one occasion in 1862, the paymaster, on his regular rounds to pay the troops, found all the officers away on a hunting trip. When the Department Commander heard about this, he ordered the post closed. George Vincent, an early resident of the vicinity, said that in 1884 the blockhouse and soldiers' quarters had been moved to Gardiner and their timbers used in rebuilding a sawmill. All that was left to mark the spot was the residence of H. H. Barrat. The buildings that once were identified as "Barrat's Landing" have long since disappeared.

Letters that the Drew brothers sent to their mutual friend, J. W. Nesmith, then (1860s) Oregon's state senator to Washington, D. C., reveal interesting personal and political problems. Following are some excerpts:

Fort Umpqua, Ore., April 14, 1861

". . . We are making an effort to obtain the back rent from the War Department for the fort location, $2,500 . . . all that will have to be done about the rent of the post here is to have the account audited by order of Sec. of War—at least that was the intention when the lease was made—that we are entitled to rent from the time the post was located, Aug. 1856." (E. P. Drew)

❖   ❖   ❖

Fort Umpqua, March 8th, 1862

". . . Nearly all the cattle have either perished or were drowned in the December freshets. Everyone who can get away is off to the Salmon River mines. We get mail here about once a month . . . Jesse Applegate is talked of, or is being considered for, governor on the Union ticket."

(J. W. Drew)

❖   ❖   ❖

Fort Umpqua, Aug. 26, 1862

". . . Since enclosed was written, our mail has arrived with dates from east by letter to the first of July, 1862. Our dates from Sacramento are Aug. 18, so the great "over-land humbug" is one month behind. (The writer here is referring to the overland daily mail service established in the summer of 1860, with the California Stage Company.) (J. W. Drew)

The First Lighthouse

The failure of Umpqua City to materialize as a commercial center did not discourage public interest in establishing aids to navigation at the mouth of the Umpqua. At least eight vessels had been lost between 1850 and 1858. The *Bostonian, Caleb,*

Curtis, Roanoke, Achilles, Noosa, Almira, and the *Fawn* were lost at or near the Umpqua bar.

Joseph Lane, who was sent to Congress in 1851, secured an appropriation of $15,000 for light signals at the mouth of the river, $15,000 for buoys at the approach to the harbor, and $40,000 to erect a fireproof customhouse at that place. Three and one-half years later an additional $10,000 was granted, but it was four years after the first grant that the first components of the light reached the Pacific Coast aboard the United States revenue cutter, *Shubrick*.

Actual construction on the lighthouse got under way by 1855. Progress was hindered when materials were stolen by the local Indians and it was 1857 before the last panel of glass was fitted into the lantern. For lack of judgment, or other reasons not known, the light tower was erected on the sand near the shore. During the 1860-61 flood, erosion caused by the elements undermined the structure, which later collapsed. Fortunately the lantern escaped injury and was salvaged.

From 1863 to 1888, the mouth of the Umpqua was without a lighthouse or adequate channel markers. The only guidepost at the bar entrance was a second-class buoy. For many years after the tower collapsed, its location appeared on foreign maps — which was reported to have caused the loss of two vessels through the miscalculation of their course.

In October of 1888, an appropriation of $50,000 was granted by Congress to re-establish lighthouse service at the mouth of the Umpqua. A site was selected (the present location) and declared government property by executive order in 1895. While the survey was in progress, bids were advertised for the construction of the tower and all necessary buildings, dwellings, barns, oilhouses, cisterns, and metal work on the tower unit.

A bid of $12,000 was accepted for the unit which was completed eleven months later. In September of 1891, a bid of $17,879 was accepted for the construction of the buildings. Five months later, word was received from the contractors that they were unable to continue work. After much legal maneuvering, another bid of $20,000 was accepted on April 20, 1892, for the completion of the keeper's dwelling and other unfinished work. The tower was completed in August of that year.

Because of the failure of the original contractors to fulfill their agreement, additional costs had used up the first allotment of $50,000. During the fiscal year of 1895, two oil-houses were built and a fence placed around the cleared ground at the station site; furnaces for heating the dwellings were also installed. The following fiscal year, a judgment of $4,000 was obtained against the contractors and their bondsmen. In January of 1898, the judgment was settled for $600, which was accepted by the Treasury.

The conical tower was sixty-five feet above ground level, and 165 feet above water. The lantern was 210,000 candlepower and was visible for nineteen miles. It gave two white flashes of two seconds, then three eclipses of three seconds, followed by a red flash of two seconds. The station is listed in the Pacific Light District as Number 825, and has served faithfully for more than sixty years, with the exception of two hours on February 24, 1958, when an over-heated oil stove caused a fire in the structure.

First Lifeguard Station

The first lifeguard station at the mouth of the Umpqua was established in October 1891. The buildings were erected on or near the site of Umpqua City, and John Bergman was the first keeper. He received his appointment with the instructions to have the station fully manned by the 1st of March 1892. For the first two years the crew numbered seven men; in 1893 the number was increased to eight. Members of the first personnel were local men: John Lawson, William Lorhum, William M. Anderson, William Smith, Henry Boltman, Peter Cowan, Ewald Glass, and George Perkins.

Their equipment consisted of one Dobbins self-righting and self-bailing lifeboat. The craft would right itself when upset by means of air tanks placed at either end in an ingenious way, throwing the center of gravity high when the boat was turned over and making it top-heavy. When bottom-up it rested on the air tanks and the heavy bottom would turn as if hung on an axis in the same manner as a wheel with a heavy weight attached.

Any water left inside the craft was expelled by a self-bailing contrivance. The weight of the water inside the boat would activate the outlet valves, and would close them when the pressure was released. A smaller boat was used where the larger one could not be transported because of its weight. The "surf boat" was hauled on a "beach wagon" when the services of the crew were needed elsewhere.

A "breeches buoy" lifeline was used to communicate with stranded vessels. A small brass cannon, called a "Lyle" gun after its inventor, fired a projectile carrying a small line over to a stranded ship. This line was used to haul out a three-inch hawser to the wreck, where the sailors made it fast to a mast; then the lifeguard crew on the shore would tighten the cable with a capstan. A "life car" was secured to the hawser with traveling blocks and pulled back and forth as often as necessary.

There was, in 1962, one remaining landmark left of the old lifeguard station on the east shore—the practice pole. This was a pole placed in the ground a suitable distance from the station to simulate the mast of a ship in distress, on which the crew practiced the breeches buoy technique.

Lighthouse and Coast Guard Consolidated

In December 1939, the coast guard and lighthouse service were put under one head, with a commissioned coast guard officer in charge. The combined stations are now staffed by twenty enlisted men from the coast guard service. The old conical light tower and some of the signal unit buildings are still in service. Separate units have been constructed on the site (declared government property in 1891) to house the personnel on duty, complete with mess and living quarters. Instead of kerosene for light, electricity is used. A stand-by diesel-powered unit is installed in the base of the light tower, should the commercial source of power be interrupted. The mooring dock for the two modern lifeboats is in the same location as the "store-houses" mentioned in the Paine and Mann transaction in 1851.

Although Umpqua City has ceased to exist as a town, the aids to navigation existing in its place are vital to the economy of the entire Umpqua basin.

Entrance to Bar Deepened

In the summer of 1923, seventy-three years after the *Samuel Roberts* entered the Umpqua River, a project to deepen the bar was launched by the United States Corps of Engineers. Richard W. Williams was appointed resident engineer, with headquarters at Winchester Bay.

When Mr. Williams was interviewed, in the spring of 1962, he recalled the steps necessary in building a huge breakwater straight out into the Pacific Ocean. His first job after getting organized was building a trestle along the north shore of the river just outside the bar. Equipment was assembled and work progressed under the supervision of Claude Fullhart, construction foreman. A standard-gauge railroad track was laid over the completed sections of the trestle-work to accommodate special dump cars, which were shunted about by a small steam locomotive. In this manner, huge boulders, weighing from six to eight tons, were dumped on either side of the trestle. The larger boulders were placed on the outer side and the core was filled with smaller ones.

Wharves were built near the mouth of the river to receive the large scows which brought the material from nearby historic "Brandy Bar." The boulders were blasted out of those huge sandstone bluffs referred to by Captain A. Lyman. This part of the work was performed by a civilian contracting firm. Rocks from the quarry were loaded aboard the scows on wooden skips, a sort of sling, and a weigh-master at the wharf checked and weighed the loads—which were required to be a certain percentage of core and outside rock. After the material was weighed, it was placed on a dump car and taken out to the construction site.

Williams recalled that, while he was working on the jetty, two schooners, outbound and loaded with lumber, grounded just inside the bar and broke up. The lumber was salvaged by the engineers and used for trestle work. There was a stretch of bad weather during the winter of 1924-25, and the cold and ice floes made work both dangerous and difficult; but the ordinary tides did not give much trouble as construction of the trestle was done during the ebb flow. In this manner the first section of the north jetty at the mouth of the Umpqua River was constructed. Work halted in 1927 when the appropriation ran out. Mr. Williams did not recall the amount expended.

In 1942 another section of the jetty was built a half mile beyond where Williams left off, with Kern and Kerby as contractors. The procedure they followed was similar to that employed by Williams, except that they poured concrete over the rocks. Two engine crews were used for this work; one crew would go early to get the forms ready; the second crew would haul the rock. Both engines would haul a car of concrete for the pour, which took from three to four hours at the lowest stage of the tide.

Rollie Letsom of Drain recalled the difficulties encountered. He said that they began their day at about 4:30 a.m., or according to the stage of the tide. The early hour gave them an advantage over weather conditions, which were more favorable in the early morning. When a "Sou'wester" came up they really got drenched because the engine faced the ocean. On one occasion they lost their oil cans from the cab when an unusually large wave broke over them.

A south jetty has since been added and the Umpqua bar is as safe as any along the Oregon Coast.

CHAPTER VI

Gardiner

Some historians, when writing about western Douglas County, state that the site of Gardiner was first claimed by Captain George L. Snelling, master of the wrecked schooner *Bostonian*; others claimed that Rufus Coffin, one of the crew, was the first claimant. Whoever it may have been, Gardiner developed into a thriving community along with Scottsburg and Umpqua City.

The first recorded legal owners, or claimants, were James T. Cooper and his wife Harriet. Umpqua County records reveal their sale of the "Gardiner Claim" of 320 acres in Township 21 S., Range 12 W., in sections 15 and 22, to Addison C. Gibbs on February 21, 1857, for the consideration of $100. (Record of Umpqua County Deeds, Book "A").

Addison Crandall Gibbs was a native of East Otto, Cattaraugus County, New York. He studied law in New York and was admitted to the bar in 1849. In the fall of 1850 he came to Oregon on the *Kate Heath* as a member of the Umpqua Land Company. The colonists elected Gibbs to serve in the Territorial legislature at the first regular elections in 1852. When a custom office was established at Gardiner, he was appointed collector for the southern district. He carried the mail from Yoncalla to Scottsburg from 1853 to 1857, either in person or by deputy. The old mailbag used during this period has its place among other historic heirlooms in Hedden's Store at Scottsburg.

Around 1863, Gibbs sold nine acres of his claim to Gardiner Chism, David Maurey, and Captain George Bauer, who erected a sawmill on the property; Horace J. Mead installed the machinery. Two years later, Gibbs sold the rest of his claim to Abel Pasco Fryer and Captain Josiah B. Leeds, who laid out the present town of Gardiner. The location, nine miles upriver from

Umpqua City, accounts for its continued prosperity. Its lumber industry is still flourishing because of the abundant stands of spruce and fir timber on the hills bordering the Umpqua River and its tributaries below Scottsburg.

Gibbs, who moved to Portland, continued to serve Oregon and became its war-time governor from 1862 to 1866. He died in London, England, in January 1877, and was buried in Portland, Oregon, July 9 of that year.

Leeds bought out his partner Abel Fryer, in 1881, and sold his holdings to George S. Hinsdale, who in turn sold an interest to W. F. Jewett. In that same year fire broke out in the engine room of the sawmill and flying embers ignited the nearby buildings, almost destroying the town; the estimated loss was $52,000. The mill was rebuilt with timbers from the old military post at Umpqua City. Hinsdale, Ned Breen, and Leeds built another mill in 1887. Later the Gardiner Mill Company of San Francisco bought both mills.

As Gardiner grew, business houses were established. William McGee and William Wade both opened hotels; Wade's was the first, opening in 1864. A drug store was operated by T. C. Markey. (William Burdick, now retired, is reported to have been the first prescription druggist; licensed in 1920, he operated the drug store there in 1915.) The first general store to offer dry goods and groceries was opened by Ephraim H. Burchard in 1860. The first bank was established that same year. Later the Gardiner Mill Company opened a general mercantile store. Alfred W. Reed operated a tannery, a creamery, a general store, and a butcher shop.

A. W. Reed became a formidable competitor of the Gardiner Mill Company and had acquired considerable real property in the Gardiner area before his accidental death in April 1899. The author well remembers the circumstances attending the accident. On April 9, 1899, word was received at the Dimmick ferry, relayed by Johnst Levins, the Oakland-Elkton mail carrier, that Alfred W. Reed, state senator from Douglas County, and Holister

McGuire, state fish commissioner, had been drowned one-fourth mile below the Brown Bridge in Coles Valley, about seven miles below Winchester on the North Umpqua River. They had been inspecting the river with United States fish commissioner Hubbard when their boat capsized in the Brown rapids. Hubbard escaped by clinging to the bushes along the shore.

Only parts of one body were ever recovered; these were identified by a nephew, Warren P. Reed, as those of his uncle. Early in June 1899, Lew Denny, a resident of Dodge Canyon northwest of Oakland, had found a human torso lodged in the willows at the mouth of Little Canyon about thirty river miles below the scene of the accident. The senator's nephew claimed the remains, took them to Gardiner, and interred them in the Gardiner Cemetery.

In the *Roseburg Review*, under the date of June 28, 1899, the following item appeared: "A skull, believed to be that of A. W. Reed of this county, was found along the Umpqua River near the Kellogg post office by John Fryer, an old settler there. Senator Reed and fish commissioner Holister McGuire were drowned in the Umpqua River below Winchester, April 8, 1899, while inspecting the river with the United States fish commissioner Hubbard. Their bodies were never recovered except the finding of a headless trunk at the mouth of Little Canyon, thirty miles below, and seven miles above where the skull was found. From the general characteristics of the parts found, the shape and contour of the teeth, identity was accepted as that of A. W. Reed. His nephew, Warren P. Reed, interred the remains at Gardiner." (The grave was opened to receive the skull.)

After the fire of 1881, the Bath Canning Company was organized, with a capital stock of $15,000; they built a salmon cannery on the site of old West Umpqua. Ship building also flourished; the ways were situated opposite the town of Gardiner, along the south bank of the estuary, and were operated in the early 1860s by Hiram Doncaster. A number of vessels were built in this yard: the sternwheel steamer *Swan* in 1869, and the sternwheeler *Enterprise* in 1870. Sailing vessels constructed there included the *J. B. Leeds, Louise Madison, Emma Brown, Active, Hayes,* and

Pacific. The steam-propelled river tug *Umpqua* also came off the Gardiner ways. A picture of the old boat *Umpqua* was acquired by George B. Abdill of Roseburg, showing Captain Fred Earl at the wheel, engineer Tom Lawhorn at the engine room door, and deck hand Pete Nelson on the forward deck with the vessel's mascot, a dog named "Paddy." The *Umpqua's* run at that time was on the Umpqua and Smith Rivers, and judging from the cans on deck, her main cargo was milk.

Civic Development

Civic development kept pace with industry. The Reverend Charles P. Bailey organized a Baptist church congregation on November 16, 1883. He and the Reverend George Black preached for the congregation until 1886, when the Reverend W. W. Wells was called to the pastorate. A year later, a public school was established. The population at that time was about two hundred.

Masonic lodge, Number 59, was established and given a charter on December 14, 1872. Its first officers were: Robert McKinney, Worthy Master; George M. Beldrice, Senior Warden; T. C. Reed, Secretary; Joseph Roberts, Senior Deacon; and W. W. Cox, Junior Deacon. The membership roll at that time was twenty-one. Allard Walker, a rancher on Scholfield Creek five miles above Reedsport, was awarded a fifty-year membership recognition by the Gardiner Lodge in 1961.

Water Transportation

For more than fifty years after its founding, Gardiner depended entirely upon water transportation. It was impossible to get into the interior without traveling the first twenty miles by boat, and all commerce carried on with outside markets was by sea-going vessels. Logs were delivered to the mills in rafts towed by the *Bully Washington* and other river tugs. Mail boats plying the Umpqua and Smith Rivers carried passengers and produce.

Two mail routes served the Gardiner area; one to Sulphur Springs on Smith River, and the other between Scottsburg and

Gardiner. The Sulphur Springs postoffice was created on February 6, 1878, with John Cowan as postmaster, followed by Charles
Mead on November 16, 1898. Clementine Dailey succeeded
Mead in May of 1905. The office was discontinued in March
1920, and mail was distributed from Reedsport. Around 1914,
Millard Cooley was awarded a contract to carry mail between
Reedsport and Winchester Bay. This route was served by the
steamer *Eva* when the Coos Bay stage line was operating; contact was also made with the Florence stage.

Captain Thomas Elliott

Captain Thomas Elliott, a native of New Brunswick, was an
early settler and navigator in the Gardiner area. Before coming
to Oregon, he piloted his own vessel on regular trips between his
home port of New York City and San Francisco around Cape
Horn. In 1852, he moved his wife and their three small daughters, Elizabeth, Katherine, and Blanche, to San Francisco. They
came around the Horn by sailing vessel, being nearly four months
en route.

After the settlement of the Umpqua basin and the discovery
of gold in California and southern Oregon, shipping was greatly
stimulated between San Francisco and the Umpqua River, and
the captain began operating his ship between San Francisco and
the Umpqua. He then decided to bring his family to Oregon.
They left San Francisco on board his boat, the *Tacoma*, on April
15, 1865, the day President Lincoln was assassinated, arriving at
their new home on May 1.

On the trip up the coast, the captain picked up two more
passengers at Eureka, Saul Perkins and John Lyster. They had
been logging in northern California but had lost everything when
the boom holding their logs broke during a severe storm and the
year's labor was washed out to sea; they were on their way to
Oregon to make a fresh start. Saul Perkins later married Katherine Elliott, and John Lyster married her sister Elizabeth. Blanche

Elliott's first husband, P. Hartzell, was killed in a logging accident when their son Frederick was quite young. She later married a man named Varrelman, and Frederick took his stepfather's family name. At this writing Fred resides in Portland.

Captain Elliott continued to operate his vessel, the *Tacoma*, on the California run until it grounded two miles inside the Umpqua bar in 1883 and broke in two. The captain died in 1907 at ninety years of age.

John Lyster died in 1893, leaving his widow with fourteen children. Mrs. Lyster later married William Wade, who was engineer on the steamer *Swan* on its voyage to Roseburg in 1871-72. Mrs. (Kathleen) Dailey, one of the fourteen children, spoke very warmly of her stepfather: "William Wade was surely a brave man to shoulder the responsibility of taking a wife with six children." At that time the others had grown up and were out on their own. Kathleen married Ray Dailey, son of John Dailey, a pioneer in the Smith River area.

John Dailey's father, a native of New York, was killed soon after his discharge from the Union Army, leaving a widow and four children. The mother died soon after the tragedy and John, the eldest, had to begin shifting for himself at an early age. His first job was driving a tow-horse on the Erie Canal. After wandering from place to place, he arrived in Corvallis, Oregon, in the middle 1860s, and, in 1870, came to Gardiner with several other young men. There he found employment in the mills. Five years later, he married Sarah Rowan from Ottawa City, Canada, and moved to the P. P. Simmons donation claim, twenty-five miles up Smith River. The Daileys soon increased their holdings to 2,000 acres; he took a 160-acre timber claim and she a 160-acre homestead. In 1906, they sold their timber holdings and built a new house on Smith River. The Perkins, Lysters, and Daileys are among the descendants of Captain Thomas Elliott. Many other families living in Douglas County and other parts of Oregon can no doubt claim similar relationship to early pioneer navigators who made Gardiner their home.

The Pyritz Family

One other pioneer family that merits mention in the Gardiner pioneer annals is that of Charles Pyritz. Mr. Pyritz married Caroline Juhkee in Steinfort, Germany, in 1847. They migrated to America in 1872, first to New York by sailing vessel; then to Omaha, Nebraska, by rail; then on to San Francisco and the Umpqua, where they settled on Scholfield Creek in 1874, above the Arthur and Charlie Walker places. There, daughter Lizzie was born. Later on they moved up Smith River above the John Dailey place.

The author was personally acquainted with six of the nine children of this union: Henry, Albert, Carl, Ralph, Lizzie, and the youngest girl, Sarah. Ralph Pyritz married Alice Larkins from the Green Valley community and the author married her sister, Sarah. Lizzie was married to Michael Dolan in 1904 and lived on Smith River until the death of her husband, when she moved to Gardiner where she now resides.

River Men

Captain Josiah B. Leeds, once part owner of the town of Gardiner, operated the "fast sailing *Francis Helen*" between the Umpqua and San Francisco in the early 1850s. Captain Henry Wade, first mate on the *Swan* on its historic voyage up the Umpqua to Roseburg, and Jacob A. Sawyers—his understudy—were both experienced fresh-water navigators, qualified to navigate inland waterways. But Captain Jimmie Graham was probably known by more people than any of the other early river men. He was born March 4, 1865, in Brooklyn, New York. His parents came to Oregon when he was two years old and settled at Gardiner. His father was killed in an accident on the Coquille River, when there was an explosion in the boilers of the boat on which he was employed as engineer. Jimmie followed his father's profession and took up navigation.

He married Minnie Sagaberd on August 10, 1892. Miss Sagaberd was born in Bolt Hogon, Germany, in October 1868. She had come to Douglas County in 1872 with her parents at the age of four years. Jimmie spent his active life navigating the Umpqua and Smith rivers; he was engineer on the sternwheel steamer *Eva* under Captain Neil J. Cornwall. When Cornwall retired to assume other duties, Jimmie succeeded him as captain. He was employed in this capacity until he retired in 1911; he died on May 10, 1934. When interviewed in October 1965, Mrs. Minnie Graham was residing with her daughter, Mrs. Katherine Gilbert, in her home at Gardiner. Mrs. Graham had just celebrated her ninety-seventh anniversary.

Mrs. Graham's two brothers, Frank and Henry Sagaberd, were with Captain Graham on her runs between Scottsburg and Winchester Bay; Frank was engineer and Henry was mate and deck hand and succeeded Captain Graham when he retired in 1911. The *Eva* was dismantled soon after Captain Graham retired and the gas boat *Atlas* was used in her stead. The helm of the *Eva* was saved and is now in the Pioneer Room of the Reedsport Bank.

Captain Neil J. Cornwall, son of the Reverend J. A. Cornwall, had charge of the river boats and the Gardiner Mill Company's tug boats. In 1915, the tug *Hunter* was in service and Captain Cornwall piloted sailing vessels in and out over the Umpqua bar. While performing these duties Gard Sagaberd was his engineer. Gard, a third brother of Mrs. Jimmie Graham to take up navigation in the Gardiner area, acted as engineer on the river boat, "Juno No. 1," as well as on the "Hunter."

One of Gardiner's early tug boats, the *Fearless*, was wrecked while crossing the Umpqua bar in 1889. The disaster did not become known until the next day, when the debris washed up on the beach. The crew of eight, with her master Captain James Hill, was lost. One member had made it to shore and crawled up on the beach out of reach of the waves, but was too exhausted to survive. Captain Hill's wife was the former Allie Palmer, daughter of P. P. Palmer, who built the Palmer House Hotel at Scottsburg. They had three sons: James, Albert, and Ralph.

The wrecked *Fearless* had an interesting background. Around 1856 a small steamer, the *Newport*, the first to enter Coos Bay, arrived there to transport coal and passengers for Patrick Flanagan and Amos E. Rogers of the West Port coal mine. The *Newport* (formerly the *Hartford*) was wrecked near Coos Head, but her engines were salvaged and transferred to a small teakwood schooner and christened the *Fearless*, which was taken to the Umpqua.

When the Southern Pacific Railroad Company built a line from Eugene to Coos Bay in 1915-16, it bypassed Gardiner. The town of Reedsport was being promoted at that time and subsequently drew off much of Gardiner's business, as the railroad bisected the new town. Also, the opening of timber stands in southern Douglas County drew lumber and plywood mills to the interior valley.

In the last few years Gardiner has staged a comeback. In 1961, the International Paper Company started installation of a $3,000,000 pulp mill, taking advantage of the available freshwater supply trapped behind the sand dunes in Siltcoos and Tahkenitch lakes. The project took state legislation to clear the way to impound the water and install a pipeline for an outlet. Meanwhile Gardiner stands serene, proud of its pioneer history.

CHAPTER VII

Scottsburg

Scottsburg, because of its location at the head of tidewater and the gateway to the interior of the Umpqua River Basin, received the first consideration among the four townsites selected by the Umpqua Land Company. The town, as first developed, had three divisions: upper, middle, and lower town. Today it has the appearance of being pushed into the river by the high wooded hill to the north—squeezed into a strip of land about one hundred yards across as the widest place and about 300 yards long, narrowing to a point at either end.

Though limited by its geographical location, Scottsburg is historically the most important town on the lower Umpqua. More business was carried on there than at any other town in the Oregon Territory at that time. No piece of ground in the state, comparable in area, can claim more distinguished men as its one-time citizens, or boast of a greater number of "firsts" than Scottsburg.

The original plat showed three main streets running parallel to the river; Commercial Street, which has long since given way to the erosion of the river; Main Street, which is now Highway 38; and Pacific Street, of which no evidence of former existence remains. There were thirteen cross streets: First, McTavish, Elk, Calapooia, Lane, Snelling, Sportsman, Chism, Jackwith, State, Jack, Nelson, and Yoncalla.

Some of the "Firsts"

The cabins of Levi Scott and Dr. E. R. Fiske were the first two permanent buildings. Dr. Eugene R. Fiske came to Oregon with the Klamath Expedition as a shareholder aboard the *Samuel Roberts* in 1850. He took an active part in the early development of Umpqua County, serving on road-viewing assignments and

84

practicing medicine at the same time. Dr. Fiske married Charlotte Grubbe, daughter of Benjamin J. Grubbe of Wilbur. They moved to Salem in 1863, where the doctor became an important factor in medical affairs in the Willamette Valley. He was also a member of the first faculty in the Willamette Medical Department, which founded the earliest medical school in the Pacific Northwest.

Three men, McTavish, Allen, and McKinley, opened the first store in a tent made from the sails of the wrecked schooner, *Bostonian.* Captain Snelling erected the first permanent store building, a pre-fabricated zinc house brought around Cape Horn. William Sloan opened a store on his land which was later called "lower town." Winchester, Paine and Company built a general merchandise store on Main Street in "middle town." Joseph Putnam and F. S. Crosby both opened hotels; Samuel S. Mann, whose later activities centered on Umpqua City and Coos Bay, operated a general merchandise store; Isaac N. Hall, one of Umpqua County's first commissioners, opened a grocery store. These were but a few of the business houses in Scottsburg the first year of its existence.

A. G. Walling, a Portland publisher and Oregon historian, writing in 1888, said that in the first year of Scottburg's existence, fifteen business houses were engaged in wholesale and retail business. It was a common sight to see five hundred pack animals in the streets waiting for their loads of supplies and mining machinery for southern Oregon and northern California.

The first postoffice in the Scottsburg vicinity was called Myrtle City; it was established on June 30, 1851, with Levi Scott postmaster. The office was discontinued on July 27, 1852. On October 8, 1851, the present Scottsburg postoffice was established with Stephen F. Chadwick, appointee. There were two postoffices operating concurrently in this area from October 8, 1851 to July 27, 1852. Postmasters at Scottsburg after Chadwick were: Loyal P. Brown, Ralph Lord, George S. Hinsdale, James Lyster, John Hedden; and Emma Hedden from 1915 to 1960, with forty-five years of continuous service.

In 1850, Alexander E. Rackliffe, a shareholder in the Umpqua Land Company who arrived aboard the *Kate Heath*, took a donation claim on Long Prairie, four miles east of Scottsburg, and built a sawmill at the mouth of Mill Creek, a little below Sloan's claim. John Sherritt is credited by some writers on southern Oregon history as having built the first sawmill in the Scottsburg vicinity. According to sources examined this is hardly possible. Old Umpqua County records reveal that Rackliffe borrowed money on his mill in 1851; besides, Sherritt did not cross the plains until the late summer of 1852. He settled in lower town that fall and opened a large wholesale and retail business. When Rackliffe sold out in 1853, it is possible that Sherritt bought and operated the mill in connection with his other enterprises. Whoever owned it, the flood of 1860-61 took it away.

The First Newspaper

By early winter of 1850, Scottsburg was well established. The trade with the mines in southern Oregon and the immigrant demand for supplies insured its prosperity. In 1854, Scott established a weekly newspaper, the *Umpqua Weekly Gazette*, the first in the Territory south of Salem. Until that time the *Oregon Statesman* in the Willamette Valley was the only news medium published within one hundred miles of the new town.

Scott bought some second-hand printing equipment in San Francisco and had it shipped to Scottsburg by boat. He engaged Daniel Jackson Lyons, son-in-law of Joseph Putnam, to edit his paper. Lyons was a native of Cork, Ireland, born March 23, 1815. His early education prepared him for the Catholic priesthood, but his career was terminated by the accidental loss of one eye. After his accident he turned to secular employment as a brush and broom maker to support himself. Despite the handicap, he studied extensively, taking music as a sideline.

Lyons migrated to America and settled near Louisville, Kentucky, still following his trade. He married Virginia Fayette Putnam and, with his family, crossed the plains in 1853. Settling at

Scottsburg in 1854, he acquired a part interest in a hotel run by
Levi Scott. This association led to Lyons' appointment as editor
of the new newspaper. Because of the strain on his remaining
eye he was slowly losing his sight, and Mrs. Lyons had to be his
"eyes" and do his writing. The Lyons had ten children, some
adopted. It is said that with all her work and having to write
her husband's editorials, she found time to teach a school for the
small fry in Scottsburg. She held the classes in her own home.

The policies of the *Umpqua Weekly Gazette* were stated in
the first edition: "Democrat in politics, in policy, Democratic."
It claimed devotion to literature, agriculture, mining news, and
general intelligence. The first editorial was a masterpiece:

> "The launching forth of our little bark on the waves of
> public opinion, and unfolding our sheet to the breeze, we
> trust that one and all will come forward and extend to us,
> not only kindness and leniency, but the necessary support
> to keep our boat afloat and in proper trim. The prospectus
> of the *Umpqua Weekly Gazette* has already been extensively
> circulated, and all know the grounds we intend to occupy.
>
> "Liberality and justice is our motto, and our columns
> shall remain free from the stain of political acrimony and
> sectional abuse. We call particularly on farmers to put their
> shoulders to the wheel, as men do in all civilized nations
> who make up the bone and sinew of society, and by their
> products furnish the nucleus, not only for the manufacturer,
> but for the commercial interest of all lands. We will wind
> up this article, not with a promise of things we never intend
> to perform, but with assurance of doing everything in our
> power to render our sheet useful and agreeable."

This "sheet" could be had for five dollars per year, or three
dollars for six months. Advertising space was reasonable; a square
of ten lines cost two dollars for one insertion, with a reduction
on yearly rates. From the pages of this folio we can recapture
much of the spirit of the times. Editor Lyons recorded some interesting historical events which, together with human interest

stories, provide an insight to the way of life in old Umpqua County in the early 1850s.

Some entertaining advertising appeared in the first issue. *Gazette* readers were informed that George Haynes & Company were in the general merchandising business at "575 Main Street"; Isaac N. Hall, the county's first commissioner, had groceries for sale; and the firm of Merrit, Openhimer & Company had everything. The latter were wholesalers in "Dry goods, Groceries, Provisions, Hardware, Boots and Shoes, Clothing, Cigars, Liquor, etc." Note was made of the "Scottsburg House," a hotel run by Joseph Putnam (Lyons' father-in-law). Allen & Lowe Company, commission merchants from San Francisco who had offices in Scottsburg, also advertised. Samuel S. Mann had a "lot of groceries and kindred stuff" which was entirely "new" and purchased at terms so favorable that he could "not fail to suit the purchaser." The Crosby Hotel was personally superintended by its proprietor, F. S. Crosby, who declared that the table was always supplied with the best the market could afford, and choice "Liquors and Cigars" were always available at the bar. (In 1865, Mr. Crosby became an ardent temperance worker.) William E. Lewis had a boat shop on Mill Creek on the Umpqua River and was an expert workman and spar maker. Hinsdale and Company, wholesale dealers in general merchandise, were located on the corner of Main and Nelson streets.

The *Gazette* also announced boat schedules. The fast-sailing schooner *Francis Helen*, Josiah B. Leeds, master, sailed May 1, 1854. McTavish, Allan, and McKinlay, the ex-Hudson's Bay men, were operating boats on regular schedule between Scottsburg and Winchester Bay and announced that the *Bully Washington* would make tri-weekly trips to the mouth of the river.

There were other items under general information. We learn from the *Gazette* that the cost of taking the United States census in 1850 was $1,316,027; that the Millerites of Boston had declared the world would be destroyed in 1854; and that a grampus, a member of the whale family, had arrived on the Umpqua. Mr. Lyons noted from the appearance of the fifty-foot mammal, that "it must have run out of provisions rounding the Horn and put in at the Umpqua for supplies. Several attempts were made to capture the creature but to no avail. It made its way as far as Sawyers Rapids; being not too well impressed with the country, it returned to its native haunts." Lyons added another item as an afterthought, "Word has been received that a whale has washed ashore south of the Umpqua River, providing the natives with an ample supply of blubber, which they devour with the gusto of ravenous wolves."

In the third issue, names appeared of those to whom contracts had been awarded by the county court for the construction of the bridges along the new road between Scottsburg and Elkton. The successful bidder for the bridge across Elk Creek at Elkton was T. D. Winchester. Other bridges were awarded to John A. Fryer, Sr., a Mr. Cassey, Captain William Hathaway, William Golden, and Clark Hudson.

Cost of Living

The cost of living in that period can be estimated by prices quoted in the *Gazette*. Current prices of staple groceries were: flour, 7c per pound; bacon, 22c; butter, 37½c; sugar, China, 12c—crushed, 17c; tea, 60-65c; coffee, 17-20c; dried apples, 15c; brown soap, 14c; soda, 50c; saleratus (baking soda), 15c; pepper, per box, $5.50-$6.00.

Lyons, a champion of good roads, said of those to Scottsburg: "They are but trails, and travelers description of them are prefaced with horrid oaths and violent imprecations." He deplored the fact that Elkton had only a political existence but was still named as the county seat.

The Folding of a Newspaper

D. J. Lyons was a brilliant man, well educated and gifted. His paper was well composed and, in his editorials, political issues of the day were intelligently discussed. He also possessed the traditional Irish sense of humor. At the end of the first volume, he severed his connection with the *Gazette*. In November 1854, G. D. R. Boyd purchased one-half interest in the *Gazette* and carried on as editor (with William J. Beggs as printer) until September 1855, when the plant was sold to William G. T'Vault and two other men named Taylor and Blakely. The press and equipment were shipped by muleback to Jacksonville in southern Oregon, where the *Table Rock Sentinel* was established with William G. T'Vault as editor. The first issue of the *Sentinel* appeared on November 24, 1855.

Gradual loss of vision had precipitated Lyons' retirement, but despite blindness he continued his brush and hotel businesses; and, in 1880, he turned his musical talent to account, frequently giving what he called "walking concerts" along the pack trail between Scottsburg and Drain and as far south as Empire City. On these trips he was led by a boy taken from an orphanage. Lyons died at Marshfield (now Coos Bay) at the age of sixty-nine, on August 8, 1895. It was at his house, in the upstairs bedroom facing east, that the second term of district court was held, with Judge Matthew P. Deady presiding. Joseph Knott, of the Bunton Gap-Wilbur community, was tried for murder at this session.

The transfer of the newspaper to Jacksonville seemed to portend the decline of Scottsburg. By 1852 the town had reached the extent of its growth. Trade into southern Oregon was greatly reduced by the opening of a road (now Highway 199) from Crescent City, California, to the mines in the Rogue River country. Goods that formerly passed through Scottsburg now went through Jacksonville.

By 1856, the number of stores in Scottsburg was reduced to two. The high water of 1860-61 took one of these and washed away all of lower town and all the mills and improvements on the main river. No flood then on record had had greater volume since the winter flood of 1844. Now the Umpqua rose forty feet above low water at ebb tide at Scottsburg. However the setback of the volume of trade and the disastrous flood did not end Scottsburg as an important factor in the future prosperity of the lower

Umpqua basin. Cyrus Hedden, the owner of the remaining store, continued to operate his business, which still continues under the firm name and with the third generation. More will be said of this remarkable pioneer family. Scottsburg and the House of Hedden are now synonymous, only spelled differently.

The House of Hedden

Cyrus Hedden, founder of the mercantile dynasty at Scottsburg in 1851, was a native of Newark, New Jersey, born in 1820, one of a family of sixteen children. At the age of twenty-one he joined a wagon train at Terre Haute, Indiana, bound for the California gold fields in 1849. His wagon train followed the Salt Lake route to California without incident other than the privilege of watching a fight, at a safe distance, between two Indian tribes along the Platte River in Nebraska.

He worked in the mines awhile before going to Portland, in 1850. There he was recruited with eight other men in the summer of 1851 to establish a settlement at Port Orford along the southern Oregon Coast. His cousin, Captain William Tichenor, had been commissioned by the post office department to establish a settlement on the coast in southern Oregon, and survey a route into the interior to facilitate mail delivery into southern Oregon and northern California.

The recruited colonists were transported to this location aboard Captain Tichenor's steamer, the *Seagull*, June 9, 1851. Tichenor left Hedden and his companions at Humboldt Bay and continued on to San Francisco, hoping to enlist some more recruits for his project. Two days after the *Seagull* sailed, Hedden's party was attacked by a band of Indians. The men retreated to a large rock in the bay, later named "Battle Rock," and fortified their position with a four-pound cannon which had been left with them by Tichenor. Their commander, J. M. Kirkpatrick, took the necessary arms and stores onto the rock. The cannon was placed on the high rock, which became an island at high tide—a small creek ran by its base.

During the siege, four white men were wounded, and twenty Indians were killed and fifteen wounded. The defenders were running short of ammunition and hoped for a chance to escape. The opportunity came when the Indians engaged in a war dance down the beach. Taking advantage of their temporary absence, the men on the rock made their escape. They kept to the woods by day and emerged on the beach by night. After eight days of rigorous experiences and little food, they arrived at the mouth of the Umpqua, where they were kindly received in the settlement there.

Hedden returned to Port Orford in August in time to take part in an exploring expedition into the interior under William G. T'Vault. A party of twenty-four set out on the 24th of August with rations for ten days. After traveling about fifty miles from the ocean toward the Rogue River, they became confused, lost their way, and their food ran out. Some of the men turned back at this point, but T'Vault was determined to continue. Nine men remained with him; they were Loren L. Williams, Patrick Murphy, A. S. Doherty, Gilbert Brush, Cyrus Hedden, John P. Holland, T. J. Davenport, Jeremiah Ryan, and J. P. Pepper.

The Good Samaritan

> *"Greater love no man hath than this, that a man lay down his life for a friend."* John 15:13

On September 9, they came to the headwaters of the Coquille River. There they abandoned their horses and hired some Indians with canoes to take them to the mouth of the river. On the morning of the 14th, they were attacked by a large band of natives at present Bullards Park, about one mile from the mouth of the Coquille. In the melee that followed only five escaped. Davenport made his way to the woods but it was never satisfactorily confirmed whether he made it to safety. Brush—who lay unconscious in the bottom of a canoe from a paddle blow that had split his scalp and nearly severed an ear— was taken by a young Indian, who had brought them down the river, to the south shore.

T'Vault, who was swimming, was picked up and taken to the south bank. Both men escaped and made their way to Port Orford on the following day.

Williams and Hedden, who had jumped into the shallow water at the beginning of the fight, managed to reach the woods toward the north, but not before Williams received an arrow in the back that ranged downward toward the right groin. Hedden was badly clubbed but both men escaped after giving a good account of themselves. Hedden tried to remove the arrow but it broke and a part of the shaft and the head remained in Williams' body.

Having passed through the territory the previous June, Hedden started with his wounded companion in the direction of the Umpqua River, forty miles away. Williams, suffering from the portion of the arrow still in his body, begged his companion to let him die, but Hedden insisted that he go along. They suffered severely from cold and hunger. Williams was barefooted and clad only in the remnants of his shirt; their only food was salal berries and mussels, a salt-water mollusk found on the rocks along the beach. After nine days of agony for Williams and fatigue for both, Hedden, half-carrying, half-dragging his companion, reached Winchester Bay. Historian H. H. Bancroft records that the brig *Almira* was lying in the harbor, with Captain Gibbs in command. The men were picked up and taken to present Gardiner, where Williams' wound was dressed. So severe was his condition that his friend Hedden provided living quarters and nursed him for three years before he could care for himself. As soon as Williams was able to travel he was taken to Scottsburg.

Hedden had made his headquarters there and operated a blacksmith shop until he opened a general merchandise store in 1851. In the fall of 1854, he married Margaret Sawyers, daughter of John Jacob Sawyers. They were the parents of four children, John N., Hulda, and two girls who died in infancy. Cyrus Hedden died in 1911 at the age of ninety-one.

Loren L. Williams

Old Umpqua County owes much to Loren L. Williams, born in Vermont in 1831. His parents moved to Michigan in 1833, where he lived with his father and mother until fifteen years of age. An unseen force seemed to possess this unschooled and inexperienced lad, causing him to join a party of trappers and hunters and eventually become a skilled frontiersman.

Williams' long illness caused by his arrow wound kept him at Gardiner City from September 1851 to January 1852. In a later account, Williams wrote: "I was put aboard a boat in the charge of Captain Edward Spicer in January and moved to Scottsburg where I remained for several months. The arrowhead worked its way out four years later on the opposite side of the groin, abscessing several times in the meanwhile. The wooden shaft didn't appear at the surface until February 1859." Dr. E. R. Fiske, who was practicing medicine at Scottsburg in 1852, examined Williams' wound and suggested: "Let nature pursue its common course."

Williams lived in Umpqua County until it was merged with Douglas County in 1862. He was treasurer for the county for two terms, and twice elected county clerk. After the consolidation of the counties, he was elected three times and appointed twice as clerk of Douglas County. In 1863 he became captain of Company H, Oregon Volunteer Infantry, and served for three years. Meanwhile he established Camp Wright on Silvies River in Harney County.

Williams traveled extensively after his retirement from public life, visiting various parts of the United States and several British possessions. On March 25, 1881, he died in San Francisco at the age of fifty years, after a short illness. He was interred in the Odd Fellows Cemetery at Roseburg.

The Heir Apparent

There is an old adage: "Some men are born great, others achieve greatness, while others have greatness thrust upon them."

None of these may apply to John Nicholson Hedden, but there are a number of reasons to believe that the place and time in which he was born may have helped to establish the position he held in the lower Umpqua basin.

He was the only son of Cyrus and Margaret Hedden, born on May 1, 1856, the second white child born in Scottsburg. His parents were of a hardy pioneer stock of which the predominant family characteristic was loyalty to their neighbors and friends.

At the age of sixteen, John tried steamboating as a prospective career, working under Captain Henry Wade on the small craft plying the Umpqua and Smith rivers. He received initial experience aboard the historic sternwheeler *Swan* when it made history by ascending the Umpqua as far as Roseburg, in February 1870. Accounts of the voyage vary and give rise to many controversial points, but following is the generally accepted account of the incident—based on these sources: *History of Oregon, Southwestern Counties, 1888,* by A. G. Walling; *Sternwheelers up the Columbia,* by Randall V. Mills; *Passing of District 66,* by Mary Wells; newspaper clippings from the *Roseburg Plaindealer,* 1871; letters from Mrs. Ray Dailey, Reedsport, stepdaughter of William Wade, engineer of the *Swan;* interview with the late John Sawyers, son of Jacob A. Sawyers ("Uncle Jake"), mate on the *Swan.*

Steamboating on the Umpqua

According to historian A. G. Walling, the possibility of navigating the Umpqua River above tidewater was taken seriously enough by some prominent citizens living in the interior valley to lead them to form a stock company. This company was incorporated for $12,000 and called the *Merchants and Farmers Navigation Company.*

The officers were: J. C. Floed, president; Arthur Marks, treasurer, both of Roseburg; J. E. Walton of Winchester, secretary; T. R. Sheridan and D. C. McClellan, also of Roseburg, and James C. Hutchinson from the Oakland area, directors. In the fall of 1869, they procured the small sternwheel steamer, *Swan,* and hired Captain Nicholas Haun to ready it for a voyage up the Umpqua, hopefully as far as Canyonville. Haun selected as his crew Jacob A. Sawyers, mate; Henry Wade, pilot; William Wade, engineer; John Hedden, fireman; and Bob Beckham and a man whose name was not recorded, as deck hands.

Captain Haun's orders were to navigate the river to Roseburg or farther, and take on and discharge freight along the way. This was technically carried out by trading staple groceries and tobacco for eggs, bacon, and garden vegetables. This was required in case they should solicit Federal aid to improve the channel. They were expected to navigate a hundred miles of fast water with an average fall of 3.5 feet per mile, an over-all fall of 506 feet from Canyonville.

The voyage began on February 10, 1870. Mrs. Ray Dailey of Smith River, a stepdaughter of William Wade, wrote: "The boat ran under its own power when there was water enough; the crew put out lines and used blocks and winches over the shallow places. Communications were slow, but the people of Roseburg knew that the boat was coming. It arrived at Roseburg on Sunday morning after church had begun, and the whistle started blowing. I remember hearing our pastor J. N. R. Bell say some ministers thought that the people should stay for the sermons, but he himself grabbed his hat and was the leader from the church."

Excitement ran high along the river. Whole communities turned out to watch the vessel's progress. The late Kearney Emmitt of Coles Valley, then a boy of around ten years, nearly ran himself breathless trying to keep abreast of the craft as it passed his father's farm. C. H. Maupin of Kellogg recalled that the trip upriver was slow, but the downriver passage was exceedingly fast. He was plowing in a field next to the river when the boat rounded a bend about a mile above his place, and before he realized it the craft was out of sight one-half mile below. Miss Mary Wells wrote in her memoirs that the *Swan*, on its return trip, tied up for the night at Mills' Ferry, and a dance was held aboard to celebrate the occasion.

Difficulties Encountered

The *Swan* was reportedly built by Hiram Doncaster in a small shipyard across the river from Gardiner, in 1869. Randall V. Mills, in *Sternwheelers up the Columbia*, gives no dimensions of the craft other than it was rated at 131 tons, a wooden-hulled shallow draft sternwheeler, powered by a pair of horizontal steam engines. The original owner was the *Umpqua Steam Navigation Company*.

The historic vessel made its first attempt to ascend the river in January 1870. She met with some difficulty about one mile above Scottsburg when her rudders were broken by striking a submerged rock. The boat was tied to a tree on the bank while the crew made repairs, which took a full day. The voyage continued to Mills' Ferry, now the site of the Esther Wells bridge, six miles southeast of Elkton. Here her boilers were giving trouble, and as the water was getting low, the captain took the craft back to Gardiner and postponed the voyage three weeks.

According to Mills, a second start was made on February 10, and the voyage was completed in eleven days; however, other sources say fourteen. When the *Swan* arrived at Roseburg, the water level dropped and stranded the boat on a sand bar for two days; then the river rose and floated the vessel free. Captain Haun had the distinction of being the only man to navigate successfully a vessel the size of the *Swan* from Scottsburg to Roseburg under its own power. He reported to his employers that the expenditure of a few hundred dollars to clear the channel would enable a craft the size of the *Swan* to pass the rapids except in seasons of very low water.

Public Interest Aroused

The navigation company began immediately to form future plans for continued operation. It retained the services of Captain Haun to supervise the construction of a special craft which was supposed to have features incorporated in its hull to meet the difficulties encountered in navigating swift water. This craft was the *Enterprise*; its estimated cost was $8,000.

Public interest in the venture was voiced by the *Roseburg Plaindealer* in 1871, which declared: "A little improvement in navigation is more apparent than real. By confining the water to one channel by means of blasting and wing dams, the estimated cost for improvement would be about $75,000." George H. Williams, then senator from Oregon, introduced a bill in Congress for this amount in January 1871, but it failed to pass.

Meanwhile, two officials from the United States Corps of Engineers, Colonel Williams and Lieutenant Herren, had been detailed to make a survey of the river to ascertain its navigability. They reported that the river could be made navigable seven months of the year, with a depth of four feet at low water, for about $22,000; also that a steamer could carry freight to Roseburg for twenty dollars per ton, and the annual saving in freight would compensate the expenditure of improvement. Upon this recommendation, Congress authorized an appropriation of $22,600. The fund was made available and a contract was let for removing obstructions from the most dangerous rapids; W. B. Clarke of Millwood was awarded the job. The work was carried out and Clarke was paid $14,000. So far as known, the balance of the grant has never been drawn. At an interview in 1960, Rush R. Clarke, son of W. B., confirmed that his father did this work, but could not name the amount of money involved. Walter Threlkeld, of Milwaukie, Oregon (ninety-three years old November 1, 1966) remembered when Mr. Clarke did some blasting in the channel of the Umpqua in front of his old home just below the Bureau of Land Management access bridge at Tyee, about ten miles below Millwood.

The Oregon and California Railroad

In March 1871, the *Roseburg Plaindealer* stated: "We are confident that before two years have passed, Roseburg will have steam communication with the coast seven months in the year.

Robert Minter

Gardiner, "The White City," as it appeared in 1914, looking east from Leeds Island.

Representatives of three pioneer families. Center is Mrs. Minnie Sagaberd Graham, born in Bolt Hogan, Germany, in 1868. She came to the Umpqua country with her parents in 1872, and celebrated her ninety-seventh birthday anniversary on October 12, 1965. On her right is Mrs. Agnes Warren, granddaughter of Captain Thomas Elliott, who moved his family to the Gardiner area in April 1865. On her left is Mrs. Elizabeth Pyritz Dolan, who came to the Scholfield-Smith River area with her parents in 1874. Standing is Mrs. Katherine Graham Gilbert, daughter of Mrs. Minnie Graham.

"Battle Rock" Port Orford in Curry County, where Cyrus Hedden and eight companions with-stood a ten-day siege by the Rogue River Indians in June 1851.

The boat landing at Scottsburg around 1906. The steamboat appears to be the *Juno* The gas boat, *Comet*, belonged to Jacob A. Sawyers. The hull of the old *Bully Washington* the first steamboat to appear on the Umpqua River (1853) lies buried in the silt at the bas of the wharf.

Farmers! Plant Grain!" Before two years had passed, the *Plaindealer* was boosting the Oregon and California Railroad. Nevertheless, the navigation company went ahead with their plans, and a freight schedule was worked out. Rates from Gardiner to Scottsburg were three dollars per ton; to Calapooia, ten dollars; to landings above, fourteen dollars; downriver rates were one half the upriver cost.

So far, success seemed assured. In February 1871, the *Enterprise* started on her maiden voyage and ascended the river to Sawyers Rapids, which she could not navigate because of low water. The navigation company then disposed of its cargo there, returned to Scottsburg, and no further attempt was made to navigate the Umpqua above tidewater for commercial purposes.

"Where Do Old Boats Go?"

As to the fate of the *Swan* and *Enterprise*, the most complete report, furnished by George B. Abdill of Roseburg, is probably found in the personal memoirs left by J. H. Dixon: "I got into a sawmill at Coles Valley which I ran for two years, selling it out and getting into the steamboat business. This boat (*Swan*) had come up the river to Roseburg. We had opposition as there was business for only one boat. I succeeded in merging the companies (evidently meaning the navigation company and its boat *Enterprise*), running one boat (*Swan*) to Coos Bay, disposing of it for half what it cost, running the other boat (*Enterprise*). We were fast getting on our feet when the Oregon-California Railroad came to the valley and took our business. Then we had a boat and no business. We sold the *Enterprise* to the People's Transportation Company of Portland, and they wrecked her on the Umpqua bar. (February 20, 1873) They took the machinery out and built the *Beaver* with it."

When the writer interviewed the late John Sawyers, son of Jacob A. Sawyers, in 1962, John said that Henry Wade, pilot on the *Swan*, was captain on the *Enterprise* on her maiden voyage to Sawyers Rapids, fourteen miles above Scottsburg, but could not recall the names of the crew. Other sources name Godfrey

Seymour as engineer, assisted by William Wade; and state that
Peter Nelson, Robert Hood, a Mr. Taylor, and Ned Breen were
deck hands. As these men were all citizens of Gardiner at that
time, it might explain the variations in examined records. The
size of the *Enterprise*, reported 270 tons rating (nearly twice that
of the *Swan*), may have been the reason for her failure to navigate the Sawyers Rapids.

John Hedden, Business Man

After steamboating on the Umpqua and Smith rivers for five
years, John Hedden decided to polish up his education. For sev-
eral years he attended the old Umpqua Academy, founded by
Dr. James H. Wilbur, and, in 1876-77, attended the National
Business College at Portland. Upon graduation he returned to
Scottsburg and went into partnership with his father, Cyrus
Hedden, and for more than forty years directed the financial end
of the business.

Hedden's store was reported to carry everything from pins to
threshing machines. This was literally true. Cyrus Hedden ordered the first threshing machine to come to the lower Umpqua
basin for John A. Fryer; it came around the Horn. The exact
date was not learned, but it was known to be in use in the late
1850s. The old separator found its way to the Henry Ford
Museum near Detroit, Michigan. Thomas Higginbothom, its
last owner, received $400 for the ancient relic.

In May, 1966, the writer was browsing around among the
merchandise carried by the store's founder, when he saw a package of small hat pins that had been in stock when Cyrus Hedden
was active in the business. The package cover stated they were
manufactured in Germany and were of the finest steel.

One of the most unusual lines of merchandise carried was
patent medicines, still on display for show purposes only. Emma
Hedden, the present owner, said that a collector had offered as
much as $100 for a single item. For the sake of curiosity, a list
was made of the different kinds of "sure cures" on exhibit. The

list discloses: "Colt's Emulsion, 'Good for Everything'; Cod Liver Oil with lime and soda; Ayer's Sarsaparilla; Celery Compound; Foley's Kidney Cure; Tanalac, a 'Splendid Tonic'; Dr. Murphy's Tonic; Mrs. Wilson's Soothing Syrup; Parker's Hair Balsam; Uncle Sam's Horse Liniment; Lydia E. Pinkham's Vegetable Compound; Dr. Pierce's Favorite Prescription & Gold Medical Discovery; Kennedy's Laxative Cough Syrup; Wells and Richardson's Dandelion Butter Color." All of these wonderful remedies bore "revenue stamps" issued to Cyrus Hedden and Son.

One showcase contains a violin given to Emma Hedden by Horace J. Meade, the millwright who installed the machinery in Gardiner's first sawmill in 1858. Beside the showcase, in the midst of modern merchandise, is a home-made cradle in which John had spent many happy hours.

Consultant and Banker

Ranchers for miles around depended on John to see them through the lean years. In days when cash was scarce, he was their bulwark between success and failure. Like his father, he accepted produce at the prevailing prices; if the price went up before the commodity was shipped to the wholesale house, the customer received the benefit — if the price went down, John stood the loss.

When sailing vessels came up the river to Scottsburg for their cargoes of piling and lumber, they usually carried flour, sugar, or salt for ballast, but some just carried rocks. The commodities were sold to the merchants free of freight charges. When John received goods in this manner, he continued a custom introduced by his father, in passing on the saving to his customers. Had John been a greedy man, the settlers of the lower valley would have been at his mercy because he had no competition that really counted.

John Hedden never refused assistance if the case merited it. If he owed a man, he expected to pay him and required the same courtesy of those that owed him. In 1905, when the Southern

Pacific Company started to build a branch railroad to Coos Bay via Drain, Elkton, and Scottsburg, he acted as banker, cashing pay checks for the construction gangs. At that time he carried thousands of dollars in gold and bills on his person. And, he had a keen sense of real estate values. Over the years he acquired several valuable farms; most if not all are still owned and operated by members of the Hedden family. The worth of these farms today verifies his good judgment.

As an Entertainer

Had John chosen a literary career, he might have rivaled Mark Twain in humor and satire. Hedden's Store served as a sort of clubhouse where the town's male population gathered to discuss the issues of the day and tell jokes, whichever seemed the order of the evening. John was always ready to listen to the jokes of others but could take the trick when it came his turn. He was a gifted entertainer but, like most persons, there were select cronies with whom he liked to jest. A sample of his humor was found in an old scrapbook belonging to Mrs. Charles G. Henderer of Elkton. In it was a letter he had written (undated) to "Uncle Job" Hatfield, extending him an invitation to join the Scottsburg band:

Dear Uncle Job:

We are about to start a band and want you to join us. Weatherly has ordered a floot, $125. I have ordered a trumbone, $280. Now we want you to have a big brass horn in "B" flat. You can get one for $175 and I think Aunt Mary (Burchard) told me she wanted to get a piano, can get one for $175, bird's-eye maple and rosewood. Now come in and see the musical instruments and you will say the book man is not in it with them. Think you could trade your old Kentucky rifle for an organ?

The candidate for circuit judge is here tonight, he is not pritty but they say all ugly people are good so he must be first class. If the ugliest man in town was going to be hung I would not have to take to the brush as long as he was here. . .

Another letter [also undated] was found in the old book, but it was along scientific (?) lines. It read:

Dear Uncle Job:

I have been asked by O. L. Williams, the editor of the *Gardiner Gazette*, to have you send him the weather forecast for January, February, and March, based on your findings after examining the melt of a hog. I hear that you are going to butcher out your way next week. Please note carefully the position of the hog when it dies. If the tail points toward the westward there will be prevailing winds from that direction for the next three months. I hear that Thode Andrews has butchered a bull and from his findings there will be a hard winter. I am sure of this, anyway, for those who have to eat the bull.

Yours, JOHN.

It would be hard to evaluate the degree of influence that John wielded, but it is certain that his contribution to sound economy cannot be lightly brushed aside. He served his generation honestly and well, and died on October 20, 1941.

Emma Hedden

When John Hedden passed away, his oldest daughter, Emma, was the next to carry on the business that her grandfather had founded. The store is now in its fourth building but the business, like the old gray mare, "ain't what she used to be." It is not so important to community life as in former days.

Emma Hedden's father had been appointed postmaster at Scottsburg on May 25, 1882, and served in that capacity until February 12, 1915, when his daughter Emma was designated postmistress; this position she held for forty-five years until her retirement in 1960.

Besides her duties as postmistress, she assisted her father in the store by keeping books and waiting on customers. By 1933, John was close to eighty years old, when Emma assumed responsibility. The store over which Miss Hedden presides is unique, to say the least. This uniqueness is in the way she displays her merchandise. The stock consists of staple groceries, some confections, stationery, school supplies, a limited variety of dry goods, costume jewelry, and novelties much the same as found in small neighborhood stores. Her store furniture—tables, shelves, and showcases—are leftovers from former days, lending a quaint mixture of yesterday with today.

Echoes from the Past

A grandfather clock, nearly eight feet tall, keeps watch over a barrel butter churn and a hand coffee mill, wall telephones, and a child's toy wood-burning stove. This odd assembly is mixed in with items which may be found in any city supermarket. The grandfather clock is reported to be 400 years old, and it looks it. It had belonged to a Captain Darling, a lighthouse keeper called the "Patron Saint" of Scotland. Members of the Darling clan brought it to early Scottsburg. It passed to the Rule family, relatives of the Darlings, in 1800. A painting in the right-hand corner of its square face represents the colonies of Great Britain. There is the likeness of a graceful woman and an anchor in the foreground; the background shows a full-rigged ship with the caption, "Great Britain, Mistress of the Sea." Miss Hedden bought the clock from a relative, Mrs. D. L. Rule of Elkton.

Other heirlooms share equally quaint surroundings. A horse collar and an old grain cradle, their uses unknown to many, hang on the wall together with barley forks, crosscut saws, cant hooks, and other items familiar only to the store's former patrons. This apparently careless display has its advantages—tourists who visit this pioneer place of business invariably buy some item just so they can say, "I bought this at Hedden's Store in Scottsburg."

The counter over which the day's business is transacted is a museum in its own right. Pigeonholes and drawers literally bulge with records of the early settlement area; there are even the books kept by the store's founder. And pictures of pioneer citizens have their own honored place among these records of the past.

With all this antique atmosphere, though, the present Hedden's store lacks the old-time aroma. It is remembered as a place of smells; they were fairly nudging one another, sometimes knocking each other down. There was cigar smoke, contending with the hearth of the "Bonanza" heating stove, which provided tobacco-chewers with a target — and both carried a knock-out punch. Shelves of current brands of pepper, cinnamon, cloves, sage, allspice, with their individual containers, added color and flavor.

In the storeroom in the rear, wooden syrup buckets, vinegar barrels, kerosene containers, binding twine, new harness, and coal tar, all blended their individual odors to make the place "smell just like Hedden's Store." The writer got his first pair of rubber boots there when the store was in its second building; also schoolbooks. The books carried the Hedden hallmark for months. When the writer was attending classes at the Hedden Bluff school in 1904, he used to let his schoolmates smell his books—they liked the smell of "Hedden's Store."

An Anniversary Observed

In 1950, Scottsburg staged a centennial ninety-nine years after Cyrus Hedden established his store. It was estimated that between thirteen and fourteen hundred people took part in the festivities, and dignitaries from all over Douglas County were present. A parade was put on by the participants, many of whom were dressed in costumes that had been worn by their ancestors. Some of the garments were over one hundred years old. A pioneer exhibit was set up in the windows of Miss Hedden's store and in the community church, displaying items reminiscent of the early history of Scottsburg.

Hedden's Store, in that historic town at the gateway to the Umpqua Valley, calls to mind the early settlers who were served by its founders, a pioneer family who helped to lay the foundations for law and order in old Umpqua and Douglas counties. Their store, like a venerable patriarch, sits at the entrance of the valley, happy and contented with the memories of bygone days.

CHAPTER VIII

Elkton

When the Umpqua Land Company was exploring possible sites for the establishment of towns, it selected one where old Indian trails converged at the mouth of Elk Creek (River); here the future town of Elkton was located. The Hudson's Bay "Fort Umpqua" was its neighbor across the river.

When Umpqua County was organized in 1851, Elkton was named county seat. This location was on the property of James F. Levins, who had arrived in Oregon from Illinois in 1850 and taken a 640-acre donation claim almost equally divided by Elk Creek. His claim embraced the townsite on the north side of the stream. Levins donated to the new county 160 acres for its specific use, but the gift was not officially accepted; it was not until the Levins property passed to other owners that the town of Elkton was surveyed and platted. However, the community had a postoffice designated as Elkton, established on September 26, 1851, with David Wells as postmaster. The settlement of this historic area kept pace with other towns and communities in the Umpqua basin.

The Hudson's Bay Company had already occupied this area as early as 1836, establishing a trading post which was called "Fort Umpqua." This date has been verified from biographical data of William Glen Rae, son-in-law of McLoughlin. Quoting *The Umpqua Trapper*, Volume II, November 1, 1966:

> "After attending the building of a new fort in the Umpqua country in the summer of 1836, Rae was appointed to the management of the Kootenay post for the fur trading season of 1836-37."

This fort was constructed on the west side of the Umpqua near the confluence of Elk Creek with the Umpqua River. The area seemed to have had particular significance for the early explorers; in their diaries, many used it as a landmark to describe their location in the Umpqua country. Among them were John Bernie, a Hudson's Bay employee who was in the area in 1818; and David Douglas, the English botanist, who explored the area between 1828 and 1832. In May 1845, Lieutenants Henry J. Warre and M. Vavasour—British Royal Marines who were sent out by the British Government to check possible defense of the Northwest — visited Fort Umpqua. Their report noted: "Fort Umpqua comprises 640 acres, of which fifty acres are under cultivation, forty-six horses, sixty-four cattle, forty hogs, representing a total value of 2,020 pounds sterling."

Captain A. Lyman, of the *Samuel Roberts*, visited the fort in 1850; his description is more detailed:

". . . An old Frenchman, M. Gagnier, treated us with great politeness. I took a tramp to see the country and was well paid. From the top of a hill which I ascended I got a magnificent view, the scenery was truly picturesque. The fort is built of sticks (or logs) set on end, or what is called a stockade. Within the enclosure are two or three log houses. There was formerly a great business carried on here in furs with the Indians, but at present it don't amount to much.

"Mr. Gagnier is assisted by one white man and a few Kanakas [Hawaiians] and Indians. He cultivates about fifty acres of land, wheat, corn, potatoes, and most kinds of garden vegetables. Mr. Gagnier has an Indian wife and one son."

After the coming of the first wave of immigrants to the area, W. W. Chapman leased the fort property from Hudson's Bay chief factor, Peter Skene Ogden, through the years of 1853-56. It was hoped that by renting the property to an American, the practice of the shooting of their cattle by settlers could be controlled. Following Chapman's lease, Israel T. Nicklin gained possession of the land by redemption on October 14, 1856; his parents, John and Sarah Nicklin, inherited the claim and sold it to

Thomas Chapman on August 11, 1857. Chapman sold to Robert M. Hutchinson on December 9, 1857, with county records listing the transaction as including "The fort site and improvements." Hutchinson sold, on April 30, 1868, to Henry Beckley and John L. Smith. Later Smith sold his interest to Beckley, and the fort site is still in the Beckley family.

The Hancocks

The first white settlers in the Elkton area were William and Elizabeth Hancock, who were natives of Lanchestershire, England. After their marriage they had moved to Australia, where they lived for nine years before coming to America. They arrived in San Francisco on July 4, 1850, took passage to Scottsburg in the late summer, and arrived there in early December. Traveling by horseback over the old pack trail, they proceeded to Elkton, the new Umpqua Land Company townsite at the mouth of Elk Creek. They took a donation land claim of 640 acres, two miles east of Elkton, where three generations of their descendants have since lived. That portion of the old homestead where William and Elizabeth Hancock built their first house is still owned by one of their descendants.

The Wells Clan

The three Wells brothers, Ira, Dr. Daniel, and William W., came to the Oregon Territory with the 1847 immigration over the southern route opened by Applegate and Scott the previous year. Ira and his wife, the former Anna Elizabeth Chandler, spent the winter with the Eugene Skinner family in the Willamette Valley. Mrs. Wells was a native of Germany, born on the Mayan River in Prussia, July 22, 1822. She came to America with her parents at the age of sixteen and settled in Illinois where she met and married Ira.

In the spring of 1848, Ira took a donation claim near present Cottage Grove. In 1849, the hostile attitude of the Indians prompted him to move his family to Scotts Valley. In the fall of

1850, Ira had selected donation claim No. 56, 640 acres, on the Umpqua River one mile south of Fort Umpqua, on the opposite side of the river. In the spring of 1851, he moved his wife and four children to the land on which he reared a large family.

Ira's youngest son merits mention. Francis Franklin Wells, born on the old homestead, November 8, 1859, was a progressive farmer. He brought the first steam-powered threshing outfit to the lower valley, had the first binder, the first cream separator, and the first registered stock in the Elkton area.

Dr. Daniel Wells selected claim No. 38, containing 640.72 acres, two miles northwest of Fort Umpqua on the north side of the Umpqua. Seven years later he sold his claim to Daniel M. Stearns and bought a portion of the Edward Spicer place four miles east of Scottsburg, at what is now Green Acres at Wells Creek. As a physician, he decided he should be near the center of the settlements to better serve those who might need medical care. Dr. Wells was killed by a horse near The Dalles in 1864, and was survived by his wife and four children.

George Wells, son of Dr. Daniel, was born on the original homestead on July 14, 1851, the first white male child born in that section of Umpqua County. Anna Augusta Sawyers, daughter of Andrew Sawyers, born December 25, 1850, was the first white girl baby born in the lower Umpqua Valley. Captain George L. Snelling presented each with a silver cup. George spent most of his eighty-odd years around Elkton. He recalled that he was an eye witness to the assassination of General E. R. S. Canby by Captain Jack's Modoc warriors in 1874. The general was shot from ambush as he was carrying out a mission under a flag of truce. Young Wells, a mule skinner in the pack train detail, secretly watched the proceedings and in this manner witnessed the ambush.

George Wells and George Dimmick were companions on a cougar hunt in the early 1880s. As told by Wells, they had treed a cat and Dimmick shot at it, but only succeeded in wounding the animal. The cougar jumped from the tree and attacked them. Dimmick became excited and jammed his repeating rifle trying to reload. Wells, with presence of mind, grabbed the big cat's tail and took a few turns around a small tree while Dimmick beat it to death with the rifle. And, said Wells, "If you don't believe it I can take you and show you the tree."

William W. Wells chose a location about one and one-half miles northwest and on the same side of the river from Fort Umpqua; claim No. 41, containing 321.35 acres. William was a lawyer and took an active interest in public affairs after the organization of Umpqua County. He taught the first session of school held in the Elkton community; it was conducted at the home of his brother Ira. His only textbook was a blue-backed Webster speller. All the children of the community were invited to attend. William also became the first school superintendent of Douglas County after its merger with Umpqua County. His land holdings were purchased by Charles G. Henderer in 1856, and became a part of the late John Henderer estate.

Charles G. Henderer, Sr.

Another pioneer taking a circuitous route from his birthplace to the Umpqua Valley was Charles G. Henderer, a native of Bavaria, Germany. Mr. Henderer entered the United States by way of New Orleans in 1847. He worked on the levees or at whatever job was available. Eventually making his way to Independence, Missouri, he engaged in the carpenter trade there.

In 1849, he went to California where he had success in mining. In 1850-51, he came to Oregon and located a donation land claim about three miles west of Elkton, approximately one mile below the claim of Dr. Daniel Wells. He sold this claim to Henry G. Brown in 1856 and bought the claims of William W. Wells, Edward Griffin, and William Hilbert; these were directly across the river and a little southeast of his old claim. The three farms gave him approximately 926 acres.

In 1858, Henderer returned to Independence, Missouri, and married Emmaline F. Meador, November 28 of that same year. On May 4, 1859, they started for Oregon. They took the Applegate-Scott route through southern Oregon, then the old military road through Mehl Canyon to the Krumm donation claim at Hedden Bluff (which was then the Cyrus Hedden property). Camping there overnight, they arrived at their new home on September 9.

Four children were born to them: Mrs. Caroline Safley, Mrs. Fannie Anna (John) Hedden, Charles M., and John Job. John married Nettie Traylor, July 2, 1890; she was a daughter of James Traylor, an early pioneer.

After the death of his father in 1898, John J. purchased the interests of the other heirs and so became the sole owner of the home place. John and Nettie Henderer were the parents of seven children, only three of whom survive at the present time: Mrs. Arthur (Fannie) Clemo, Mrs. Lawrence (Una) Smith, and Mrs. Carrie Ross. Fannie and Una reside on portions of the old home place and Carrie Ross lives several miles west of Drain.

Henry Beckley

Henry Beckley, a native of Indiana, arrived in the vicinity around 1859. Miss Mary Wells, in her memoirs, said he came to Oregon with the Hall party, (the Hall party came over the southern route) along with four brothers by the name of Smith, one being John L., who later was associated with Beckley in several business enterprises around Elkton.

Elkton did not gain the stature of a surveyed town until 1878, when Beckley, John L. Smith, Daniel Stearns, Harrison B. Hart, and Levi Beckley formed a company and platted and officially recorded a townsite. At that time Elkton, as a town, had a population of 350, some of whom were the family of Henry and Mary Beckley; they had ten children: seven sons and three daughters.

Henry Beckley was elected state representative from Douglas County in 1898. He died from a heart attack on September 17 of that year, on his way to Salem to take his seat in the September term. Mrs. Beckley died on May 12, 1921; both are interred in a surface vault in the family plot in the Elkton Cemetery.

Henry G. Brown

Another pioneer of the Umpqua Valley chose a rather roundabout way to reach Oregon. Henry G. Brown was born in Coos
County, New Hampshire, January 15, 1833. As a young man, he
took passage from an unnamed port on the east coast to the
eastern side of the Isthmus of Panama (before the canal). Carrying his possessions on his back, he walked across the isthmus to
a port on the west coast to take passage again, this time to San
Francisco. Many young men of his day were not daunted by
hiking the forty-two miles with a pack on their backs. Then, instead of entering Oregon by boat, he traveled up through the
Sacramento Valley and over the Siskiyou Mountains through
southern Oregon to Scottsburg, where he arrived in 1851.

Brown later went into the mercantile business with four other
men; the concern was called Brown, Drum and Company. He
married Patricia Stearns, whose brother, Daniel M. Stearns, was
a member of the firm. After this company was dissolved he operated a pack train over the pack trail that was opened to Oakland to connect with the California Trail leading into southern
Oregon.

In 1856, he took a homestead of 160 acres four miles west of
Elkton. That same year he bought the adjoining Charles G.
Henderer donation land claim of 163 acres, eventually increasing
his land holdings to 1,600 acres. As an elected state representative on the Republican ticket in 1882, it is said that he served
with distinction. He was the father of five children: Samuel H.,
Hattie S., Helen M., Francis Caroline, and Martha. Upon his
death his son, Samuel H. Brown, took over the management of
the farm, where he resided until his death. Two of his children,
Grace Brown Agee and Henry Brown, became co-owners of the
old home. The estate was settled so that each inherited approximately 800 acres, Grace receiving as her portion, the old home-
site. Henry's part included his present home on Paradise Creek
at the foot of "Big Hill," about nine miles below Elkton. In 1956,

the Oregon Historical Society presented Mrs. Grace Brown Agee with a certificate designating the Brown farm as a century farm.

The Haines Clan

By 1863, Elkton had developed into quite a little village; new families were coming in; one of these was the Haines clan, headed by Alfred Haines the First. His twin sons, Joseph A. and William W., had preceded their father to Oregon by eleven years. They had come to Scottsburg in 1851, but had later gone on to Curry County.

Alfred the First was a native of New Jersey, born in 1803. His first wife, a Miss Luper, died leaving three children besides the twins: James, Susan, and Rebecca. On December 24, 1840, he married Sarah Dixon and, in 1862, he crossed the plains by mule team, coming to Scottsburg over the southern route and via the military road from Wilbur. He moved to Elkton that same year and bought 160 acres two miles southeast of town for the consideration of $400; it was the old Stuttard place. (The spelling is given in Government Donation Land Claim Records.) Mr. Haines later bought seventy-two acres for which he paid one dollar per acre at a forced sale.

Alfred and his wife had a large family: Caroline, Lewis C., James A., Mary E., Alfred Benton the Second, Sarah, Josephine C., Edward E. "Ed," and Jonathan C. Seven of these were of school age at the time of their arrival in the Elkton area. Alfred the First lived on this property until he died in 1888. His widow capably managed the farm.

Edward E. Haines, son of Alfred the First, was born on the old homestead in 1862. He began his business career at eighteen years of age by purchasing a stage line between Drain and Scottsburg, which he operated four years. He had five children by his first wife, Mary Butler, daughter of Rufus Butler; they were Maude, Florence, Homer, Walter; and twins, Ruth and Ruby. Afterwards Edward and his wife were divorced and "Ed" married Alice Adelaide McNeil; their children were Lydia, Harry,

Lawrence, Opal, E. Melvin, and Aleene Alice. More will be said later concerning Ed's activity in the lower Umpqua Valley.

Alfred Benton Haines, older brother of Ed, was born in Whiteside County, Illinois, in 1844. He came to Oregon with his parents in 1862. In 1864 he enlisted in Company K, 1st Infantry, Oregon Volunteers, and served with his regiment in the Indian uprisings; he also served as Indian Agent on the Klamath Reservation for two years. Mr. Haines was the fifth postmaster at Elkton from 1871 to 1876. In 1873, he married Martha Ransom, daughter of William Clark Ransom. After his marriage he bought the old farmstead, where he carried on the Haines tradition of raising large families. His children were Benton Alfred the Third, Mabel, Mildred, Nannie, Ned or J. E., Blaine, Ivan, Oliver, Agnes, Edith, Dorothy, and Jean.

With such prolific families as the Haines's, it would be impossible to bring all their descendants down to the present generation, nor is it the purpose of this manuscript to do so; but an exception is made: Josephine Haines Thornton, daughter of Alfred Haines the First, has a daughter, Mrs. Catherine Gray of Grants Pass, Oregon, who celebrated her 100th birthday anniversary on December 22, 1966, and that deserves space in any manuscript. This information was furnished by Mrs. Josephine Haines Bloodgood, of Portland, who is a grandniece and namesake of Mrs. Josephine Haines Thornton. Mrs. Bloodgood made an elaborate birthday cake for Mrs. Gray, and had it flown to the rest home in Grants Pass where Mrs. Gray resides.

Eustace Schad

Any history about Elkton would not be complete without mentioning Eustace Schad—he was as much a part of the Elkton community as the town itself. Born in Hamburg, Germany, in 1848, he came to America at the age of eleven years, with his brother Philip, eleven years his senior. Philip took a homestead in Mehl Canyon, along Mehl Creek, which meandered through small meadows, making a nice little farm—but at that time quite isolated from the settlement at Kellogg two miles away.

Philip was accidentally killed in 1868, but Eustace continued to operate the place. Meanwhile, he acquired a neighbor: his sister Gertrude and her husband, Amos Teal. Their homestead joined Schad's on the north. Eustace married Sarah Levins, daughter of James F. Levins, and they moved on to his father-in-law's place on Elk Creek in 1873. For thirty years he grew prunes, raised grain, and kept a small band of sheep and a few cows, hauling his grain to market at Scottsburg, seventeen miles distant.

In 1900, Schad was awarded the mail-carrying contract on the Oakland-Elkton route, which service he performed for eight years. He stated with pride that neither he nor his son Elmer, who relieved him occasionally, had once in those eight years failed to get the mail through to Oakland on time. This indeed was remarkable considering the condition of the road during the winter months, the trip being twenty-seven miles each way, six days a week. During good weather Schad used a light wagon drawn by "Pansy" and "Dolly," two faithful sorrel mares. He endeared himself to his patrons with his ever-obliging services. Eustace died on January 1, 1916.

Anthony Binder

Another pioneer family which contributed to the development of the Elkton community was that of Anthony Binder. He was a native of France, coming to America at the age of sixteen. In early life he was listed as a stonemason. Hannah Grabers, who became his wife, immigrated to America from Germany with her brother when she was fifteen years old. The two settled in Iowa, where she met and married Anthony Binder. They lived near Montgomery, Iowa, for a number of years, where their oldest son Charles was born in 1863. In 1882 they came to Oregon and purchased the former Daniel Wells donation claim from Daniel M. Stearns, who had increased his holding to 1,240 acres. Binder gradually increased it to 1,600 acres.

Anthony and Hannah Binder had seven children: Charles, Mary, Joseph, Amelea, John, George, and Frank. When their father retired, Charles and Frank purchased the home place in partnership, and it continued to be farmed, by the first and second generations, for some eighty years. The writer has a vivid recollection of Anthony Binder after his retirement. When rather a young lad, he had the privilege of eating the noon meal at the Binder home. Anthony Binder was then an elderly gentleman with a long white beard, sitting in front of the fireplace, smoking an unusually long-stemmed pipe.

Anthony's son John re-activated the old Elkton gristmill in 1901, and operated it for several years. He made a good grade of soft wheat flour under the trade name of "Pride of Elkton," which retailed at one cent per pound. Several others have operated the mill through the years; Gilbert Binder, John's son, was the last to run the business, which was closed down in 1924.

Nels Rydell—Blacksmith

The Scandinavian countries contributed to the personnel of the Umpqua country in the persons of Nels and Ida Pearson Rydell. While both arrived in the United States from Sweden in 1876, they apparently had no former acquaintance until they met in Chicago, Illinois; here they were married. Nels worked in an iron foundry for six years before coming to Oregon, in 1882, and taking a homestead on the summit of Hancock Mountain; the old pack trail and stage road passed by the house.

"Paddy," as Nels was called by hosts of friends, moved his family to Elkton in 1895, to establish a blacksmith shop, at which trade he was a master craftsman. He owned the first gasoline engine to come to Elkton, a Mitchel, Lewis, and Staver, three-horsepower. This engine was used to operate his drill press and other shop tools. As a byline he kept a feed stable and a few horses which he hired out occasionally.

The Rydells celebrated their golden wedding anniversary on July 20, 1926, with many descendants of early pioneer families attending, dressed in costumes of that period. The Rydells were the parents of three sons: Walter, Clyde, and Chester, each of whom became a respected citizen of Douglas County. Chester, who married Mona Cheever, great-granddaughter of Ira Wells, died suddenly from a heart attack in 1959. Clyde, former county road patrolman for the Elkton road district, is now retired and lives on his ranch—the former A. E. Rackliffe donation claim on Long Prairie. Walter chose merchandising. He, with W. W. Kent of Drain as an associate, established a general merchandise business in Elkton around 1915. He also worked in the Elkton Mercantile and Development Coop. In 1935 he was manager of the Western Auto Supply store in Bend, Oregon. When interviewed, in 1960, he had retired and was living with a daughter in Springfield.

Paddy retired from active life in 1936; he died in 1942, his wife having preceded him in 1934. She had been a devout Christian, but during the last months of her life she was bedfast and unable to attend church services. The writer sponsored a group of young people who came to her home and sang the old hymns of the church; one she always requested was "Abide With Me."

Charlie Weatherley

Ansel Weatherly came to Oregon in 1850, soon afterward marrying Sarah Wells, daughter of Ira Wells. Through some process of property transfer he gained possession of the Aseph Wells donation land claim. According to George W. Dimmick, Aseph Wells was Ira's father. It was on this land claim that Ansel and Sarah Weatherly reared their eight children. They were: Fred S., who married Esther McCollum, daughter of John Mc-Collum of Kellogg; Charlie, who never married; Mina, wife of David Higginbothom; Clara, wife of William Cheever; Phil, who married a Miss Jones of Oakland; Ella, who married Price Finley; Delbert, who married Ethel Traylor, daughter of Henry Traylor; and Pearl, who married a man named Branstetter, an engineer for the Southern Pacific Railway Company on the Shasta Division.

Members of this pioneer family lived their lives generally without fanfare but the life and vocation of one of the boys, Charlie, deserves special notice. Charlie was born on the old homestead in 1867. As an adult he was slight in stature, about five feet eight inches in height, weighed about 140 pounds, growing slightly bald as he grew older. He had a cheerful disposition and seldom ever displayed anger. His voice was rather high pitched and feminine, and this often made him the object of practical jokes.

One of these almost had a tragic ending. The Elkton Mercantile Company kept a limited selection of caskets on their second floor. One day Charlie and several of the local pranksters were ambling about the store and, either by accident or previously arranged plan, the party arrived in the casket department. Charlie was forced, or persuaded, to try one for size. The lid was closed over him and left down for a few minutes, but when the jokers opened the cover poor Charlie had passed out either from fright or lack of air. He quickly recovered, but it was difficult to say who was more shaken, Charlie or the jokers.

Charlie delighted in cooking; when the family was growing up, his sister Ella detested housework and would frequently change duties with him. In the early 1900s, Charlie decided to open an eating house. His talent for preparing plain food was almost unbelievable, and he was always immaculate in appearance. The Weatherly Eating House was soon made famous from Portland to San Francisco by his customers who were the "drummers" or traveling salesmen who passed through Elkton in the stage-coach days. The schedule of stages both ways, from Drain to Scottsburg, put them in Elkton around noon. Having dinner at Charlie's was hailed with enthusiasm by the passengers; prices were one dollar for traveling men and fifty cents for local customers. His menus varied from day to day, but whether the meat course was baked or boiled ham, fried chicken with country gravy, or stewed chicken with dumplings as light and white as new snow, it would be accompanied by mashed potatoes, fluffy as feathers.

The old-fashioned cruet stand decorated the center of the table, where the guests were served family style. Charlie did all the cooking, serving, and dishwashing and kept the premises spotless. He was not a politician or a successful financier, but he surely knew how to satisfy a hungry man's appetite. He never married, but dearly loved children. Around 1935-40, when a young couple separated, Charlie took their two small boys and cared for them as well as a mother could. Later their mother persuaded him to let her take one for a visit, and while with her the child ate some blue vitriol and died; this nearly broke Charlie's heart. Elkton lost a good citizen when he passed away in 1942.

School District No. 66 Established

In 1857, a school district was formed and a school board selected. A log schoolhouse was built on a parcel of ground donated by Ira Wells, located between his place and that of his father, Aseph Wells; it was 3½ miles south of present Elkton. The new district was numbered 66, and through the years scholars from as far away as Kellogg and Hedden Bluff attended classes in this building. William W. Wells taught the first term, followed by William H. Spencer; Anna, Dave, and Dan West, all children of Calvin B. West; L. L. Williams of the Indian battle on the Coquille River in 1851; John Marshall; Kitty Cartwright, daughter of Darius B. Cartwright, proprietor of the "Mountain House Hotel" (located along the Territorial Road near the present Lorane in Lane County); and Caroline Haines, daughter of Alfred Haines the First.

By 1872, the school-age population had increased to where it was necessary to provide a larger building. Arrangements were made with Mrs. Sarah Haines to use the vacant Thomas Stuttard house; this was also a log building and heated by a fireplace. William Wells taught the first term in this building. Some of the teachers who followed him were: Caroline Haines, Sarah and Anna Booth, and Peter P. Palmer.

Masonic Lodge No. 63 was given a charter in 1874 and was also meeting in the Stuttard house used by the school district. When this arrangement proved unsatisfactory, the Masons pooled their resources with those of the school board and a new two-story building was erected along the county road about one-half mile north of the little log building. The Masons met in the upper room until they built their own hall in Elkton. Around 1900, the old rough-lumber schoolhouse they helped to build was replaced by a nice frame building, which served the district for many years.

Anna Minter McCulloch taught in the new school building in District 66 in 1902. At the fiftieth wedding anniversary of Mr. and Mrs. Oliver Haines, September 17, 1961, Mrs. McCulloch was one of the many guests present. She was asked to stand and receive honor as their early teacher. All those present who had attended her classes stood with her—fifteen of her former pupils, all over sixty years of age.

In 1874, three new school districts were established. Elkton was Number 34, Hedden Bluff Number 86, and Kellogg Number 54. District 66, though greatly reduced in area, still retained its identity in the Wells-Haines community south of Elkton. The last schoolhouse built in this district was erected in the 1920s near the site of the little log building; the new building was referred to as the "Muddy Flat" school.

District 34 Established

The first school sessions in Elkton District 34 were held in 1878, in a small building on the main-traveled road through town. In 1895, a new two-story schoolhouse was built. Mrs. Anna Stark, daughter of James T. Cooper, was probably the first principal, as she taught there in 1896. This item appeared in the *Roseburg Review*, June 1897:

> "The first commencement of the public school at Elkton took place here June 25, which rendered the following program: Band music; Invocation, J. A. Smith; essay, "Idleness

Is the Rust of the Brain"; address, "The Sources of a Nation's Wealth," Roy Wells; song, "Starry Waves," Minnie and Meneta Belle; essay, Luella Hosington; declamation, "Cripple Ben," Ida Robison; song by the choir; address, "Memory," Frank Binder; instrumental music, Meneta Belle; Recitation, "The Old Sergeant," Sallie McGuire; band music; essay, "Things That Cost Nothing," Bessie Cully; Declamation, True Legion of Honor, Fannie Benedict; address and valedictory, Peter Nash Jr.; presentation of diplomas by G. W. Benedict; song, "Our School-boy Days"; choir; closing remarks by J. A. Smith.

"The above program was very interesting. The people should be thankful to Prof. W. Wright for his skillful energies in bringing our school to the front." (The article was signed, *Uno*.)

The Reverend John H. Mulkey, who supplied the Christian Church pulpit, was principal in 1900. Ella Roadman and Ray Henderson, both from Wilbur families, taught there in 1904. When the local districts consolidated into a union high school district in 1929, a fine unit was constructed a little below the main part of town and the first school buses began operating in District 34. In 1942, a new grade school unit was built one-half mile below town; this modern facility serves three times the territory as did old District 66.

After eighty-five years and serving four generations, the last term of school in District No. 66 closed in 1929; the building was razed and the lumber used for other purposes. It is notable that the first center of education was in the Elkton area; now, after more than a century, the Elkton community is back where it began—the educational center for the three districts was carved out of old District No. 66.

Growth of the Elkton Community

Though the Elkton location was designated as county seat in 1851, and a post office was established on the 26th of September of that same year, the area continued as just a rural community until 1878, when the site was surveyed and platted by a group of interested business men led by Henry Beckley. Thomas Levins was postmaster at that time. He was granted a license by the 1876 Douglas County Court to operate a grocery store. This was the first business venture in this community of 350 persons.

In 1879, Harrison B. Hart and George W. Dimmick opened a general store north of the sawmill. Later this business was purchased by C. W. Baker and Joseph Emery, who sold it in 1884 to Henry Beckley and J. W. Stark, Beckley later buying out Stark. After Beckley's death in 1898, his heirs operated it until 1899, when it was purchased by James G. Lyons. When Lyons died, around 1906, two of his older children, Mary and Max, operated the store a short time before closing the business.

Julia Wells' store (founding date not learned) was a competitor of all these general stores. Tom Bledsoe and Robert Hedden (no relation to the Scottsburg Heddens) bought out Mrs. Wells in 1906. About this time, or a little earlier, William Moore of Drain opened a general store. There were now more stores than Elkton and the surrounding community could support. In 1908-9, all these businesses were incorporated into a co-operative store, the Elkton Mercantile and Development Company, which had been promoted by Bledsoe and Hedden. Robert Hedden was appointed manager, with Mary Lyons and Walter Rydell assistants.

John Binder re-activated the old gristmill in 1901. Jess Schad operated a drugstore (date uncertain); Price Finley, a livery stable; Joe and Martha Robison, a hotel; and Mr. Robison ran a tin shop on the side. A church house was built by the Baptist denomination in 1885. A Mr. Hickethier, photographer from Drain, had a tent office during the summer; his pictures record many of the activities around Elkton during this period of its growth.

Dr. Cole, a physician with his office in his home, was replaced by a Dr. Gray around 1906-07; his office was also in his home, which was in the William Stark residence one-half mile from the main part of town, along the Scottsburg road. Dr. Gray filled his own prescriptions and according to his diagnoses, everyone had liver trouble, for which he dispensed a foul-tasting brown-colored liquid. He also pulled teeth. Dr. E. J. Wainscott, now a successful physician in Roseburg, started out in Elkton in 1904-05.

Sarah Wilburn had a candy shop and also sold "soda pop" in glass bottles—which had a cap held down by a wire spring. When the cap was removed, the customer had to be alert to get a drink before the pop fizzed out on the floor.

The stage line had a barn in Elkton, where relay horses were stabled. In the winter when the roads were muddy, the lead teams would be entirely covered with mud splashed on them by the wheel horses. When teams were changed, the incoming horses were forced to wade in the river until the mud was washed off, before it had time to dry. Horses working under these conditions developed what was called "mud fever," which caused the hair to fall off, the skin to crack, and sores to develop.

Several of the drivers during the stage-coach days were local men. Some of the earlier ones were: Jacob "Little Jake" Sawyers; Arthur Mack; Ed Patterson; Bob and Ed Grubbe; Bill Levins, and his son Charlie Levins. The youngest driver, and one of the last to make the schedules, was Alex Sawyers of Drain, who began driving when only twenty years of age. At this writing, he is the only one of the group living.

Proposed Railroad

Elkton almost had a railroad. The Oregon and California Railroad Company surveyed a proposed line from Drain to Coos Bay via Elkton and Scottsburg in 1885-86. Nothing was done toward construction until the summer of 1905. For some reason work was halted after about four miles of track was laid and considerable work had been done grading and two tunnel bores started.

The Whipple brothers, William and Lloyd N., from Mysillo, Connecticut, did the initial survey for the route. They had married sisters, Lilly and Allie Isabelle Greene. William married Lilly and Lloyd married Allie Isabelle. They moved their families to Oregon in 1887. William settled permanently at Ashland, Oregon, while Lloyd took a homestead three miles north of Drain. In 1893 Lloyd moved his family to Drain to give them educational advantages. Ten children were born to Lloyd and Allie Isabelle Whipple: Ralph William, Ernest George, Robert Lloyd, Dessie, Pearl, Carrie Bee, Nellie, Marjorie, and Hugh Glen. One of their son's name is not recalled. Lloyd N. Whipple died December 27, 1934; his wife, March 31, 1942. This pioneer family contributed much toward the development of the respective communities in which they made their homes.

Brass Band

Elkton even had a band. This news item appeared in the *Roseburg Review* in 1896: "Elkton supports a brass band. . . The members range in ages from 7 to 14 years, but all have ability and promise to be a credit to our little burg."

The social life of the Elkton community changed little over the years, until the advent of the automobile. People have come and gone; mostly gone, as the present population is less than half what it was in 1878.

CHAPTER IX

Winchester

The town of Winchester, about ten miles south of Sutherlin on Highway 99, was one of the townsites selected by the Umpqua Land Company in 1850. Its growth was less explosive than that of Scottsburg, but it later gained importance as the county seat of Douglas County when the latter was created in 1852.

The early history of the Winchester site appears in a letter written by Thomas Smith on June 5, 1908, at the request of George H. Himes, then curator of the Oregon Historical Society:

". . . Daniel Hasty located on the north Umpqua River in 1848 and built a small ferry boat with the expectation of a large emigration that fall which did not arrive, but it came in good play to cross gold seekers that fall, but the trouble was very few of the gold seekers had any money to pay their ferryage.

"John Aiken and Thomas Smith bought out Mr. Hasty after he had started for the California gold mines. We [Aiken and Smith] overtook him on Deer Creek (now Roseburg) and bought him out and returned and located in May 1849 and I have been a resident ever since. . ."

In the fall of 1850, Winchester, Paine and Company bought the ferry. After their purchase of the townsite, the land company employed Addison R. Flint to survey and lay out the town.

Flint was an accredited civil engineer who had been assisting in a railroad survey in Chile. Coming to San Francisco in 1849, he became associated with the Umpqua Land Company, an associate of Winchester, Paine and Company. In October 1850, he arrived in Scottsburg aboard the company's schooner, *Kate Heath.* He proceeded to Winchester where he made his home until 1858; then moved to Roseburg. There he continued in his profession, establishing section corners and boundaries, and laying out roads. He surveyed Roseburg for Aaron Rose in 1854 and also subdivided Scottsburg for Levi Scott. His name appears on many abstracts of title to properties in Douglas County. When county government was established, he was selected county clerk, and he was Winchester's first postmaster, appointed on November 3, 1851.

Flint was also helpful in establishing schools and religious institutions. The first school session at Winchester was conducted by a Mr. Eason in a lean-to under an oak tree on Thomas Smith's land. The first Sunday school there was held in Flint's house. Flint and Dr. Calvin C. Reed assisted Benjamin J. Grubbe in organizing a Sunday school at Bunton's Gap, three miles north of Winchester. And Flint was the second principal of old Umpqua Academy, located at Wilbur about five miles from Winchester; he was also on the Academy's first board of trustees.

Dr. Calvin C. Reed, M.D.

Dr. Reed spent only five years of his life in Douglas County but he left a lasting impression on society in the upper Umpqua Valley. He and his wife, the former Almira Brown, crossed the plains in 1850. Mrs. Reed drove a specially built wagon. One of her horses died along the road and was replaced by a cow; with this mixed team she crossed the Cascade Range over the Barlow Route. Traveling down the west slope, her remaining horse fell over a bluff and was killed. A few hours after the incident Mrs. Reed gave birth to a daughter, whom she called Bianca. Eighty-five years later, in 1935, Bianca Reed Hill was queen mother at the Eugene Sunset Trail Pageant. She led the parade, riding in the same wagon in which she was born.

When Dr. Reed arrived in Oregon, he settled at Winchester and, in 1851, built the first gristmill in that part of the Umpqua basin. It was situated about one and one-half miles above the present power dam. Its site may be identified by the angle of the old millrace, which is still in evidence.

The doctor's three sons had learned flour-making in Missouri. When they finally decided to move to Oregon, their millstones were shipped ahead around the Horn and were waiting on the wharf at Scottsburg when they arrived. The stones, three feet across and from eight to ten inches thick, were packed to the site by mules, each stone slung on poles between the animals. As yet there was only a pack trail from Scottsburg, which connected with the California Trail at Bunton's Gap, about three miles north of Winchester. Dr. Reed died in 1855 from over-exertion in rescuing an employee who had fallen into his millpond.

The mill was washed away by the high water in 1861 and was never rebuilt. The stones lay in about twenty feet of water near the old site until 1947, when a motel owner at Winchester salvaged them and installed one on either side of the entrance to his grounds. They are now at the entrance of the O. C. Brown Park and Playground near Dixonville east of Roseburg, having been placed there in 1952 through the efforts of Dr. Reed's grandson, Carl Hill. O. C. Brown, who was superintendent of public schools in Douglas County for many years, donated the parksite for a children's playground. His widow, a granddaughter of Dr. Reed and a sister of Carl Hill, set aside a sum in her will for development of the site.

Carl Hill

Carl Hill is a son of William G. and Bianca Reed Hill. He taught school for twenty years, then went into politics and served several terms in the state legislature, two years on the state game commission, and six years as county judge of Douglas County. He now lives in retirement at his home southeast of Dixonville. The Hills have a son, Robert V. Hill, a physician in the United States Navy.

After Roseburg was officially designated county seat of Douglas County in 1854, Winchester was just another village similar to Elkton and Scottsburg, a supply center for the surrounding ranches. In recent years, though, the lumber industry has stimulated growth; several large sawmills in the immediate vicinity contribute to the town's prosperity. Winchester has also become famous as a fishing resort and an ideal location for retirement.

Just below the power dam, at the site of the old ferry, are two modern concrete bridges serving Highway 99 and Interstate Highway 5. Both bridges span the river side by side (for north and south traffic), where the old trail to California led across the river. The Southern Pacific Railway bridge crosses the river about one hundred yards farther downstream.

CHAPTER X

Oakland and Sutherlin

The Oakland area was made history-conscious by the Reverend J. A. Cornwall, of the 1846 immigration, when his and another family by the name of Campbell wintered on what is now Cabin Creek, a short distance north of present Oakland. They had been overtaken by a violent storm in the Umpqua Valley in November of that year and had wisely built a cabin for protection until the spring of 1847, when they continued their journey to the Willamette Valley.

Historian Bancroft notes: "Oakland, a few miles south of Yoncalla, was laid out in 1849 by Chester Lyman, later a professor at Yale College. This is the oldest surveyed town in the Umpqua Valley."

Reason Reed and his wife Nancy filed claims on 640 acres of land in the vicinity of present Oakland in 1850, probably the first white people to settle permanently in that area. They built their house about one mile south of the present town — a two-story frame building with a fireplace at either end. The house stood for many years at the lower end of what is now identified as Stearns Lane, a landmark of early Umpqua County. When the Oregon and California Railroad built their line through Whitmore Gap, two miles south of Oakland, it passed within fifty yards of the old house.

After the Reed house had been abandoned as a residence, hoboes used it as a way station on their treks north and south. They tore the old building down piece by piece and used the lumber as fuel in its own fireplaces until only the chimneys remained, standing gaunt and lonely like monuments in a neglected cemetery; even these tumbled down in 1930. All that is left today to mark this site is a pile of rubble overgrown with briers.

Emma Hedden

Left: Cyrus Hedden, the founder of the "House of Hedden" as he appeared around 1900. The business that he founded in 1851 is still conducted by his granddaughter Emma Hedden.

Right: On the counter over which the day's business is conducted at Hedden's is a journal kept by the store's founder; a shot pouch carried by Miss Hedden's maternal grandfather, Charles G. Henderer; and, sharing the foreground, Cyrus Hedden's gold-headed canes, and a child's toy potato masher and rolling pin that belonged to Emma's mother.

Left: Echoes from the past in Hedden's store. A 400-year-old grandfather clock, reported to have belonged to a Captain Darling, known as the patron saint of Scotland. The old timepiece keeps a watchful eye on two beer steins in the window and an early-day wall telephone.

Right: Emma Hedden, owner of the present "Hedden's Store." Miss Hedden is proud of her pioneer ancestors, and has the right to be.

"King of all he surveys." In the 1880s, a driver of a horse-powered threshing rig was a special person, not unlike the old-time stage drivers. This is a typical harvest scene in the Umpqua Valley in the early settlement period.

The entire population of lower Wolf Valley in 1904. From left to right, back row standing: Susan Clayton, Rae Clayton, J. Boyd Rader, Walter Threlkeld, Hiram S. Powell, W. F. Powell and his son Leland, Mrs. R. Threlkeld, James Bartram, Ewing D. Powell. Second row standing: Mrs. Rea Clayton, Mrs. J. Boyd Rader, Mrs. G. C. Powell, G. C. Powell, Mrs. W. F. Powell, R. Threlkeld, Leonard Bateman, Mrs. James Bartram, and Mrs. Ewing D. Powell. Children standing left to right: Kenneth Clayton, Virgil Clayton, Inez Clayton, Warren Powell, Edna Powell, Myrtle Powell, Orville Bartrum, Etta Bartram. Seated: C. Pichette, Elmer Bartram, and Henry Pichette.

Dorsey S. Baker, M.D., came to this section in the fall of 1851. His claim was across the Calapooia River, north of the site of old Oakland. When Douglas County was created, the Calapooia was the boundary between Umpqua and Douglas counties. This left Dr. Baker's house in Umpqua County. His home was used as a voting place for the newly-organized voting precinct of Green Valley, and he served on the first election board, receiving two dollars per day for his services. County and United States District court were held in his house after the county business had increased to the volume where a central location was needed.

For several years the doctor kept a store where the Territorial Road, or Applegate Trail, crossed the Calapooia. He later built a gristmill and established a thriving trade in flour, freighting it by mule pack train to the mines in southern Oregon. The old water turbine that furnished his power now rests in a small park south of Stearns' hardware store at present Oakland. Thomas Banks operated a blacksmith shop near the mill's location.

David C. Underwood came to the Oakland vicinity in October 1850. He had arrived at Scottsburg from San Francisco with others of the Umpqua Land Company aboard the company's schooner. He reached the interior valley in company with A. C. Gibbs, A. R. Flint, and Joseph Knowles. They had walked to Oakland from Scottsburg over the pack trail that had been recently opened. Thomas Smith of Winchester, who was at Scottsburg with a pack train, transported their luggage.

Underwood took a donation claim near what is now Chenoweth Park at Oakland. Umpqua County later built its courthouse on his property. The road that led past the site may still be observed if one cares to penetrate the thick shrubbery growing in that area.

Underwood became the first postmaster of Oakland, receiving his appointment on February 21, 1851. He was elected county judge in 1858 and served Umpqua County until 1862, when it merged with Douglas County.

W. P. Powers came to the Oakland vicinity in 1850 and constructed a sawmill in the English settlement east of Oakland. He built the first frame house in the area from lumber cut at his mill. That same year, Harrison Pinkston, Raymond Venable, Morgan Williams, William Patterson, Allen Venable, P. C. Parker, Preston Rice, a Mr. Shoupe, and a Mr. Crosby settled in Green Valley, five miles northwest of Oakland. In 1851, Joseph Knowles, along with Ira Rice, W. S. Rice, Isadore Rice, Wessly Allen, Frederick Thiele, W. S. Tower, and John Cannady, settled in what is now called Rice Valley. All of these men crossed the plains with John H. Medley in 1850.

John Medley did not come to Oakland until 1852. He was the grandfather of Charlie Medley who operated a furniture store in later Oakland. When John arrived in the area, he settled west of Reason Reed. His claim eventually became the property of Stephen Deloss Goff, about three miles northwest of the present town.

Ed Young, a patriarch of old Oakland, was the father of Gearry Young, a prominent businessman and banker in Oakland in the late 1890s and early 1900s. Gearry's mother was the former Delia Whitmore, daughter of George Whitmore, who came to Oakland in 1857. The first recorded deed to property in "old town" was made in his favor; it was located at "C" or Main Street at First. Although the town was originally laid out to sell in parcels, it was not officially surveyed until 1861 by J. W. Perit Huntington. The Reason Reed land was bought by Alonzo Brown in 1871. He laid out a new townsite in 1872, when the Oregon and California Railroad bypassed the old town.

The new town—with its shipping facilities and its location in a rich farming and stockraising area—was early developed as a commercial center. Its growth was stimulated by the need for a centralized market for the produce grown in the interior valley.

Oakland was never a large town in population, but its economic influence was felt throughout western Douglas County. More wool, grain, prunes, and turkeys, have passed through its warehouses than through those of any other town of its size in Douglas County. Thousands of hogs, sheep, and cattle have been shipped from its stock pens. Automotive transportation and modern methods of farming have eliminated its livestock market, but its wood-processing plants now play a prominent role in the economy of the town. Oakland's face has been changed by highways but there is still evidence of former days. The architecture of many of its buildings calls to mind the men who erected them and helped to develop that area of Douglas County.

Sutherlin

Sutherlin, a more recently established town three miles south of Oakland, is situated in the western end of Sutherlin Valley. This section of Douglas County, one of the several farming districts adjacent to early Oakland, came into being around 1910. The Luce Land Company, a development project promoted by an eastern real estate firm, subdivided the valley into five, ten, and twenty-acre fruit tracts. Small investors, particularly those in the low income bracket, were induced to put their life savings into what the promoters claimed was a safe investment, but the plan did not materialize as promoted because the ground at that time was not adapted to fruit growing. Some investors went bankrupt; others just lost interest. In recent years the lumber industry in southern Douglas County has made the town a prosperous community.

Sutherlin Valley proper is about one mile in width and extends eastward ten miles to the foothills of the Cascade Range. The town and the valley derived their names from the first settlers, John Franklin Sutherlin and his family, pioneers of 1850. The Sutherlins were from Greencastle, Indiana, and claimed relationship to Benjamin Franklin. Sutherlin and his wife, the former Sarah Carmichael, were the parents of ten children, and the clan has done much toward populating the valley that bears its name.

Fendal, the eldest son, graduated from DePauw University at Greencastle, Indiana, in 1845. He paid his way through school doing janitorial work at the college during the school year, and conducting an itinerant clock and watch repair service during vacation. He crossed the plains to Oregon with three other young

men and arrived at Portland in the fall of 1847—three years before the rest of the family came west. It is reported that when
the young men were at the Snake River, their stock stampeded
and swam the stream. Fendal followed them on foot and drove
them back to camp. Being too exhausted to swim back across the
river, he solved the problem by grabbing the tail of the last ox
to take to the water and was towed safely across.

In 1849, Fendal went to California, but returned to Amity,
Oregon, in 1850, to teach a term of school. While at Amity he
received word that his father and family were on their way to
the Oregon Territory. Fendal met the party in the Blue Mountains and escorted them to the Willamette Valley over the Barlow
Pass. They spent the winter at Max Porter's place at Rickreall,
came to the Umpqua Valley in the spring of 1851, and settled
about three miles southeast of Reason Reed.

In the fall of 1851, Fendal bought squatter's right to James
T. Cooper's claim, southeast of the present town of Sutherlin.
Cooper adds a bit of interesting information concerning his
acquaintance with Fendal Sutherlin. In his memoirs he wrote:

> "I took my first claim where Fendal Sutherlin now lives,
> in 1850. Fen took up the Bushby place in 1850 where Rose-
> burg now is, and I went from my place on the swale (local
> identification of Sutherlin Valley in the early days), on foot
> to help him build a cabin. Fen didn't put in an appearance.
> I had my tramp without any dinner and I made my way
> back to Aiken's house (at Winchester) and found them all
> in bed."

Fendal married Lucy Richardson who had arrived in Oregon
with her parents in 1849. It is reported that she rode her favorite
mare, "Kentucky Belle," most of the way across the plains. The
mare later became famous as the dam of several outstanding race
horses in the Umpqua and Willamette valleys.

Like his father, Fendal raised a large family, and many of his
descendants still reside in Douglas County and throughout the
state. The house he built on the south side of the valley is still

standing. Fendal, his wife, and a number of their children are buried in the family cemetery situated about two miles east of their home on the south side of the valley that had been their home for fifty years.

When John Franklin Sutherlin came to Oregon, he was a wealthy man even by today's standards. He is quoted as saying that he did not come to Oregon to acquire land but to get his boys away from the influence of evil companions. He carried $16,000 in gold across the plains in a false bottom of his wagon, and $10,000 hidden in a flour barrel. His reasoning was that, if he were held up, the bandits would find the lesser sum and be satisfied.

John Sutherlin contributed some interesting facts pertaining to social and financial conditions existing in Douglas County at the time of his arrival. The part he played in the community's economic life is revealed in a letter, dated 1858, to his brother, Owen Sutherlin, living at Greencastle, Indiana. The letter indicates that he had always had money to get whatever he desired, and that his ten children, who accompanied him to Oregon, when old enough, were comfortably settled on land all within twenty-five miles of his home. Before his death he had bestowed $1,000 in cash upon each child, in addition to other property.

Sutherlin's sources of income were varied. He seems to have made extensive loans to settlers all up and down the Umpqua Valley at the high rate of twenty-five per cent interest. He established a sawmill soon after he arrived, and leased it. He engaged profitably in fruit growing; ten acres of his land were planted to 500 apple trees, 200 peach trees, also pears, cherries, and plums. He sold his apples in the valley for $1.50 per dozen and 75¢ a pound at the mines in southern Oregon. Any produce sold at the mines had to be freighted in by pack train.

He did well at farming as the land was new and required little cultivation; crops could be had within two to three years from one planting, such as wheat, oats, or barley — which re-seeded the ground from grain lost in harvesting. Wheat and corn brought $1.25 a bushel, and hired help could be had for $1.50 a day with board.

Stock, except work animals, were allowed to run at large and shift for themselves winter and summer. Sutherlin didn't bother to keep a regular riding horse, which would require feeding; he simply went out on the range, caught one, rode it all day, and turned it loose at night.

It appears, though, that John F. did not succeed in getting his boys away from evil influence after all, by bringing them to Oregon. According to his report, robbery and murder were the order of the day and traveling alone was unsafe. It was a regular custom for men to go armed for self-protection, not only from Indians, but from whites. But evil was not allowed to continue unopposed. Dr. James H. Wilbur, founder of the Umpqua Academy in the town that now bears his name, conducted what Sutherlin called "considerable preaching at our school house." There were also camp meetings, organized by itinerant circuit riders; these were held in tents pitched under oak trees near where the Fair Oaks church building now stands.

From all accounts, John Sutherlin came under the influence of Dr. Wilbur's preaching. He specifically mentioned the circumstances of the meeting at which he made commitment to unite with the Methodist congregation. He also mentioned the conversion of one of his neighbors, "Cap Hall."

John F. and Fendal Sutherlin were both colorful characters. The elder Sutherlin and his wife Sarah are interred in the family plot beside their many descendants; their resting place is marked by a large reddish-marble monument.

Part Three

GOVERNMENT AND TRANSPORTATION

CHAPTER XI

Organized Government

In the early days of the colonization of the Northwest Territory there was no organized government of any kind. Great Britain and Russia, as well as the United States, were interested in gaining possession of that vast area between the Canadian border to the north and the California line, extending from the Pacific Ocean to the Rocky Mountains. What authority the Hudson's Bay Company had over the company's employees and the fur traders was the sole law exercised at that time.

In February 1841, when Ewing Young, of the historic cattle drive, died and left a sizable estate to be administered, the need of some form of organized government became evident. It was at his funeral that the initial steps were taken toward creating such a body.

Between 1841 and 1843 meetings were held by those of the pioneers who were interested—committees were appointed to investigate the necessary procedure. The question came up as to which form of government would be acceptable to all the settlers —political, provisional, or independent. The French-Canadians and some Americans were at first in favor of the independent form. George Abernethy of Oregon City advised that if the United States extended its jurisdiction over the area in four years it would not be expedient at that time to form an independent government. A committee was appointed to contact those interested and bring their report to a meeting May 2, 1843 at Champoeg. This meeting was organized by the election of Ira L. Babcock as president, George W. LeBreton, W. H. Gray and W. H. Willson, secretaries.

The report of the committee was in favor of a political organization to continue until such time as the United States should establish a territorial government. The voters were rather confused as to the wording of the report and on the first balloting it seemed as though it had been rejected. Even when the "ayes" and "nos" were called for the chairman couldn't get a clear count. George W. LeBreton suggested a standing divided vote. Those in favor go to the right side, and the opposition go to the left. W. H. Gray seconded the motion; it was so ordered. Joseph L. Meek was the first to step to the right side. Others followed and the count showed that the majority favored the provisional form of government. George Abernethy was elected the first provisional governor April 8, 1844.

George Abernethy, financial manager of the Methodist Mission, who was elected to head this provisional government, took office on July 14, 1845. He served until March 3, 1849, when Joseph Lane assumed office as the first territorial governor of the Oregon Country. Lane served until June 18, 1850, when he resigned to take his elected seat in the United States Congress.

Zachary Taylor, who succeeded Polk as president, appointed John P. Gaines, a citizen of Kentucky, to be governor in November 1849, but Gaines did not arrive in Oregon until August 15, 1850. Territorial Secretary Kintzing Pritchette served as governor until Gaines arrived on the scene.

Gaines, with two other government officials—General Edward Hamilton, the new territorial secretary; and James E. Strong, who was replacing Chief Justice Bryant—left New York on the government vessel *Supply*, in November 1849. They arrived in San Francisco in July 1850. Here they transferred to the steamer *Fallmouth* for the Columbia River. It took them nearly eight months to make the journey around the Horn. During this time, Strong's five-year-old son died aboard ship off the coast of South America and was buried at sea; Governor Gaines's two daughters, aged seventeen and nineteen, also died on board ship of yellow fever.

Governor Lane had already started to organize the judicial branch of the new territorial government by issuing a proclamation dividing the territory into three judicial districts. Chief Justice of the Territorial Supreme Court, O. C. Pratt, helped in this and was assigned to the second district. It included southern Oregon from Linn County south to the California line, and east from the Willamette River to the Snake River. Judge Pratt served this area, unaided, for two years during the transition from provisional to territorial government.

Judge Pratt, a friend of President Polk, was a well-versed jurist. A native of Ontario County, New York, he entered West Point in 1837; but in 1840 he resigned his cadet-ship to study law. He was admitted to the bar by the New York Supreme Court in 1840. Seven years later he crossed the plains to California, and in 1848 he came to Oregon, where he became a member of the Territorial Supreme Court.

No new counties had as yet been created in the district assigned to Justice Pratt. During the legislative session of 1850-51, Governor Gaines issued a proclamation creating Umpqua County. Its boundaries were the Calapooia Mountains on the north, the Cascade Range on the east, the California line on the south, and the Pacific Ocean on the west.

When the governor created the new county, he made the necessary provisions for the framing of its government. He designated Jesse Applegate's house in Yoncalla, Reason Reed's house near Oakland, and a John Aiken's house in Scottsburg as polling places. Seventy-four votes were cast throughout the county. The first political convention to organize was held on June 11, 1851, under an oak tree on the property of James F. Levins of Elkton. (Umpqua County Record Book "A").

When the votes were counted they showed that Edward P. Drew of Umpqua City was favored as territorial representative; J. W. Perit Huntington of Yoncalla was county clerk; Henry Jacquith of Long Prairie, sheriff; Adolphus Germond, treasurer;

and Benjamin Gould, Isaack N. Hall, and William Golden, county commissioners. They determined their length of term in office by lot. Golden drew the one-year, Hall the two-year, and Gould the three-year term. Elkton was named county seat but was never established as such by law.

Umpqua County records show that county and United States District Court sessions were held in private homes, woodsheds, store buildings, hotel rooms, and schoolhouses, all the way from Yoncalla to Scottsburg. This hop, skip, and jump procedure was inconvenient for the recording clerks who had to move their office equipment, consisting of a ledger, quill pen, a bottle of ink, a pair of saddlebags, and a good horse. The next meeting place was arranged before adjournment of regular sessions. From the appearance of the first record book, the clerk put in considerable mileage.

After Umpqua County was created, the U. S. District Court held its first regular session in the new county at Yoncalla, in the home of Jesse Applegate, in March 1852, Justice O. C. Pratt, presiding. J. W. Perit Huntington served as deputy U. S. marshal, and Jesse Applegate as clerk pro tem. R. C. Boyce was acting U. S. district attorney.

Their first item of business was the impaneling of a grand jury. The men selected were: Lindsay Applegate, John M. Scott, Robert Cowan, Solomon Williams, Joseph Cline, Thomas Owens, William H. Wilson, John Long, Reason Reed, Oliver Jefferies, Charlie Applegate, William J. J. Scott, Robert Smith, Dr. James Cole, Harrison Pinkston, William Cox, and William Hayhurst.

The second session of the U. S. District Court was held in the house of James F. Levins at Elkton, on June 6, 1853, with the Hon. Matthew P. Deady, a native of Talbot County, Maryland, presiding. Deady had read law under Judge William Kennon of St. Clairsville, Ohio, from 1845 to 1848. He had been admitted to the bar by the Supreme Court of Ohio in 1847, had come to Oregon in 1849, and had settled at Lafayette in Yamhill County. He was elected to the legislature from that county in 1850 and appointed to the supreme court in 1853, where he served until

Oregon was admitted to the Union on February 14, 1859. Meantime he had served as district judge in the southern district. The second session of the U. S. District Court held at Elkton was his first appearance as judge in his appointed district.

At this term a special session was ordered held at Scottsburg on July 29 to try Joseph Knott, from the South Umpqua area, on a murder charge. The trial was held in the house of D. J. Lyons, the Hon. M. P. Deady presiding, Joseph Knowles was sheriff, Joseph G. Wilson, deputy U. S. marshal; Columbus Simms, territorial prosecutor; and Hiram Dunlap, clerk. Knott was acquitted for lack of evidence.

With the judicial branch of the county government established, it took longer to get the administrative arm operating because Umpqua County was divided into five counties in the January term of the legislature in 1852. The division that affected Umpqua County most was the creation of Douglas County from the southern portion of the Umpqua River basin.

Douglas county boundaries, as of 1852, were Calapooia Creek to the west and the four mountain chains which define the eastern and southern watershed of the river basin. The polling places of the new county, designated by the governor, were all within this area; they were Reed's house at Winchester, Knott's in the South Umpqua Canyon, and Roberts' in the South Umpqua Valley. Winchester was named county seat. The laws which established the administrative branch of the county government were adopted at Winchester on April 14, 1852. Flemming R. Hill called the convention to order and Addison R. Flint was appointed clerk. The county commissioners were selected and their terms in office decided by lot. J. E. Danford drew the short term which ended two months after appointment. W. F. Perry drew the term which expired at the next general election in 1853, and Thomas Smith's term expired in 1854. F. R. Hill was appointed sheriff and held office until the next general election.

After organization, Douglas County's court business was carried on in W. J. Martin's store at Winchester, and the U. S. District Court met in a room over J. E. Walton's store. The proprietors received three dollars per day rent, which was the regular sum set by Umpqua County for use of private buildings and schoolhouses. At the first session after organization, the Douglas County court spent most of the day granting licenses and dividing the county into voting precincts. A justice of the peace was appointed for each precinct until the next regular elections.

The voting precincts were: Calapooia, Winchester, the area that took in Wilbur; the North Umpqua; Coles Valley, Deer Creek, now Roseburg and vicinity; Lookingglass, the territory west of Roseburg; Myrtle Creek, south of Roseburg; and Canyonville, in the extreme southern portion. The justices of the peace were: Winchester, C. Barret; Deer Creek, Henry Evans; Lookingglass, W. B. Skinner; Myrtle Creek, H. B. Bryant; and Canyonville, Burnett.

The first business transacted by the Umpqua County court was similar to that of Douglas County: granting licenses and dividing the county into voting districts. At its December term in 1851, five voting precincts in Umpqua County were defined and election boards named: Amos E. Rogers, A. C. Gibbs, and Samuel S. Mann for Gardiner; John Hudson, Job Hatfield, and William Sloan for Scottsburg; Dr. Daniel Wells, William A. Smith, and Thomas Levins, for Elkton; Dorsey S. Baker, Xenophon E. Scott, and D. C. Underwood for Green Valley; and Oliver Jefferies, Robert Cowan, and Jesse Applegate for Yoncalla.

As the business of Umpqua County grew with the expanding settlements, district and county courts were held in the house of Dorsey S. Baker in old Oakland, until a courthouse was provided. When the counties consolidated in 1863, all Umpqua County records were moved to Roseburg, the county seat of Douglas County.

The old record books from which the preceding information has been gleaned still exist. Loren L. Williams, who was Umpqua County's clerk at the time of the merger with Douglas County, wrote in the record book of deeds, below his signature, the old county's epitaph: "Umpqua County died, July 5, 1863."

CHAPTER XII

Roads, Ferries, Bridges and Mail Service

After an efficient county government was organized, people began to clamor for results from its commissioners in the way of improved transportation through the construction of roads, building of bridges, establishment of ferries, and better mail facilities. These were uppermost in the needs expressed by the settlers along the upper river.

In 1850 a pack trail was opened from Scottsburg to Oakland via Elkton, Kellogg, and Green Valley, to connect with the Territorial Road coming in from the Willamette Valley on the north. The volume of business carried on with the mines in southern Oregon and the demand for an outlet to market made it necessary to widen the trail to accommodate wheel traffic. It fell to Umpqua County to bear nearly all the cost of construction, as the worst sections of the trail were within its boundaries.

When the first county court met at Elkton in December 1851, the primary task of the commissioners was to consider road petitions. One of the first reviewed was that presented by Jesse Applegate and twenty-four co-signers, asking for a county road from Scottsburg to settlements on Elk Creek and the northern branches of the Calapooia. (The trail from Elkton to Drain was not widened until 1872.) Another petition was presented by B. J. Burns and twenty-three others to locate a county road to connect Winchester on the Umpqua River with Scottsburg. J. W. Perit Huntington and thirteen others petitioned for a location of a county road from the house of William Sloan in Scottsburg, to the house of Thomas Smith at Winchester, passing by the house of James F. Levins in Elkton. A fourth petition was presented by James Levins (not James F.), asking for a county road to begin at his house south of Elkton and terminating where the road

143

from the Willamette crossed the river, passing the house of Adna Barnes Kellogg at Pleasant Plain (now Kellogg), and connecting the settlements along the Umpqua River with Winchester.

Some of these petitions overlapped, and it was left to the discretion of the commissioners to authorize the most practical ones. Jesse Applegate, John Long, and Job Hatfield were appointed, with J. W. Perit Huntington as surveyor, to locate a road beginning at the most convenient point on the usually traveled road from the Willamette Valley, to serve the Calapooia and Elk Creek settlements, and terminating at Andrew Sawyers' house at the foot of "Big Hill" (Paradise Hill), five miles below Fort Umpqua, property of Hudson's Bay Company. This section is now Highway 38 from Scottsburg to Drain, via Elkton. They were ordered to meet in December to survey and lay out the road on the nearest and best route.

The route petitioned by James Levins was ordered surveyed and located. Dr. E. R. Fiske of Scottsburg, Xenophon E. Scott of Green Valley, and W. F. Bay of Elkton, with Richard Lannitt as surveyor, were given instructions to begin at Scottsburg and lay out a road to the ranch of Andrew Sawyers, bypassing the section allotted to Applegate's party. The remainder of their route was from Elkton, through Kellogg, Little Canyon, and Dodge Canyon, to Sutherlin.

Dr. Fiske's crew reported in April of 1852 that their survey had been completed. They had located a route over Marvin Hill and through the remaining portion of the petitioned course, and reported it to be practical at all seasons of the year. However, the party recommended passing through Dodge Canyon instead of Green Valley, it being nearer.

The county court divided the territory, approximately 1,400 square miles, into six road districts. The Scottsburg district embraced the western part of the county from the lower end of Long Prairie, southwest of Elkton, to the Pacific Ocean. Dr. E. R. Fiske was appointed its first patrolman to oversee construction. The Long Prairie district was somewhat smaller, ending at the foot of "Big Hill," or what is now Paradise Creek; Henry Jack-quith was the first supervisor.

The Elkton district extended from Paradise Creek at the foot of Big Hill to the mouth of Little Canyon, thirty-five miles of hills and two crossings of the Umpqua River. Charles G. Henderer of Elkton was made responsible for this territory. It was later divided by the county court in 1853 by establishing a line from east to west between the houses of Aseph Wells and Zacheus Levins; the north portion was called Elkton, and the southern part, the Trenton district—later Kellogg.

The Green Valley district took in the territory south of the Trenton district to the southern boundary of Umpqua County and east to the Cascade Range. When Douglas County was created, all territory east of the Calapooia River was given to Douglas. All that remained of the Calapooia district was assigned to Harrison Pinkston of Green Valley.

The Yoncalla district was bounded on the south by Green Valley, on the north by the Calapooia Mountains, on the east by the Cascade Range, and on the west by the Elkton district; Warren N. Goodell of Drain was appointed patrolman.

When Umpqua County was first created, it included a part of what is now Lane County; this district followed along the northern county line to the summit of the Calapooia Mountains and along the Scottsburg district boundary to the place of beginning; David Lucas was its first supervisor.

Actual work on the roads began in 1853.

In 1854, a five-mill property tax (a mill being one-tenth of a cent) was levied and a one-dollar poll tax was added. All males over twenty-one were subject to this tax, which could be paid in cash or by working two days on the road in their district. The *Gazette* observed, in 1854, that between $7,000 and $8,000 was subscribed by private citizens toward opening the Scottsburg-Winchester road. The county treasurer's report in 1858 showed there was on hand $3,656.15 and 8 mills to pay the expenses of its government.

By 1855 the pack trail from Scottsburg to Oakland had been replaced by a road of sorts. It seemed that the *Gazette* liked to needle the county commissioners: "Pack trains now share the narrow trails, dignified by the name of roads, with freight wagons." The sarcasm evidenced by the *Gazette* was hardly justifiable as there was so much to accomplish with so little money. There were men in the position of supervisors dedicated to their jobs, and the settlers donated many a free day of labor to help out the scanty treasury.

Elkton Road District

There were two road supervisors, each in his generation, who deserve credit as road builders, namely, Edward E. Haines of the Elkton district and Roy Fisher of the old Trenton-Kellogg area.

At the age of eighteen, Edward E. Haines bought a stage line between Scottsburg and Drain, which he operated for two years. Most of his early life he freighted over the makeshift roads from Drain to Elkton and Elkton to Scottsburg. He was supervisor of the Elkton road district for a number of years; with the help of his two oldest boys, Homer and Walter, he managed the farm and directed the road work.

Heavy road construction equipment in Haines's day consisted of a specially built road plow and a V-scraper; this was simply two 2-inch by 12-inch planks bolted together to form a V, which was used to smooth the road and fill the ruts made during the winter months. Lighter tools were picks and shovels operated by hand and oiled by elbow grease. Few sections of the county roads were hard surfaced. Creek or river gravel was used as it came from the pit. It was hauled on farm wagons equipped to handle one cubic yard at a load. Farmers were paid at the rate of four dollars per day for themselves and team, and the driver had to help load by hand shovel; consequently little gravel was hauled, as tax money was scarce.

Haines carried the mail over these roads between Oakland and Elkton for more than sixteen years. When he first began, around 1920, three round trips a week were made with a horse-drawn vehicle. During the rainy season he deliberately drove with two wheels in the drainage ditch so that the tracks left by the wheels would keep it open. When this failed, he stopped, and with the shovel he always carried, opened it by hand.

Around 1930 the roads were improved to the extent that Haines could use an automobile.

Roy Fisher, a native of Kellogg and son of Henry and Mary Maupin Fisher, was born around 1883. Early in life he took an active interest in community affairs, giving support to school and church activities, and was an advocate of better roads. He was appointed district road patrolman around 1910. When Douglas County streamlined its road program, Fisher was named road patrolman over several districts, which included Elkton, Kellogg, Tyee, and Green Valley. He held this position until his retirement in the 1950s; he died in 1964.

Retired roadmaster and county surveyor of Douglas County, Floyd C. Frear, when interviewed in 1961, told some details about the roads once patrolled by E. E. Haines and Roy Fisher:

"The most important road in connection with the history of Douglas County is no doubt the Elkton-Sutherlin State Highway 125, as the route from Kellogg follows the route as constructed by Colonel Joseph Hooker about 1855. When I traveled the Elkton-Sutherlin road in 1917, one could only drive an auto for three or four months in the year as it was axle-deep in mud for the balance of the year. Elmer Schad, who carried the mail around 1910, said that one winter his saddle horse bogged down passing through Dodge Canyon. Beginning at Elkton, I laid out the section from the cemetery at Elkton to Roy Wells's house. This was opened by Wells and Cathcart in 1924. I next laid out from the Kent ranch down the Alfred Haines hill to the present Smith Ferry bridge. Clyde Rydell built this section about 1926. I also laid out the Smith Ferry section in 1930 to the top of Kesterson hill, the worst section of the road. In 1914 Roy

Fisher built this section from the Kellogg bridge to the Cobb ranch. This was partly built by donation work. Roy Fisher donated the right-of-way. Fisher, Cap Maupin, and others donated work to open the road from Cobb ranch where the road intersected the military road.

"It has been improved by the 1921 bond issue and special road taxes voted each year by various road districts and market road funds. It was designated Market Road No. 10. Roy Fisher built through the rock bluff just north of the Ross Hutchinson ranch from Deep Gulch to Yellow Creek. Green Powell built through Little Canyon. Little Canyon was laid out by M. B. Germond and Harvey L. Epstein and built by the 1917 bond issue and a special tax fund about 1919. In 1920 I laid out a section from Marvin Hill through the Settle and Bartram ranches to Crawford Hill. This was built with the 1917 and 1921 bond issue and special taxes in 1922. This section was so bad that for one-half mile it was built of 'corduroy.' [Corduroy was split puncheons eight to ten feet long, laid crosswise of the road.] In 1932 I relocated the road from Highway 99 to the mouth of Little Canyon. In 1933 the State Highway Commission adopted the Elkton-Sutherlin section as a secondary road to Elkton. One could drive it in an hour or less—a distance that used to take all day in winter by horse stage."

The section laid out by Dr. E. R. Fiske in 1852 is now a standard width two-lane highway, paved the entire distance from Interstate Highway 5 at Sutherlin, to the Anna Chandler Wells bridge at Elkton.

Floyd Frear—Roadmaster

Floyd C. Frear was a native of Factoryville, Pennsylvania, born on June 10, 1888. He received his training as a civil engineer at Scranton, Pennsylvania, and came to Oregon in 1908. His first work was for the city of Roseburg during its first paving job in 1910. In 1917 he became assistant to Milton B. Germond, then surveyor for Douglas County.

Frear's first assignment under Germond was to lay out the Loon Lake road to the Umpqua River at the mouth of Mill Creek in 1917. He and his viewers, John I. Chapman and Johnst (short for Johnston) Levins, camped for ten days under the trees in November weather. Luther Judy was road patrolman of the Loon Lake district at that time. Germond laid out the Loon Lake road to Golden Falls in 1908; his viewers were Maurice Webber and Rafe Dixon.

Frear laid out the Bullock road on the west side of the Umpqua from the steel bridge at Kellogg to the bridge at the mouth of Little Canyon. He also laid out the road from this point to the Short ranch (the old Hutchinson place); his viewers were A. L. Aikens and Grant Clayton. The chain men and swampers were volunteers: Fred Bullock, Ross Hutchinson, Tom Higginbothom, Robert Minter, Ernest Short, and Edgar Madison.

From 1933 to 1936, Frear laid out the Smith River road from Gardiner to the North Fork of Smith River. Harvey L. Epstein, county surveyor, laid out the section from the North Fork to Sulphur Springs in 1932.

The Umpqua Ferry county road was located in the fall of 1919. It originated at the Umpqua store in Coles Valley and terminated at the site of Ewing Powell's old homestead house. Oscar Edwards laid out the section from the Powell house to the mouth of Little Canyon.

When Germond died in 1920, County Judge D. J. Stewart appointed Frear county surveyor and roadmaster. In 1921, Frear surveyed one of the most needed links in western Douglas County, the road between Scottsburg and Reedsport. A preliminary survey had been made by E. L. Robinson in 1916, and a $550,000 bond issue had been voted by Douglas County in 1917, of which the Scottsburg-Reedsport road was to receive $75,000. Frear later recalled that Judge Stewart—en route by boat from Scottsburg and observing the high rock bluffs—remarked, "It's impossible to build a road there!" Consequently no work was started then. However, in 1921, George K. Quine was elected judge and a bond issue of $1,000,000 was voted, to be used for several projects already under way, including the completion of U. S. 99 and Coos Bay Highway 42. The bond issue was divided among thirty-five county roads, including both highways. Reedsport voters were promised $200,000 if they would vote for the issue, which they did. George Quine, Ed Weaver, and Robert Long comprised the county court.

Three assistant engineers were selected: Jess Cole, Spencer Hinsdale, and Rupert Kline. Frank Kernan of Reedsport was contractor on the "dike" section. The first two miles out of Reedsport, this link passed through low, swampy ground. Instead of keeping along the nearby hills, the county court was persuaded to place the highway along the river and build the road on top of the soil dredged up. Thus a drainage ditch was made and the owner of the land through which the route passed had a large section of his land reclaimed from the marsh. This section has always been referred to as the "dike section." The Christmas week flood of 1964 did much damage to this stretch of pavement.

Frear started the line from the Schofield Road and continued to Dean's Creek on the dike, to the upper end of the Hinsdale property. Other contracts were let shortly thereafter from Dean's Creek to Scottsburg; the road was opened to traffic in 1923.

Side Roads

In 1921, Frear laid out a road from the Henry Beckley ranch to the old John Rhodes place at Hedden Creek. He re-located the old military road from this point through Mehl Canyon to connect with the Bullock road in 1946.

The Henderer road, from the Beckley place through to the Abel Fryer donation claim, across the Umpqua River at Paradise Creek, was laid out in 1935-36. Some information concerning the continuation of this road was contributed by Floyd H. Weatherly in a letter dated November 1964:

"The road coming from Scottsburg on the south side of the river through the Sagaberd place was built around eighteen years ago (1946) by Howard Hinsdale as a logging road. It followed the river seven miles up to the Lutsinger place, which is directly across the river from the old Long Prairie schoolhouse. Then it went up in a southwesterly direction onto the mountain connecting with the bridge road and came out through the old Gard Sawyers' place to the Henderer road. [The "bridge" road crossed the river at this point over a low-water bridge bolted to the bed-rock, connecting with Highway 38. After the timber in that area was hauled out, the steel frame was salvaged.]

Last year a new road was put in by the Bureau of Land Management, from Lutsinger Creek, up past our house [Floyd H. Weatherly] for ¾ mile along the river, then turned up the mountain. It runs south of the Charles Hedden place [the Abel Fryer donation claim] and connects with the Henderer road at the old John Sawyers place. It is 5 and 1/5 miles long. The original road was transferred to the Long Bell Lumber Company, and then to the International Paper Company, which owns part of the road, and the balance by easement. We are hoping to get the county to take it over and connect it with the Henderer road by using the B. L. M. road up the river to a point where it goes up the mountain, about three miles from the Henderer road."

If this is accomplished there will be two good roads, one on either side of the river; the one on the north side paved all the way from Scottsburg to Elkton, the one on the south side paved halfway.

In 1922, Frear re-located and laid out the road over Hancock Mountain. Of a $1,100,000 bond issue, $15,000 was allotted for this project. F. F. Wells and August DeGnath, with Frear and Quine, examined the old railroad tunnel at Elk Creek as a possible route, but estimated the cost to be too great. A 5 per cent grade was built over the mountain and surfaced with 2 by 12 inch planking. Del Weatherly was grading foreman for the east side and also for the Henderer road; Chris Hansen was grade foreman on the west side. Many switchbacks were necessary to keep the grade at a 5 per cent maximum. (The State Highway Commission eventually used the old tunnel, as discussed in Chapter VIII.)

In 1934-37, Frear laid out the Anlauf-Lorane re-location of the old Territorial Road from Anlauf to the Lane County line. This was the first road opened from Lane County to Oakland by Jesse Applegate in 1846-47. The Douglas County section was finished in 1938. P. M. Morse, county surveyor from Lane County, laid out the road from the county line to Lorane several years before Douglas County built its section. The Douglas County end was built with special taxes, W. P. A., and an appropriation from the general road fund. The project was finished while County Judge Huron W. Clough and Commissioners H. H. Roadman and R. L. Stearns were in office.

Oregon's Military Road

The belief held by some that the military road through the Umpqua Valley from Scottsburg to Myrtle Creek was the first road opened to wheel traffic after settlement began, is erroneous. Umpqua and Douglas County records, supported by the National Archives, Record Group No. 77, Roads 118-132, show that a county road was in service two years before the military road was located.

In 1850, when Joseph Lane succeeded Samuel R. Thurston as Territorial Representative, he turned his attention to the construction of roads throughout the interior. He made his first request for federal assistance at the first session of Congress in 1852, by introducing a bill for a grant of $40,000 for roads throughout the Territory. Although no significant objections to this request were raised in that session, it was held up until January 1, 1853, before being signed into law by President Franklin Pierce.

Of this grant, $20,000 was allotted to locate a military road from Camp Stuart in Jackson County to Myrtle Creek in the Umpqua Canyon of Douglas County. This assignment was given to Major Benjamin B. Alvord, assisted by Jesse Applegate; the road was surveyed and located in the fall of 1853. They spent $5,000 trying to avoid the Umpqua Canyon. Failing in this, they used the remaining $15,000 to improve the route through the canyon and the nearby Grave Creek hills, as located by Applegate and Scott in 1846. This work was contracted to Jesse and Lindsay Applegate and Jesse Roberts, all from Yoncalla.

At the first session of the 33rd Congress, in 1854, an additional appropriation of $20,000 was made to extend the military road from Myrtle Creek northwestward to Scottsburg. When the extension of this section was authorized, Jefferson Davis, then Secretary of War, selected John Withers, a first lieutenant, 4th Infantry, U. S. Army, stationed at Vancouver, to supervise construction. Davis stated in his orders:

"Your object will be first to secure a practicable wagon road between the points indicated, and then to devote the remainder of the funds at your disposal to the improvement of the most difficult places, aiming to make the road uniformly good throughout its length. You are authorized to have the work done by contract or to employ hands for the purpose. The former is believed to be the preferable mode, particularly if persons residing along the line, and thus interested in the success of the work, are willing to undertake it at a moderate rate."

Lieutenant Withers surveyed the route from Myrtle Creek to Scottsburg, divided the construction work into sixteen sections, and advertised for bids in the Scottsburg *Umpqua Weekly Gazette*. Handbills were also circulated in the settlements describing the labor to be placed under contract.

Upon reviewing the bids, Withers discovered that Jesse Applegate, as spokesman for the Yoncalla and Elkton citizens, had submitted proposals to build along a different route from his survey. Although the bids were lower than those accepted, these were rejected by Withers as not being the shortest and best route in accordance with the advertisements. This rebuff aroused the residents in both communities and they engaged W. W. Chapman, an Elkton lawyer, who protested directly to the Secretary of War, and obtained an injunction to stay operations on two segments of the road. (One segment in question was the route through Mehl Canyon.)

Withers secured the services of Attorney Stephen F. Chadwick and had the injunction set aside. Chapman retaliated by delaying the improvement upon the section for which he, personally, had a contract, until threatened with having the courts declare his bonds forfeited. In the spring of 1855, Withers made a tour of inspection and declared that the road was "as good a wagon road as any in the country and will greatly facilitate the transportation of any government supplies to Fort Lane (Camp Stuart), by the way of Scottsburg."

Colonel Joseph Hooker

During the winter of 1857-58, plans were made to concentrate on improving roads in southern Oregon—which had been impossible during the previous season. Lieutenant C. H. Mendall, of the topographical engineers of the U. S. Army, employed Colonel Joseph Hooker, in 1858, to oversee the improvements to be done on the military road in southwestern Oregon. Colonel Hooker was at that time residing in the Rogue River country as a private citizen.

The work on both sections of the road was to be under the immediate supervision of Colonel Hooker. He began by organizing two labor parties in San Francisco and dispatching them by steamer to the mouth of the Umpqua in the first week in April of 1858. Hooker decided to have part of the work done by contract. Robert M. Hutchinson contracted for a bridge over Deer Creek at Roseburg; Adna and Lyman Kellogg, and Hill & Company were also given contracts. Hardy C. and Thomas Elliff had a contract for $8,000 to build thirteen miles of road from Jacksonville to Cow Creek; David W. Ranson and Jep Roberts were the contractors for the bridging.

Crews of from twenty to forty men concentrated their work in the Umpqua Canyon, which, because of heavy rains, was almost impassable. Much of the route had to be re-located; the vertical walls were blasted away to make a road bed where Canyon Creek had previously been used as a road. After the removal of sizable mud deposits that had accumulated during the rainy season, permanent improvement of the drainage was provided for by culverts. This section was now declared to be, "An excellent road, sixteen feet wide with timber cleared from thirty to sixty feet; it was practicable for a six mule team."

On the Scottsburg end, a party of men had completed about fifteen miles of construction by August 1, when the Fraser River gold strike caused most of them to leave the job. However, Hooker was able to recruit two new groups, one near Roseburg and the other at Myrtle Creek, and with the aid of several civilian contractors completed the necessary repairs by early fall of 1858. Whenever the military road through Douglas County is currently spoken of, it is called the "Hooker Road," and is so designated by the State Highway Commission.

The route of the military road from Scottsburg to Hedden Bluff, twenty miles above Scottsburg, followed the county road to Sawyers Rapids, where it crossed the river. From this point it passed through the John and Abel Fryer, S. H. Allensworth, John E. Gardiner, and John Jacob Sawyers donation claims to cross a secondary ridge of the Coast Range.

The grade over the backbone of this ridge between the Walker district and Hedden Bluff was so steep that Jake Sawyers and John Letsom became stalled on the hogback with their threshing machine in the summer of 1899. When the front wheels of the rig passed over the ridge, the fan housing would not clear, and a portion of the road bed had to be dug away before they could proceed.

The distance from the John Rhodes place at Hedden Bluff to Gottlieb Mehl's mill, on the creek that now bears his name, was five miles. This section of the road followed along close to the river to avoid the bluffs and ridges. Small streams and deep gulches were bridged, but these bridges had to be replaced after every high water; windfall trees and earth slides were a constant menace. Sometimes the road would be blocked to wheel traffic from four to six weeks.

Larger streams, such as Fitzpatrick and Mehl creeks, had to be forded, which was nearly impossible through the rainy season. From the Mehl Creek crossing, the military survey followed along the east side of the creek, past the Abe Langdon homestead to where it crossed through a gap in the main divide between Mehl Canyon and the Umpqua River. Here it dropped sharply for one mile through the Ziba Dimmick land to Robertson's crossing, twenty-three miles from Scottsburg.

It is not generally known but, for one whole generation, this section of the old military road was the only available route, except the route around by Elkton—eight extra miles between Hedden Bluff and the settlement at Kellogg. In the winter the two miles up out of Mehl Canyon were knee-deep in mud.

An alternate route ran from the Abe Langdon place to the toll ferry at Kellogg. This route was not laid out by the military. A man named Smith, who operated a blacksmith shop, shod horses, and repaired wagons for the freighters, had a claim between Mehl Creek and Dimmick's toll ferry; presumably he laid out this route. It followed up a spur running east away from the creek and connected with the Elkton-Winchester road just above the old schoolhouse at Kellogg. Traces of this road can still be seen.

From Robertson's crossing, the military survey meandered southeast past John J. Kellogg's home. From this vantage point the old grade is plainly visible to where it intersects the Elkton-Winchester road at what was then the Barney Kellogg house, now commonly known as the Cobb ranch. The old county road bypassed the bluff just south of this point by going around it past the Henry Fisher place and coming to the river at the Ross Hutchinson ranch a mile or so up the river.

The county and the military survey followed the same route to the top of Marvin Hill, from where it left the river at the mouth of Little Canyon. In his report to the Interior Department, Lieutenant Withers wrote: "Sandstone formation commences with Little canyon, the point where the road enters the Coast Range of Mountains, and is principally confined to them. The hill region which the road passes appears to have been disturbed by volcanic action, the crust of the earth being broken up and mixed together and sometimes reversed in their orders." This formation made road building in this section extremely difficult.

After the military survey intersected the Willamette Road at Wilbur, it took up the route re-located by Alvord and Applegate in the autumn of 1853. The military road in Douglas County is usually associated with that section between Scottsburg and Wilbur.

Ferries and Bridges

As the volume of traffic into southern Oregon increased, it was apparent that roads were only a part of the transportation problem. The county road crossed the Umpqua River three times between Scottsburg and Winchester. Since bridges at these points were financially unfeasible, ferries were used. The crafts were flat-bottomed scows, about forty feet long and from twelve to fourteen feet wide, with the bottom sloping up at either end. The side, or gunwale, of the earlier boats was about thirty inches deep by four inches thick, hewn from large fir trees.

A four-inch lip, or offset, was left on the bottom of each gunwale to receive planking laid crosswise to form the bottom and deck. When sawmills began operating in the settlements, the gunwales were sawed and the boats decked over. A gunwale from the first boat used at the Crescent Ferry at Kellogg lay half-buried in the sand at the site of Dan Maupin's house on the Childer's place, ten miles below the old ferry slip, as late at 1912.

Equipment used to operate these ferries was simple. A three-quarter inch steel cable was stretched from bank to bank and anchored at either end to a winch, or windlass. The windlass was constructed from tree trunks, usually oak, about eighteen inches in diameter, cut in ten-foot lengths, with a fork at one end. Two of these forks were set in the ground about six feet apart. A roller, or drum, was fitted in the forks with the ends of the cable wound around it, with hand spikes inserted in offset slots at either end and scotched by a crossbar to keep the cable from unwinding. This arrangement allowed the cable to be raised or lowered according to the level of the water.

Two large wooden blocks with six-inch steel sheaves were placed on the cable. These were attached to the ferry boat by one-inch hemp ropes from twenty to thirty feet long, passed through a ring in the deck, or wrapped around a banister. By shortening the bight at one end and lengthening it at the other, the force of the current caused the boat to move from shore to shore. To make the return trip, the order was reversed. When the current was not strong enough to move the craft, the boat was manned with long sweeps, or oars, and sculled across. This was the custom followed by settlers who maintained private ferries without cables.

In 1850, only two ferries were operating on the river between Scottsburg and Winchester; one was at Hope's Elbow, four miles below Elkton; the other, the Hasty and Corryell Ferry at Winchester. In the fall of 1851, Edward P. Drew established a toll ferry on the Elkton-Winchester road, six miles southeast of Elkton, called the Trenton Ferry. He was granted a special license by the county court in December of that year, requiring him to pay a fee of three dollars per month for the first three months. When the April term of court convened, a yearly fee of $125 was set. By this time, five ferries were operating in Umpqua County; three on the Umpqua, one on Elk Creek at Elkton; and one on the Calapooia River west of Oakland. Toll charges were fixed at the same session: for a man on foot, 12½¢; a man on a horse, 25¢;

for each loose horse, mule, cow, or steer, 25¢; for a wagon, 75¢; and for each animal attached, 25¢; for each sheep or hog, 6½¢.

Levi Gant, who owned the land on both sides of the river where the Trenton Ferry was operating, challenged the action of the court in denying him a license and granting one to Drew. The court took the position that a license had already been granted to somebody else, and therefore it could not reverse its decision. Gant petitioned for a hearing before the District Court. He was represented by A. C. Gibbs, and Drew by his brother Joseph. Judge M. P. Deady decided in favor of Gant, thus setting a precedent for the granting of licenses. Courts could not limit the number of licenses granted; the owner of the property where ferries were operated could not keep others from operating at that location. Drew recalled his petition for a license, and the court issued Gant a license binding him to the provisions regulating toll ferries.

Drew sold his equipment to Garrit and Mills in May 1852, for $1,000. Mills later sold out to John L. Smith and Henry Beckley for $2,000. After Smith's death, his estate operated the ferry until, in 1889, it became a free crossing financed by the county.

After Drew disposed of his interest in the Trenton Ferry, he established the Crescent Ferry two miles south, in June 1852. The Indians called the location "Chinnagouche," meaning Crescent. In December of that year, Drew sold a half-interest to James T. Cooper. When Ziba Dimmick settled at Kellogg in 1854, he bought Drew's interest in the ferry and the land he claimed at the site. In 1864, John A. Fryer bought Cooper's donation claim and his half of the ferry. It was operated under the firm name of "Dimmick and Fryer" until 1889, when all toll ferries were declared free. They continued to operate under contract with the county, furnishing their own equipment, tending the ferry alternately a month at a time. In the early 1900s the county bought their boats and let contracts for operation only. In 1914 the Umpqua River was bridged at the ferry site.

The ferry at Hope's Elbow, five miles below Elkton, was established by John H. Hope in 1850, the first one on the Umpqua below Winchester. Information on Hope's former activity is not available but the county records connect him with the ferry and various public services performed. His name appears on the muster roll of the Umpqua County Volunteer Mounted Riflemen in 1855. There appears to be no other public record of his activities after the company was disbanded in May 1856.

Sometime during the fall of 1850, Charles Leinfelder, one of the group aboard the *Samuel Roberts*, came into possession of a claim in a bend of the Umpqua River, thirteen miles above Scottsburg, which embraced Hope's Ferry. Leinfelder apparently was in poor health, for he hired John Endicott Gardiner to work for him.

Their working agreement, effective on January 1, 1851, was that Gardiner would work for Leinfelder for one year, and board himself and employer; amount of wages agreed on was $200 cash payable at the end of the year. If payment was not made before January 1, 1853, Leinfelder promised to convey to Gardiner 160 acres of his claim taken from the northeast part, or forfeit $5,000. Court records reveal that Leinfelder died before the end of 1851.

Gardiner lost no time in presenting his claim. The land office at Winchester requested legal proof of his right to ownership. This he furnished by producing the agreement between himself and the deceased, witnessed by A. R. Flint and George C. Brown. In 1852, Flint surveyed the claim and established its boundary. The lines were run at an angle so as to cross the river twice.

Gardiner was a shrewd trader and no doubt had some plan in mind when he followed this odd procedure in running his boundaries. The pack trail to the Willamette Valley and southern Oregon divided at Hope's Ferry; the road to the Willamette went via Elkton, and the one to Jacksonville passed through Mehl Canyon to connect with the Elkton-Winchester trail at the Crescent Ferry. In 1852, the pack-train business was booming, and it appears that Gardiner was planning to get control of the land on both sides of the river and charge toll, both for the ferry and the road. The topography of the land at this point was ideal for such a scheme, as the mountains came abruptly to the river's edge at the ferry where the trails divided. When the county fixed toll charges and the license fee were raised to $125 per year, traffic did not merit the expense, and with an open road on either side of the river there was no need for a ferry.

Still discernible is the road leading to the old ferry landing, in which good-sized trees are growing. The large fir tree named as a landmark is still standing at the ferry site. Gardiner made application for a toll license only once, in 1853. He remained in the lower valley for some years, and his name appears frequently in old Umpqua County records.

An early ferry was operated across the mouth of Elk Creek at Elkton by James F. Levins, on the Elkton-Winchester road; he was granted a toll license in 1853. This ferry was displaced by the construction of a bridge at that place, which was put in service in September 1854.

In January 1852, Raymond Venable was licensed to operate a toll ferry across the Calapooia, two miles west of Sutherlin. This ferry served the military road after its construction in 1857, being displaced by a covered bridge in the late 1860s. The U. S. Army operated a ferry at Sawyers crossing for a number of years during the height of freighting and pack-train activity, even after a route was opened into southern Oregon from Crescent City, California.

In 1857, James Laughlin established a ferry at Robertson's crossing after the military road was opened. The road crossed the river opposite Laughlin's claim but approached the river through Ziba Dimmick's land. When Laughlin petitioned the county for a toll license, Dimmick filed an objection through his attorney, Stephen F. Chadwick, claiming that the county had no jurisdiction over the military road and asking for an appeal to the District Court. The commissioners, who had cut their eye-teeth on the tangle with Drew and Gant, ordered Dimmick to present his case to them. A. C. Gibbs, counsel for Laughlin, based his defense on the Drew-Gant ruling. The suit was decided in favor of Laughlin, who was granted a license; this resulted in two toll ferries operating within one mile of each other for more than a year.

One of the more recent ferries established was at the upper end of Hope's Elbow in 1905, where the section line between the donation claims of Sawyers and Hathaway crossed the river. John Letsom operated it the first year, but he was drowned in January 1906, when he fell off the boat; Andy Hargan was appointed to finish Letsom's contract. In 1907, Alex Sawyers bid in a new contract which was renewed from term to term for twenty-seven years. The ferry was abolished in 1934, with the completion of the Henderer road. When a county ferry was established at Scottsburg, around 1917, Alex Sawyers bid in the contract, operating the ferry by hired deputy until 1930, when the highway bridge at that point was completed. Steel and concrete bridges have displaced county-operated ferries until none are left. The one Alex Sawyers operated at Scottsburg was the last to go.

Bridges

With tax money coming in, the April term of the court in 1854 allotted $3,000 for bridges. Contracts were let for six bridges between Scottsburg and Elkton, averaging $150 each; two at Golden's Creek, one at the foot of Big Hill (Paradise Creek), two on the properties of Anaheim and Henderer (the Brown place), one on the Chadwick land, and one on the Andrew Sawyers property.

The first bridge to displace a toll ferry was across Elk Creek at Elkton. In the spring of 1854, a contract was awarded to build a bridge across the creek about 300 yards above where it empties into the Umpqua. The county court consisted of Aseph Wells, Barney Kellogg, and Zacheus Levins; L. L. Williams was county clerk. Bridge specifications were spelled out by the county commissioners: 149 feet long, abutments 20 feet wide, 5 suspension stringers 16 feet apart—the center stringers to be 89 feet long and

Mrs. L. F. Clark

Mrs. L. F. Clark

Left: Jesse Clayton, patriarch of Wolf Valley, was the first permanent settler in that area. He came to Oregon in 1847.

Right: Ashford Clayton, brother of Jesse, with a grandson and his favorite saddle horse "Jim" in 1900. He crossed the plains to Oregon in 1851.

Robert Minter

Reunion (1901) of scholars who attended the early Kellogg school: Left to right, standing: Hattie Fisher, Commodore Langdon, J. Boyd Rader, John Maupin, William Howard, Jimmie Eliott, Sarah Fryer Hutchinson, Frankie Dimmick Hobbs, Fred S. Weatherly (no relation to the Long Prairie Weatherlys). Second row, seated, left to right: Louie Smith, Agnes Shambrook, Clara Moore, Esther McCollum Weatherly, Eva Howard Kinsel. Front row, seated: Emil Anderson, Robert Minter, Irma Moore. The small boy, Dayton Minter, did not attend school in the old building erected in 1874.

"Weatherly Eating House" at Elkton in the early 1900s. This small-town establishment becam famous from Portland to San Francisco because of its reputation for supplying good food. Elkton located along the Drain-Scottsburg route, was the "nooning place" for stages arriving fro either direction.

Left: Charlie Weatherly, proprietor, cook, waiter, and dishwasher at the Weatherly Eatin House.

Right: George Crenshaw, an early settler in lower Wolf Valley in the 1880s. Crenshaw was veteran of the war between the states and had spent sixteen months in Andersonville Priso

the end stringers 30 feet long. These timbers were to be at least 12 by 12 inches for the upper side of the abutment. (This abutment was a crib-like pyramid constructed from 12 by 12-inch sawed timbers laid on the ground without solid footing.) The leading stringers were to be 8 by 12 inches. The bridge was to be put in service by September 1854; the total cost of material was $2,025. T. D. Winchester supervised the construction and was allowed $750 for his services, with an additional $250 for extra labor. The commissioners ordered payment of the bridge cost at the December term of court in 1854.

A second bridge was erected at the same site in 1879, with James Ellenburg hired to superintendent construction. At the July term of court that year the county treasurer was authorized to pay him $300 for his services. The order was attested by C. Geddy, county judge, and J. R. Sheridan, county clerk. This bridge collapsed in 1909, and Walter Rydell witnessed it go down. Rydell was doing chores around his father's barn one morning when he observed a dog casually trotting across the bridge. When the animal approached the main span, the structure suddenly settled about six feet on its northern foundation; no other traffic besides the dog was on the bridge. The general state of decay prohibited repair, so a new structure was ordered by the county court.

The Last Wooden Bridge

A third covered bridge was built on the same site in the summer of 1909. C. H. Maupin of Kellogg got a contract to furnish the lumber for the new bridge. He used a small portable sawmill set up on the north portion of the Tom Maupin ranch, fourteen miles up the Umpqua River above Elkton. The lumber was delivered to the bridge site by rafting it down the river. This operation took six days because it was in July and the river was low. The material was bound in bundles at the start, and fastened with common baling wire, but the packages broke up at the first rapids. This necessitated the use of boats to keep the pieces herded into the current; the writer was one of the herders. A boom was placed across the river at Elkton, where the lumber was retrieved and stacked convenient to the bridge site at the mouth of Elk Creek, by the middle of July 1909.

This was the last covered wooden bridge across Elk Creek at Elkton. It was constructed under the supervision of an engineer hired by the county. In 1931, it was displaced by a concrete and steel structure several hundred feet above the old bridge site, where the highway through Elkton was re-located. This last bridge across Elk Creek was built, under cooperative agreement, by the Umpqua Highway Improvement District, Douglas County, the Bureau of Public Roads, and the Oregon State Highway Commission; Hargraves and Lindsay were the contractors. It was named in honor of Anna Chandler Wells, wife of Ira Wells, one of the first settlers in the Elkton area.

The second public ferry between Scottsburg and Winchester to be replaced by a bridge was the Crescent Ferry at Kellogg. In 1914 a steel bridge was built about 200 yards above the old ferry site. The steel was hauled from the railhead at Oakland, twenty-seven miles, on farm wagons. This bridge rendered forty-seven years of service, collapsing in September of 1961.

In 1962, the State Highway Commission announced the awarding of a contract for the construction of a new bridge at the cost of $600,000. This was finished and put in service in the summer of 1963. It it not possible to enumerate all the old bridges in this narrative, but those mentioned in this chapter were the keys to the development of the lower Umpqua basin.

When the Esther Wells Smith bridge was put in service in 1928, this bridge was constructed about 500 yards above the Trenton Ferry site, and was named in honor of a daughter of Ira and Anna Chandler Wells, widow of John L. Smith.

In 1926, the Umpqua River at Elkton was bridged, connecting the Henderer and Beckley roads with Highway 38; this bridge was washed away a year later. The next structure was placed higher, but the main span suffered severe damage from the Christmas week flood in 1964. This structure was repaired to the extent that only one vehicle was allowed on it at a time. A completely new bridge has now been erected over the Umpqua River at this place, the west approach of which obliterated the site of the former Fort Umpqua.*

Floyd C. Frear, the roadmaster and county surveyor of Douglas County, gave an interesting run-down on the history of the first Beckley bridge in a letter dated July 1, 1962. Because of the interesting origin of the structure we will let Mr. Frear tell the story:

"After the state built the concrete bridge at Winchester in 1922, the county dismantled the steel bridge above the dam, which consisted of a 220-foot span and two 148-foot spans. I measured them up, and the county court, consisting of George K. Quine, judge, and Ed Weaver and Robert Long, commissioners, decided to use the 220-foot and one 148-foot span at Elkton. The road district there had voted a two or three mill tax to put the bridge in . . . I had planned on having the bridge five or six feet higher, because the old-timers at Elkton gave me the flood marks. The state engineers over my protest made me lower the structure five or six feet so as to give flatter grade on the Elkton end.

"The bridge was completed in 1923 at a cost of about $20,000. I always was worried about the bridge being too low, which I was forced to lower by the State Highway Department. On February 22, 1927, high water washed the longer span down river west of Orval Beckley's; this was not too badly twisted, but the short span was carried down stream to the Sam Brown farm, where it lodged in the middle of the river and was not worth salvaging.

"The county court called the state engineers, and all met at Elkton; there it was decided the long span could be repaired. A Portland contractor, O. N. Pierce, straightened it and a new 200-foot span was added so as to put the piers farther back from the channel. Then the bridge was raised to the elevation I had recommended for the first bridge.

*A new 810-foot, reinforced concrete structure at this site was completed in the late fall of 1966; it is known as the "Mary Beckley" bridge.

"It was completed in the fall of 1927 at a cost of around $37,000. The flood that year was the worst in years; in addition to the loss of the Elkton bridge, some fifty-five other bridges in Douglas County were washed out—all the way from 12-foot spans up to 100-foot spans—and twenty-five others were damaged. The only ones not to wash away between Scottsburg and Elkton, were at Paradise Creek, Golden Creek, and Wells Creek. All the bridges between Elkton and Scottsburg were out—at that time there were nine or ten down that way."

The Christmas week flood, to which reference has already been made, exceeded all other floods except the 1860-61 high water. The recent flood washed out the approach of the Elk Creek bridge across the Umpqua on the east side; the short span lodged in the mouth of Elk Creek, evidently damaged beyond repair. The grade was then raised to the level of the main bridge and a new approach was added. (Douglas County is in far better financial circumstances—according to the 1963-64 tax assessment of $8,093,693.19—to bear road and bridge costs than it was in 1858, with only $3,565.15 and eight mills in its treasury.)

Scottsburg Bridge

The contract for the concrete and steel bridge across the Umpqua at Scottsburg was awarded in the summer of 1928. Construction began soon after the contract was awarded by the State Highway Commission, May 29, 1928, the bid being slightly under $100,000, with extras authorized by the state, bringing the total to $107,815.00. The bridge was put into service on November 1, 1929.

This structure was a part of the Pacific Highway (now U. S. 99) and Roosevelt Highway (now U. S. 101). The bridge was designed by C. B. McCulloch, then Chief State Highway Engineer. It was the first of this type constructed by the State Highway Department, being designed with a tensile member between the two top cords of each accompanying span. This distributed the live load of each span in such a manner that the weight in one span was counterbalanced by the weight in the adjoining span. Thus the weight of the total structure was considerably reduced over that of the conventional bridge of that time.

One problem in connection with the footing elevation of the north approach, specified by the engineer, was the depth of bedrock. The test probes made by the engineers indicated bedrock, but the excavation found none at the specified level. The engineers decided to drive the piling from the original plan level down to bedrock, but because it was above water level the readily available wood piling was not acceptable, since wood above water level tends to rot. At that point the state engineer specified the driving of concrete piling which had never before been used by the State Highway Department.

A considerable number of pilings were needed, and in the interest of saving time and space, a special fast-setting cement called "Luminite" was to be used. This was supposed to cure in twenty-four hours. The engineers did not believe such a brief curing time possible and specified seven days' setting before driving the piling. The first test sample, after seven days, broke the testing machine. After a similar test following a three-day cure, the twenty-four-hour cure was considered safe—as well as remarkable—and casting one day and driving the next was permitted. This revolutionary process cut the projected construction time by almost a month.

Moonshiners at Work!

An interesting side event happened while the bridge was under construction. Prior to the building of the bridge, Douglas County operated a public ferry across the Umpqua just above the bridge site. The operator was a Mr. Wakefield who ran a specified number of hours during the day but, by special appointment, made crossings at any time. Early one morning when the bridge crew came to work they observed the ferry out in the river just off the landing. They also noticed a covered van-type of truck with only its front wheels on the end of the ferry scow and its back end completely submerged in the river.

Apparently the stay-chain broke as the front of the truck was driven onto the ferry and the back wheels rolled down over the ferry slip and into the river. During those prohibition days there was quite a large business in "moonshining," the illegal manufacture of liquor. The truck was loaded with sugar and everyone seemed to know what it was to be used for; they all assumed (albeit diabolically) that the truck's owner would be legally slaughtered.

It took several hours to get the truck, the dock, and the ferry into the proper relationship with each other, during which time the cargo of sugar had dissolved and its valuable contents washed out to sea. All that was left in the truck were the empty cloth bags. Believe it or not—the owner of the truck sued the county for the loss of his sugar and won the case!

Mail Service Revived

The establishment of mail service in Umpqua County was of uppermost importance to the early settlers. Jesse Applegate and Job Hatfield went to the mouth of the Umpqua in 1850 to meet the United States surveying schooner *Ewing*.

Before the *Ewing* arrived, the *Samuel Roberts*, owned by Captain A. Lyman, had been chartered by Winchester, Paine and Company and had put in at the mouth of the river. When the Applegate-Hatfield party heard the plans of the company aboard the *Samuel Roberts*, for acquiring land and establishing towns, the importance of the mail project was forgotten.

Mail service to and from the states remained the same, with the colonists carrying it themselves. Occasionally mail was left at Hudson's Bay Company Fort Vancouver, where it was picked up by some accommodating captain of an outgoing ship. Narcissa Whitman, wife of Marcus Whitman, complained to a friend that it took two years to get an answer to her first letter home.

When the Provisional Government was organized in 1845, one of the first acts of the legislative assembly was to create a postal department and appoint as postmaster general William G. T'Vault, allotting him $50 to establish the department. The assembly also fixed the rate of postage effective at that time: letters of a single sheet would be conveyed thirty miles for 15¢; over but not exceeding eighty miles, 25¢; not exceeding 200 miles, 30¢; more than 200 miles, 50¢; newspapers, 4¢ each.

T'Vault was also the first editor of the *Oregon* (City) *Spectator*, Oregon's first newspaper. In Volume 1, No. 1, of February 5, 1846, he advertised for mail carriers, but there were no roads at that time, and no postoffices established as yet. Because the high rates of postage did not stimulate business, the plan was abandoned the next year.

The treaty of 1846 granted the United States possession of the Oregon Territory. In 1847, the Postal Department appointed as Deputy Postmaster General, John M. Shively, and as special agent, Cornelius Gillman. They immediately advertised for carriers between the first postoffices in the Oregon country—Astoria, established March 9, 1847, John M. Shively, postmaster (the first one west of the Rocky Mountains); and Oregon City, established March 29, 1847, David Hill, postmaster.

Between 1846 and 1848, the Postal Department effected a plan to subsidize a steamship line to carry mail between Panama and Oregon by way of some port in California. An agreement was reached with Howland and Aspinwall—who operated the Pacific Mail Steamship Company—to place three steamers on the west coast to put in at ports between San Francisco and Astoria—including the Umpqua River. Three vessels were built in accordance with this contract by the United States Navy: the *Californian*, the *Panama*, and the *Oregon*.

The *Californian*, carrying 12,000 letters, left New York in the fall of 1848 and arrived at San Francisco on February 28, 1849. On October 27, 1850, the *Oregon* arrived at Astoria, bringing mail from San Francisco for the first time. Other Oregon ports continued to be by-passed. Territorial Representative Samuel R.

Thurston started to investigate the long delay. Before he had solved the problem, he was succeeded in office by Joseph Lane, who found that the former Secretary of the Navy had made a side agreement with Aspinwall—if his company would take the mail by sailing vessel monthly, at or near the mouth of the Klamath River, Monterey, and San Diego, free of cost to the government, his company would not be required to run regular steamers to Oregon until after receiving a six months' notice. (As yet the mouth of the Klamath River had not been explored. The Klamath Exploration Expedition set on foot by Winchester, Paine and Company was not undertaken until June 1850.)

Under this side agreement the steamship company carried the mail past the Umpqua River to Astoria, the distribution point. The mail was then sent to Oregon City, then to Yoncalla, and from there to the lower Umpqua settlements, which included Umpqua City, two miles inside the Umpqua bar. This ridiculous arrangement added six hundred miles of travel, and many days of delay.

Mail clerks' ignorance of Oregon's geography caused further delay, and the pressure brought to bear by leading citizens of Oregon and their representatives in congress did not bring results. They did not have the authority to compel the steamship company to honor its contract, and the government could not annul the contract because of the side agreement. This intolerable situation was well defined in a letter, now in the Oregon Historical Society Library at Portland, written to Joseph Lane by J. W. Perit Huntington of Yoncalla, then clerk of Umpqua County (Umpqua harbor was still being bypassed):

"Yoncalla, Umpqua, O. T. Mar. 31, 1852

Joseph Lane,

Delegate for Oregon,

Dear Sir:

"I wish to call your attention to the insufficiency of the mail facilities hitherto extended to Southern portion of the territory and urge upon your consideration the importance of relieving us of our difficulties under which we now labor.

"You are aware that the Pacific Mail Steamship Company by the terms of their contract were bound to deliver and receive the mails at the mouth of the Umpqua River as well as the Columbia and other points, but up to this time they never have entered the former place, disregarding alike the stipulation of the contract and a special order from the Post-master General dated Sept. 25th, 1851, which required them to leave the mails at Scottsville on the Umpqua River. No such place as Scottsville exists, and Scottsburg, the place probably meant, is situated about twenty-five miles above the mouth of the river. To this point it is not expected the steamer will ascend, but a mail route has been in operation since August last from Umpqua City [situated at the mouth of the river] to Scottsburg, and there connecting with the Willamette Valley. Umpqua City from its position near the mouth of the river is a safe and convenient anchorage, is without doubt the proper place for landing the mails and there is no reason why they cannot touch there.

It is true that no official survey as yet has been made, but numerous vessels which have passed in and out of the river during the past eighteen months (the largest, a bark drawing fourteen feet of water) are evidence that the entrance is practical and few harbors are equally safe to vessels once inside. Under the present inconvenient arrangements the mails passing immediately by the mouth of the Umpqua are carried to Astoria and thence to the Columbia and by land back again to the Umpqua, making to Yoncalla an extra travel of upwards of six hundred miles, causing a delay from ten to fifteen days. This can well be avoided without additional expense by *simply requiring the P. M. S. S. company to comply with their contract.*

"The fact that no survey of the Umpqua harbor has been made has been urged by the company as a reason for non-compliance with their contract and the special order of the Postmaster-General, but the same excuse will hold good in regard to Port Orford, Humboldt Bay, and other places which the steamers have touched and to which the company makes no objections. It should also be remembered that the company on entering into their contract *were well aware* that no official survey has been made and if they deem the entrance unsafe why did they agree to deliver mails there? Having contracted to do so they should be compelled to comply or forfeit their contract.

"I trust that you will pardon the liberty I have taken in thus intruding upon your valuable time. The subject is of deep interest to the people of this section of Oregon.

"I am, Very respctly, Your Obt., Servt.,

(signed)   J. W. PERIT HUNTINGTON

Rather than improving, the situation became worse. In 1853, the steamship company succeeded in getting the distribution office moved from Astoria to San Francisco. However, their contract must have expired — or been cancelled — sometime before 1857, for when Lane was in Oregon mending his political fences that year, he gave as his reason for not getting action sooner, the fact that the Republicans had a majority in congress.

The First Daily Mail

When the Territorial road from the Willamette Valley was connected to the military road in 1858, it established a thoroughfare through Douglas County from Portland to Jacksonville, a distance of 290 miles. After the completion of this road, the settlers along it began to press their representatives in congress to use their influence on the Postal Department to create a daily mail service from Portland to Jacksonville.

By 1858, the California Stage Company had extended its lines north from Sacramento over the Siskiyou Mountains to Jacksonville. In June of 1860, the Postal Department and F. L. Stevens, vice-president of the above-mentioned stage company, signed a contract whereby the stage company, for the consideration of $90,000 per year, agreed to carry the mail and establish passenger accommodations between Jacksonville and Portland, thus giving Portland through mail service to Sacramento. The California Stage Company was formed in 1853 and had $1,000,000 in capital stock, and around 750 good American horses. It operated over 450 miles of roads.

By late summer the company had placed its equipment on the road as far north as Oakland in Douglas County, connecting there with Chase's line to Corvallis, where it linked with the Oregon Stage Company's line to Portland, thus forming the Oregon and California Stage Company.

This company made trial runs between stations on September 12, 1860, and three days later their handsome Concord coaches were ready to roll. These conveyances offered the best transportation in their day. The coach body weighed between 2,500 and 3,000 pounds, was suspended by thoroughbraces (heavy, reinforced leather straps), and was capable of carrying double its weight. Inside were three leather upholstered seats which could accommodate nine passengers in reasonable comfort. As many more could ride on the top, which was surrounded by a low iron railing—safe enough to sit upon but no protection from the rain and low-hanging tree branches.

The coaches were painted a light yellow or gold, trimmed with olive green, with "Oregon and California Stage Co." stenciled along the sides and "U. S. Mail—Wells-Fargo & Co." stenciled under the windows behind the driver's seat. A canvas-covered rack was attached to the rear of the body, accommodating the baggage and Wells-Fargo express other than the money box, which, according to tradition, was carried under the driver's seat.

At 6 a.m. on September 15, 1860, the first stage left Portland, speeding south through the Willamette Valley. Simultaneously, a section of three coaches—carrying twenty-six passengers and six sacks of letter mail for postoffices along the way—left Sacramento for Portland. The gaily painted coaches made an impressive sight as they sped over the trails which were now dignified by the word "roads."

All traffic, foot, horseback, or farmer's buckboard—even local stages—gave way to the overland mail, drawn by six white horses, decked out in jet-black harness, trimmed with silver buckles and ivory rings. Thirty-five drivers, all sworn agents of the United States, had been assigned to twenty-eight coaches. The drivers wore a touch of green and gold, the company colors, in their hatbands, which seemed to give them an air of authority.

The first stage from Portland had as one of its passengers, William Farwell, editor of the *San Francisco Evening Gazette*. When he reached Sacramento, six days and five hours later, he wrote an editorial for a Sacramento paper commenting on the occasion: "This is an important era in the history of California staging, and indeed that of the whole country. No one need subject himself to the delay of uncertain ocean mail but now can write daily. A person who has no desire to risk his life to the rough coast of Oregon, can take a quiet seat in the stage, pass through the most interesting section of the country and reach Portland at his leisure."

The Oregon and California Stage Company had a rigorous schedule to keep. Their contract with the government ran from September 15, 1860 to July 1, 1865, as specified in order number 15029, which fixed their operating time over the road. Northbound stages left Jacksonville at 2 a.m. daily and arrived at Portland three days later, from April 1 to December 1; during the rest of the year they arrived five days later. The south-bound stages left Portland at 6 a.m. daily, and the operating schedule was the same as that of the north-bound stage. Each had to average 76.75 miles every twenty-four hours.

The victory of the stage company over distance and tortuous roads was short lived. Toward the last of November, Oregon's fall rains started and continued without letup for several weeks, which changed conditions rapidly. The handsome Concord coaches got stuck in never-ending, seemingly bottomless mud holes and the company reverted to its winter schedule, replacing the coaches with "Mud Wagons." These vehicles were constructed on the same principle as the passenger coaches, but were stripped of all unnecessary equipment, making them suitable for rough service—and this was what they were giving. On the way through the Umpqua Canyon, passengers were obliged to add their pushing strength to that of the straining horses when their conveyance got hopelessly mired down. By the last of December 1860, the incessant rain had created no end of difficulties for the company. Their stages got stuck and horses became exhausted; and the drivers would walk ahead carrying the mail sacks, as the postal department penalized the management for not keeping their contracted schedules.

Mail service came to a halt when high water washed out bridges and disrupted ferries; landslides in the Umpqua Canyon carried away or covered up much of the military road upon which $50,000 had been expended. It was months before mail and passenger service was fully restored. The *Oregon Statesman* observed, in 1862, that the rainfall from October to March was 76.61 inches.

By 1865, when their original contract expired, the California Stage Company was operating over more than 400 miles of roads in Oregon. That year the company demanded an additional $50,000 for service over the Jacksonville-Portland run, but was refused, and in 1866 they sold their stock to Frank Stevens and Louis McLane, who soon sold out to W. E. Corbett, E. Corbett, William Hall, A. C. Thomas, and Jesse Carr. They operated the line under the firm name of H. W. Corbett and Company until 1869, when Carr bought the stock and ran the route until 1870. The California Coast Overland Mail obtained a contract at that time and bought Carr's stock. This company was operating in 1881, when the Oregon and California Railroad was completed and the mail contract was given to the railroad company.

Local Mail Service

In 1859, when Oregon became a state, there were 174 postoffices to service it population of 52,400. The Yoncalla postoffice was the receiving point for mail addressed to postoffices within Umpqua County, in the early 1850s. From there it was delivered to other offices by carriers. The patrons knew which days the carrier arrived at each respective office and most of them personally called for their mail immediately upon its arrival. It was the custom for whoever picked up the mail to deliver the mail of others who might live in his neighborhood. Most carriers made their tour of duty on horseback. The mail from Yoncalla to Umpqua City went over the old pack trail via Elkton and Scottsburg until the road was opened to wheel traffic in 1872.

Around 1900, route delivery was introduced. Each patron furnished a sack of durable material, marked with his name and equipped with a string or loop to hande it by or to hang over a saddle horn. Some patrons had large wooden boxes near their residences to receive the bags—others had just a hook on a post. On the trip in, the carrier picked up the bags and delivered them, with enclosed letters or packages to be mailed, to the local postoffice. The postmaster then distributed whatever mail went to each name. These sacks were delivered on the next trip, whether there was mail in them or not. The same rule applied on the in trip; the sack had to be in the box or on the hook—"no sack, no mail." Postal records reveal that the salaries for the local carriers were low, but provided a steady income if the worker had the necessary staying qualities.

Mail Contracts

The route serving the lower Umpqua Valley was established in the fall of 1851, with Addison C. Gibbs awarded the contract. The writer was unable to locate the route number.

The second route, No. 12720, as contracted with M. M. McCarver and dated April 22, 1854, commenced on July 1, 1854 and expired June 30, 1858. He left Corvallis every Friday at 6 a.m. and arrived at Yoncalla the next day by 6 p.m. A return trip was made every Wednesday, leaving Yoncalla at 6 a.m. and arriving at Corvallis by 6 p.m. the following day. This gave the distributing office in Umpqua County a weekly mail delivery. M. M. McCarver was one of the 1843 immigrants, and quite active in helping to frame the Provisional Government.

Contract No. 12722 was made with Martin Monohon on April 22, 1854, covering the same time period as McCarver's. He left Yoncalla every Monday at 6 a.m. and arrived at Umpqua City by 6 p.m. the next day. His return trip began at 6 a.m. on Monday and he arrived at Yoncalla by 6 p.m. the following day. In this early period of Umpqua County's existence, only Indian trails were traveled as the main thoroughfares. The trail between Drain and Elkton was not opened to wheel traffic until 1872. Early settlers of the Elkton area claimed that the first postoffice in that area was established in the year 1851 near the later residence of Eustace Schad on the James F. Levins property on Elk Creek, a mile or so from the site of old Fort Umpqua.

Yoncalla to North Canyonville

A contract awarding Route No. 12723 to Richard A. Forrest was made dated April 22, 1854, covering the same time period as McCarver's and Monohon's. The carrier left Yoncalla every Monday at 7 a.m. and arrived at North Canyonville (now Canyonville) next day at 5 p.m. The return trip began at North Canyonville on Wednesday at 7 a.m. and arrived at Yoncalla by 6 p.m. the next day. This route was previously served by William H. (Uncle Billy) Wilson, attested by a voucher issued by Addison R. Flint, postmaster at Winchester in 1852.

Kellogg's First Mail Service

The Kellogg postoffice was established on February 26, 1856, with John Jay Kellogg as postmaster. Legend has it that Barney Kellogg carried the mail between Kellogg and Elkton—a distance of six miles—once a week from 1856 to 1858.

The first recorded route via Kellogg was No. 12711; it ran from Oakland to Umpqua City, a distance of seventy-three and a half miles. This contract was awarded to Lewis S. Thompson, who made one round trip a week for the sum of $1,170; the duration of this contract was from July 1, 1858 to June 30, 1862. The next contract, for No. 15007, covered the same area from July 1,

1862 to June 30, 1866, and was awarded to G. W. Bartges of Scottsburg for $1,650 per year.

The next record of a route from Oakland through Kellogg to Elkton—a distance of twenty-seven miles—was a contract awarded to Lyman L. Kellogg for a weekly trip at the rate of $500 per year. Lyman carried the mail from January 1, 1879 to June 30, 1879. Following Kellogg was Hugh White of Salt Lake City, Utah, whose contract ran from October 1, 1879 to June 30, 1882. He also made a weekly round trip, but for the remuneration of $310 per annum.

According to the Maupin family's oral history, Garrett Maupin, Jr., had the mail contract from Oakland to Elkton from 1882 to 1893; but he died before his contract expired. Mrs. Leona Madison, in her work, *The History of the Elkton Community*, wrote that Bill Fisher carried the mail between 1884 and 1886, which is no doubt correct as Bill substituted for his Uncle Garrett Maupin, during the last years of his illness. As far as known, Maupin had three four-year contracts. This would bring the date up to 1894. There are two years unaccounted for. However, H. R. Dimmick, in a letter to his son "Little George," dated March 3, 1896 wrote:

"I have bought the Oakland stage line and have been running it since the 10th of January (1896), most of the time on horseback . . . the mail contract runs two years from next July" (1899). Dimmick sold out to Joe and Abe Cole in 1897. From this point the writer can fill in from personal knowledge, excepting for the dates which will be approximate. Most of the carriers from 1899 to 1964 were personally known to him.

The Coles carried the mail from July 1897 to March or April 1898, making three round trips a week . . . Abe used a light wagon in good weather; his son William carried the mail on horseback in rainy weather. Some sort of an arrangement was made with Johnst Levins, who carried the mail until July of 1900, when the route was bid in by Eustace Schad. Mr. Schad had the contract for two four-year terms. Toward the end of his second term he sublet it to Lew Denny. Several local parties took turns operating the route until 1912, among them Arthur Mode. Rufus Langdon had it before the route was taken over by Edward E. Haines.

According to the Postoffice Department's records, Edward E. Haines's first route was No. 13262; mail to be carried from Oakland to Elkton from July 1, 1918 to June 30, 1922, for which he was paid $1,129 per annum. The schedule was three round trips a week; each round trip equaled fifty-four miles. He left Elkton at 7 a.m. on Monday and arrived at Oakland by 4 p.m. of the same day. By 1921-22 the roads had been improved to the point where he could use an automobile the year around. By order of the Postal Department on January 25, 1922, his schedule was changed to six round trips a week, effective January 30, 1922. He went to Oakland through Green Valley in the morning and returned through Dodge Canyon in the afternoon.

Another order from the Postal Department dated March 18, 1922, increased his pay from the original $1,129 to $2,258. Then on May 18, 1922, another order reduced the service to three round trips a week and also reduced his pay back to $1,129 per annum. No further information is available as to when the route was again returned to the six round trips per week—which was the schedule Haines followed during the seventeen-odd years that he was on this route. Mr. Haines died in 1936.

Marjorie Spencer

Most of the early carriers over the first established routes in old Umpqua County have been accounted for, as have those over the local route that served the area of the author's birthplace. In May of 1966, he toured the old route with Mrs. Marjorie Spencer, the current carrier; her tour of duty covers 105 miles compared with the original twenty-seven in 1858, more than a century ago.

Mrs. Spencer is a daughter of Harry Baimbridge and the former Ruth Carter of the Kellogg community. Ruth Carter was an early schoolmate of the author. Marjorie Spencer has carried the

Oakland-Elkton mail for eighteen years. She is a vivacious lady, easy to talk with, interested in her surroundings, and satisfied with her job. Quoting from her letter in which she furnished the changes in her route since she took over in 1948: "I have enjoyed the route very much. The people are all wonderful and have been so good to me. The country is beautiful—I never tire of driving the roads. So many beautiful trees and flowers, and of course the river adds to the beauty (in the summer). . . . When I started to work, the mail was sorted for me and I used sacks for some people; formerly mail sacks were used for everyone. Now I sort the mail myself and sell stamps. I put the mail in order in a box with partitions for each road."

At the time Mrs. Spencer took over the Oakland-Elkton route, the schedule was similar to the one followed by Edward E. Haines. There is a gap of eleven years after Haines for which information is rather sketchy. A Mrs. Vesta Thomas had a contract during that period, the last year of which was finished by Mrs. Spencer and her brother, Dale Baimbridge. Mrs. Spencer bid in the next term personally. She lists the following changes in mileage and schedule in the route:

The first change occurred on January 1, 1952, when the Henderer Road was opened for travel from Elkton to Hope's Elbow. This made a total of seventy-four miles compared to the original fifty-four.

The next change was on October 16, 1952, when the Bullock road on the west side of the Umpqua was opened to traffic from the mouth of Little Canyon to the steel bridge at Kellogg; this increased the mileage to seventy-five and a half miles. Then on October 1, 1955, the total daily mileage was raised to eighty when the west side of the Umpqua from Little Canyon to the Robert Minter ranch was included.

On February 9, 1957, the cut-off at Union Gap, between Oakland and Sutherlin, and the added Schad road up the south side of Elk Creek above Elkton made the daily run eighty-four miles. On October 7 of that same year, the Carnes or Compton (also known as the Wells) road was added, making a total of ninety miles.

By December 14, 1957 the Maupin road from the steel bridge at Kellogg to the V. K. Holcomb place brought the tally up to ninety-five miles. Three years later, on October 15, 1960, the Henderer road was extended to the Charles Hedden farm on the old donation claim of Simeon H. Allensworth, making a total of ninety-nine miles. On August 19, 1961, the Baimbridge road southwest of Oakland was included, boosting the score to 101 miles.

Mrs. Spencer noted that, on December 7, 1963, the road by the "Solomon" place was closed by a permanent detour back to the new highway, making a total of 103 miles. Three years later, on January 3, 1966, her tour was extended to the Anna Madison place; this was a part of the James Laughlin donation claim, lying in the "Crescent" with the Kelloggs. Evidently this is the last extention for the time being, making a total of 105 miles, a fraction under four times the original mileage—and all is completed in less than six hours. Mrs. Spencer begins her tour at 8:30 a.m. and is back home, one mile south of Oakland, by 2 p.m.

Weather conditions often complicate matters. When the Kellogg bridge collapsed in September of 1961, a detour had to be used for over a year. The Christmas week flood of 1964 caused the most inconvenience though, making it necessary to go around by Drain for several trips. Three bridges across the Umpqua were closed during this period: the Tyee bridge at the mouth of Little Canyon, the Esther Smith bridge between Elkton and Kellogg, and the Beckley bridge at Elkton. This made a total of 135 miles to be covered and the use of four cars to get the mail delivered. A pickup truck was used at this time instead of the usual sedan, as it was necessary to carry pieces of lumber and a bale of hay to build up the road in sunken places by putting hay in the mud holes.

The weather is no respecter of the times. In 1966, mail carriers had weather problems as bad, if not worse, than the carriers in 1850. However, under normal conditions, Mrs. Spencer has black-topped pavement over ninety-five per cent of her route, which is much better than the 1900 corduroy road through Dodge Canyon.

Part Four

COMMUNITIES

CHAPTER XIII

Kellogg

The community of Kellogg is situated about six miles south of Elkton along the Elkton-Winchester road, now State Highway 125. The Umpqua River meanders through the area as it does through all settlements in the Umpqua basin. When the John Jay Kellogg family arrived to settle in the Umpqua Valley in 1849, a spot was selected where the Umpqua River made a large sweeping bend which formed a crescent encircling about 2,000 acres of bottom and bench land. Here Kellogg and his two eldest sons, Adna Barnes Kellogg and Lyman Lorenzo Erastus Kellogg, staked their claims within the crescent and called this locality "Pleasant Plain."

When the United States Postal Department established a postoffice there on February 26, 1856, it appointed John Jay Kellogg postmaster and called the office "Kellogg," honoring the man who was the first white settler in that area. Mr. Kellogg and his wife, the former Jane Maria Bull, were both natives of Oneida County, New York. They were married in 1823 in the Methodist church in Watertown, Oswego County, New York; and their seven children were born before the parents crossed the plains to Oregon.

Between 1850 and 1854, seven other men settled near the Kelloggs: James T. Cooper, James Laughlin, and William Robertson, who took donation claims within the crescent; Shadrach Hudson settled east and across the river from Cooper; and Ziba Dimmick took a claim on the north bank of the Umpqua opposite Laughlin. Abram G. Langdon and his brother Ansel took claims along the old pack trail to Elkton.

The Kelloggs built the first gristmill in that part of the Umpqua Valley. A brush and log dam was constructed across the Umpqua at the mouth of McGee Creek, and the beaver technique was used, weighting the brush and logs down with large stones. At low water, traces of the old dam may still be seen. The old millrace was much in evidence along the east bank of the river until recent highway construction completely covered it. In July, 1857, Kellogg was accidentally drowned in the penstock of the mill. His sons, Barney and Lyman, continued to operate the mill until it was washed away by the high water of 1860-61. In January 1881, Jane Maria Kellogg died at the age of seventy-eight. Both are buried in a cemetery plot selected by Mrs. Kellogg on a portion of the donation claim of their son Lyman.

Later this plot became a communal burial ground. A. E. Ozauf, of Scottsburg, was owner of the land embracing the burial plot in 1900. He deeded two acres of this property to the directors of School District No. 54 and their successors. When this district was consolidated with Elkton District No. 34, a cemetery association was formed. Roy Fisher, then the owner of the property, executed right-of-way to it in favor of the Cemetery Association. A board of four trustees administer the business of the corporation.

Before his death, Mr. Kellogg had written on the flyleaf of the family Bible (which dated back to 1801): "This Bible is to be the property of the youngest child I have living at my death and of their mother also." Mrs. Harriett Goff was their youngest child then living. Her youngest child left no children, but by mutual consent Mrs. Harriet Goff's grandson, Byron Goff, was given custody of the historic book from which the data of the Kellogg, Fryer, and Goff families have been taken.

Lyman Kellogg

Lyman Kellogg succeeded his father as postmaster at Kellogg and served for thirteen years. During Lyman's entire thirty years around Kellogg, he was active in civic affairs. He served as justice of the peace for the Kellogg precinct for a number of years, and when the Rogue River Indians went on the warpath in 1855, he enlisted in the Umpqua County Volunteer Riflemen, Company I, 2nd Regiment. He was mustered in at Roseburg as first sergeant. When the company was disbanded in January of 1856, he re-enlisted and was promoted to first lieutenant.

Lyman's first wife was Mary Pinkston, daughter of Harrison Pinkston, who was an early settler in Green Valley, five miles northwest of Oakland. She taught the first school session in Kellogg, which was held in the old log "fort," in 1854. This had also been used as a place of refuge in case of an Indian attack during the Rogue River uprising.

The Lyman Kelloggs were the parents of six children, two boys and four girls. One boy died in infancy, but five grew to maturity: Harry, Mrs. May Hadeen,*Mrs. Minnie Neas, Mrs. Anna McNabb, and the fourth, Fannie, of whom the writer has no record. Harry has two direct descendants who were interviewed in 1962, Mrs. Bert Hill of Oakland, and Floyd Kellogg of Portland.

Mary Pinkston Kellogg died in 1876. Three years later, Lyman sold his property at Kellogg, moved to the Oakland area, and married Mrs. Emily Neal. He died in 1882 and was buried in the Masonic Cemetery at Oakland.

Adna Barnes Kellogg

Barney's claim reached almost from river to river, closing the points of the "crescent." The east boundary passed near a high promontory still known as "Barney's Peak." Barney was twenty-three years old when he came to Oregon with his parents. His old home—on a site in the southeast corner of his claim—housed the Kellogg postoffice as different periods for nearly forty years.

*Correction for page 185, Umpqua Valley, Oregon and It's Pioneers, (October, 1967) Third paragraph the name, "Mrs. May Hadeen," should be "Mrs. Laura May Hayman."

Barney spent his entire life in Kellogg and never married. He served the community in many capacities during his active years. He died in the early 1900s and is interred in the Kellogg Cemetery. The Diamond "C" ranch buildings are located on the same site as were Barney's, where the old military road from Scottsburg intersected the Elkton-Sutherlin Highway 125.

William Robertson and James Laughlin

Robertson and Laughlin, two of the original six to settle within the crescent, sold their holdings to John A. Fryer, Sr., in 1864. Laughlin had come to public notice in 1857 when he and Ziba Dimmick had a legal bout over a ferry on the military road at Robertson's crossing. No information is available concerning the further activities of either Laughlin or Robertson.

James T. Cooper

Mr. Cooper was the third man of the original six (excluding the Kelloggs' to settle on Kellogg's Pleasant Plain.) In November 1850, he selected his first claim in what was afterwards called Sutherlin Valley. Two years later he sold this to Fendal Sutherlin and took his second claim beside the Kelloggs.

That same year he bought a half-interest in the ferry that E. P. Drew had established. The first license for a toll ferry was obtained at Elkton, then the county seat of old Umpqua County. The crossing was designated "Crescent Ferry." When Ziba Dimmick took his claim across the Umpqua from Cooper, he bought Drew's interest in the ferry. Cooper married Dimmick's oldest daughter Harriet.

As the donation land law allowed a husband and wife to claim 640 acres (and all available land in their locality had been claimed), Mr. and Mrs. Cooper moved, temporarily, to Gardiner in 1857 and claimed 320 acres, which included present Gardiner. Cooper was postmaster there from June 18, 1857 until August 1858, when they sold their claim rights to Addison C. Gibbs and moved back to Kellogg. James T. and Harriet Cooper were the parents of thirteen children. Their daughter, Anna, was reported to have been the first white child born in the Gardiner area, and her mother the only white woman living in the immediate vicinity when her daughter was born.

They were living on their claim at Kellogg, in 1860-61, when flood water took away all their buildings. The barn lodged against a clump of trees on the lower end of their farm, but the timbers were used to rebuild on higher ground. They erected their new house on the site of the present home of P. W. George, who now owns that portion of the Cooper claim. The old Cooper house had been remodeled by J. M. Engle in 1908.

Cooper sold his claim at Kellogg to John A. Fryer, Sr., in 1864, and he and his wife moved to the Wilbur community where they lived for thirty-six years and raised a large family of children. In the fall of 1900, they returned to Kellogg and moved onto the old Ziba Dimmick place with Mrs. Cooper's half-brother, Lot Dimmick. There Cooper spent his last years; he died in 1903 and was buried in the Masonic Cemetery at Oakland.

Southwestern Oregon, and Kellogg particularly, have cause to remember James T. Cooper. When he built his new house after the 1860-61 flood, he sent to his native Scotland for the seed of the shrub with the golden blossoms called "Scotch Broom." The writer remembers the original bush growing beside the road in front of Cooper's house. Now it has spread all over western Oregon and parts of Washington to the Canadian border, and promises to take root in many other areas. In June, which is its blooming cycle, the whole countryside in certain areas is a mass of golden flowers.

Harriet Cooper is remembered for her devotion in organizing Sunday schools. After returning to Kellogg in 1900, she established one that met in the district schoolhouse. Then past sixty, she walked one mile to and from her home every Sunday, winter and summer, for more than four years to give religious training to the young people of the Kellogg community. The writer attended the classes she organized and has some of the cards issued to the primary classes, some dating back to 1900, and one back to 1896; the latter was given to one of his older brothers who attended her classes held in a different neighborhood.

Shadrach Hudson

Shadrach Hudson arrived in Oregon from Cass County, Michigan, over the southern route in 1847, with his father, John Hudson, and two brothers, Clark and Joseph. They first settled in the Willamette Valley near Eugene. In 1849 they went to the California gold fields, but returned to Oregon the following year. John located at what is now Weatherly Creek on Long Prairie and built a sawmill. Clark and Joseph went to Bunton's Gap, now Wilbur, and ran sheep but did not locate claims. Shadrach located a claim of 320 acres on the Umpqua River, one mile below and east of Crescent Ferry. Shadrach operated his claim in a sort of haphazard manner as he ran a pack train between Scottsburg and Jacksonville at the same time. In May of 1858, he sold his land to Isaac Spoors for $800; in February 1865, Spoors sold it to W. R. Singleton for $700. In November of that year Singleton sold it to H. M. Martin. In April of 1878 Martin sold the claim to Martha Ann Maupin, widow of Garrett Maupin, for $1,000. The site of his claim is currently owned by Eugene Fisher, great-grandson of Mrs. Maupin.

Ziba Dimmick

Ziba Dimmick was a native of Richmond County, Ohio, born in 1816. He served in the Black Hawk War in 1832, and later moved to Illinois where he married Cynthia Ursula Hall. They were the parents of six children. Those who reached maturity were: Harriett, Hezekiah Russell, Daniel Henry, Thomas Mason, and Mary Elizabeth.

During the 1849 gold rush, Ziba came to California alone by way of the Isthmus of Panama, but returned to Illinois, in 1851. He and his wife were divorced soon after his return, Ziba keeping all the children but Mary Elizabeth, who remained with her mother. After the separation and divorce, while yet in Illinois,

Ziba married Jane Hewitt in 1852. Miss Hewitt, born in 1831, was a native of Saene, County Cork, Ireland. They emigrated to Oregon over the southern route in 1853, accompanied by Ziba's children by his first marriage. The winter was spent in what is now Lookingglass community west of Roseburg. In the spring of 1854, they moved to his claim on the Umpqua.

Dimmick was a cooper by trade but this was not a profitable business at that time and place. His main cash income was from the toll ferry and furnishing lodging for freighters and provender for their animals. It was said that, during the height of freight-carrying pack trains and freight wagons, traffic would be lined up as much as one mile on either side of the river, waiting to cross.

Ziba Dimmick fathered nineteen children, fifteen growing to maturity and rearing families of their own. The children of his second marriage were: George W., Theodore W., Susan Milita, Zenas L., Ralph E., Lot S., Mary E., Louisa A., and Francis L. So far as is known, all were born on the old donation claim, where they grew up and from where they went their different ways. Ziba and his wife lived on the old homestead until his death on November 11, 1878. Mrs. Dimmick then moved to Wilbur and spent her remaining years in the house Dr. Wilbur built in 1853. She died on April 10, 1900, and was buried beside her husband in the family cemetery at Kellogg.

Abram G. Langdon

Abram G. Langdon came to the Oregon country in 1853, with the same party as Ziba Dimmick. According to a letter written by Dimmick to his son Russell in 1865, the Langdon brothers, Abram and Ansel, joined their caravan in Missouri. Abram chose his claim along the old pack trail to Elkton, about one mile north of Dimmick. Little is known of the Langdon family history; common knowledge of their sojourn in Kellogg must be relied upon to give them their place in the annals of Kellogg.

Abram and his wife Sarah were the parents of eleven children; all except one, Alzena, died in infancy. Alzena married a Jim

Walker in the early 1880s and had two sons and one daughter. She died shortly after her youngest, a girl, was born. Etsel, the oldest boy, was raised by his grandparents and assumed the surname of Langdon. The second boy, Jesse, was cared for by his father, and the little girl was taken by relatives then living in the Yoncalla area. There is no record of what eventually became of any of Alzena's children, or of their father.

Through misfortune and mismanagement, most of Abram's property was lost. He moved off the home place around 1890 and established a home along the old military road in Mehl Canyon, about two miles northwest of his original claim. Here Abram and his wife spent the rest of their lives. Abram in his active years had taken part in the organization of old Umpqua County. His name appears frequently in its record books as serving on juries and election boards, and he was justice of the peace in the Kellogg precinct. A number of land transfers in that area also bear his name.

Mrs. Langdon died in April 1903, and Abram in August of the same year. They are buried on their old homestead beside their eleven children. There are no grave markers and the burial site is known to very few now living.

Ansel Langdon

The claim of Ansel Langdon was located about a half mile north of that of his brother, on land now owned by Keith and Myrtle Kesterson. Ansel married Nora Maupin Bunch, and they became the parents of three children: Rufus, Dora, and Commodore. The only other record available on Langdon is his enlistment in the Volunteer Riflemen of old Umpqua County in 1855. The death dates of both Langdon and his wife are unknown. Rufus died in 1934. Insofar as known, Dora (who married Everett Tooley of Coles Valley) and Commodore are still living.

Johnson Bull Goff

In the spring of 1850, at the age of seventeen, Johnson Bull Goff sailed for Oregon from his native state of New York, aboard the bark *Minerva* by way of the Isthmus of Panama. Arriving in Oregon, he engaged in the pack-train business until the military road was opened, when he began to haul freight with wagons. Meanwhile he had taken a donation claim south and adjoining that of Adna Barnes Kellogg. Goff's claim is currently owned by the Ross Hutchinson estate.

In 1857, Mr. Goff married Harriet Lucerna Ann Kellogg, the youngest daughter of John Jay Kellogg. When the high water of 1860-61 washed Goff's cabin away, the family took refuge in the old "fort" on the John Kellogg farm.

The Johnson Goffs were the parents of nine children; all but one, David Henry, grew to maturity and became respected citizens of the Oakland community and the Umpqua Valley. They were: Adna Lyman, Almira Jane, Stephen Deloss, Rosa Belle, David Henry, Winnie Grace, Irvy Jay, Roscoe Oren, and Fred Arlie. Mrs. Harriet Goff died in July 1890, and Johnson B. Goff in March 1912. They are both interred in the family plot in the cemetery on the south side of Richard's Peak, two miles southeast of Sutherlin.

John Ambrose Fryer, Sr.

Perhaps the most affluent man to have lived in old Umpqua County in the day of its organization was John Ambrose Fryer, Sr. His presence in the lower Umpqua Valley was the result of his search for his brother, Abel Pasco Fryer, who has been mentioned in connection with the founding of Gardiner. Abel had run away from his home in Oneida County, New York, to California, when he was thirteen years old. John followed in 1849, crossing the Isthmus of Panama on foot, and carrying his belongings on his back. He then took passage to San Francisco, where he made inquiries concerning his brother. Learning that a man named Fryer lived in the Oregon Territory on the lower Umpqua in the vicinity of Scottsburg, he made his way to southwestern Oregon, where he found Abe, who had taken a donation claim and was living just across the river from Andrew Sawyers.

John took a sixty-four-acre donation claim joining Abe's on the north. When the military road opened, he did a profitable business furnishing hay and grain to the freighters. He also found time to build several bridges for the county along the road to Elkton. In 1858 he married Mary Louisa Emmaline Kellogg. Five children were born to them: Charles, John A. Jr., Ora, Sarah, and Wallace.

Abe Fryer eventually went to Kansas, where he reportedly remained for the rest of his life. Before he left Oregon though, he gave John title to his land with the stipulation that he feed and care for his old dun-colored saddle horse as long as the animal lived.

John Fryer is said to have owned the first threshing machine in the lower Umpqua Valley. Cyrus Hedden of Scottsburg obtained it for him and had it shipped around the Horn in the middle 1850s. The old machine was eventually owned by John McCollum, who came to Kellogg in 1872. In the 1920s, Tom Higginbothom bought it from Fred Weatherly (the Kellogg Weatherlys) for $5. Higginbothom later sold it to the Henry Ford Museum for $400; it was placed in the museum at Detroit, Michigan, where it remained until destroyed by fire in 1960. The old machine was truly a historical relic. The sides of the separator had been used by former owners as a ledger to keep records of crops threshed and accounts received.

In 1865, John sold his ranches on the lower river to James E. and Jacob A. Sawyers. The year before, he had bought the James T. Cooper, James Laughlin, and William Robertson donation claims and moved his family to Kellogg. During the years that followed, John built up a sizable fortune with his interest in the toll ferry (together with Ziba Dimmick) and the profits made selling provender to the freighters for their horses and lodging for themselves. He got control of 1,900 acres lying within the crescent of the river, either by purchase or by inheritance through his wife.

His wife's death was recorded in the Kellogg family Bible: "Mary Louisa Emmaline Fryer died February 5, 1871, age 30 yrs., 6 months and 27 days." Misfortune began to plague John after this. By the time of his own death in 1910, he had lost practically all his property.

Fryer served Umpqua and Douglas counties in various capacities for sixty years and also was a volunteer in the Oregon Mounted Riflemen. He is buried beside his wife and four of his five children in the family plot in the Kellogg cemetery; his second son, John A. Fryer, Jr., is buried at Scottsburg.

John R. Shambrook

John R. Shambrook was the first and last resident physician in Kellogg. He was a son of George Shambrook, a pioneer of Coles Valley. Dr. Shambrook married Sarah Fryer, daughter of John A. Fryer. He had taken a homestead (later called the Stahl place), which adjoined his father-in-law's place on the east and had planned to build what he called a sanitarium, when he was drowned while returning from a professional call in 1889. He had been summoned to the bedside of Mrs. William Rader on McGee Creek. His body was recovered later at Gus Wood's place, twenty miles below the scene of the accident.

George W. Dimmick

George W. Dimmick, born July 11, 1854, was the first child of Ziba and Jane Dimmick after they arrived in the Umpqua Valley. At the age of nineteen he entered Wilbur Academy for pre-medical studies. After two years—when his career was cut short by the death of his father—it fell to George, as the eldest son, to manage the farm.

Besides running the home place, George bought the Abram G. Langdon donation claim and opened a store in Elkton (see Chapter IX). In 1898 he was appointed county treasurer of Douglas County to fill an unexpired term; he was elected by popular vote in 1900, remaining in office until 1906.

Around the turn of the century George planted Italian prunes on the Abe Langdon place. In 1898-99, Charles H. Dinniny, a former resident of Kellogg then living in Wilbur, persuaded Dimmick to try a fruit drier he was promoting called the "J. W. Mote Evaporator." A description of Dinniny's drier appeared in a June issue of the *Roseburg Review*. Insofar as known only two of these driers were ever built in the Umpqua Valley—the one Mr. Dinniny had on his place, and the one belonging to George. Dinniny's theory was good, but his drier wasn't. Two major obstacles were involved that have not yet been solved: the size of the fruit and its ripened condition; a small ripe prune dries much faster than a large green one. These factors still require a certain amount of hand sorting. George was stuck with a bad bargain but he continued to use the drier until it burned down in 1903.

In 1903-4, as administrator of his mother's estate, George sold the home place to Mrs. Elizabeth Peters and, in 1910, the Langdon place to the Kestersons. He then purchased the Sam Evans place in Coles Valley, later selling a half-interest to T. W. Cardwell. In 1916 he traded his half-interest to Norman Agee for twenty-six acres at Winston, Oregon. Several years later he sold the Winston property to Binger Herman and retired to live at Wilbur. Eventually he moved to Springfield, Oregon, where he spent the last years of his life; he died at Eugene in 1940. His wife, the former Mary Jane Otey, had died in 1938. Both are buried in the Wilbur cemetery.

Captain Henley Maupin

Captain Henley Maupin was a contemporary of George Dimmick. He was born in Lane County, six miles south of Eugene, January 22, 1855, the oldest son in a family of nine children. His parents were Garrett and Martha Ann Poindexter Maupin, who emigrated to Oregon from Missouri in 1852. This oldest boy was named after a close friend of Garrett Maupin—a Captain Henley under whom he had served in the Mexican War. Garrett had promised the captain, who had been mortally wounded, that should he, Garrett, return home from the war, he would name his first son after his friend.

The Umpqua River, a half mile southeast of Elkton, as seen from the Ira Wells cemetery. The Hudson's Bay Company Fort Umpqua was located around the bend in the river. The new Mary Beckly bridge crosses the river at this point. An historical marker has been placed at the east approach of the span on State Highway 125, commemorating the 131 years of history connected with this location.

Minnie Hargan Ware

The pioneer town of Elkton as it looked in 1925. The first political convention in Umpqua County was held here under an oak tree, on June 11, 1851. The town, or village, was designated as the county seat of Umpqua County but was never declared as such by law. This town's location, at the junction of Elk Creek with the Umpqua, was mentioned by many of the early explorers as a landmark, showing their position in the Umpqua Valley.

Mrs. Wanda Minter Chase

Left: Mrs. Mary Ann (Powell) Minter, mother of the author, with her favorite spinning wheel. She bought the instrument from Mrs. William Moore in 1885, paying for it by carding and spinning three fleeces of wool into knottable yarn. The author has been lulled to sleep on many a winter evening by the hum of the "old wheel," a counterpart of spinning devices used throughout the ages.

Right: Charles McClellan Minter, the writer's father, as he appeared in 1892 (the same year the author was born). He lost the two fingers on his left hand operating an edger saw in C. H. Maupin's sawmill in the winter of 1891. He was drowned in the Umpqua River while operating the Dimmick and Fryer ferry at Kellogg, on January 19, 1900.

The old schoolhouse at Kellogg in 1899, with Peter Nash, Jr., teacher. The scholars who attended classes that year were, from left to right, back row: Cyrus Minter, Frank Minter, Roy Fisher, Etsel Langdon, Willard Mode, Earl McCollum, Clifton Moore, Dora Langdon, Laura Corder, Hilda Anderson, Mabel McCollum, and Hattie Fisher. Front row, in the same order: Eben Mode, Walter Fisher, Emil Anderson, Arthur Mode, Robert Minter, Harold Avery Minter, Joe Mode, Willard McCollum, Graydon Moore, Addie Willan, Vella McCollum.

When Garrett returned to Missouri after the war, he moved, with his wife and two small daughters, to Oregon, settling on a donation claim south of Eugene. In 1864, he moved his growing family to Douglas County and rented a part of the W. F. Bay place, five miles south of Elkton, where he engaged in hauling freight from Oakland to Scottsburg. At that time this was a profitable business, as the valley ranchers depended on private freighters to market their wool and surplus grain through Cyrus Hedden at Scottsburg.

On one of his trips with a load of sacked wool, Garrett's wagon overturned near the head of Williams Creek, pinning him beneath the load; he was smothered to death. His thirteen-year-old son "Cap," who had accompanied his father on this trip, was thrown clear. Cap unhitched one of the work horses and rode the animal barebacked to the Charles G. Henderer farm, where Garrett's family was then living, to break the sad news. Garrett Maupin was buried in the Henderer family burial plot.

It fell to Cap to help his mother support the family, which had increased to nine children. Their names, as recalled, though not necessarily in the order of their ages, are: Mrs. Nora Langdon, Mrs. Louisa Cassidy, Mrs. Poney Elsworth, Captain Henley, Thomas, Garrett Jr., Mrs. Mary Fisher, Mrs. Bina Benson, and John. All were well known by the early settlers of Kellogg, from 1864 through the 1890s.

In 1878, Mrs. Martha A. Maupin bought the Shadrach Hudson donation claim. Cap and his two younger brothers, Tom and Garry, assumed the responsibility of running the ranch. Their first job was to build a house. Lumber was obtained from the Gardiner mill and shipped to Scottsburg by boat, then hauled to Kellogg, twenty-six miles over the old military road through Mehl Canyon. Joe Roberts did the carpenter work.

Cap helped support the family by going out of the valley to work. In his early twenties he rode the range in Surprise Valley in northern California, breaking horses for cow outfits. For two years he drove a bull-team-drawn wagon, hauling freight into Virginia City.

The three brothers eventually controlled around 1,500 acres. In 1888, the property was divided. Tom got about 1,000 acres across the Umpqua north of the Hudson claim; Garrett, Jr., got the Lyman Kellogg claim, and Mrs. Maupin, the 320 acres east and adjoining the Hudson land. Garrett, Jr., died in 1893.

"Cap Goes Out on His Own"

The year the property was divided, Cap married Ida Clarke of Millwood, daughter of W. B. Clarke. She and their infant daughter died one year later. In 1893, he married Adilla Peters, daughter of Alex and Elizabeth Peters. They were the parents of eight children: Alva, Edith, Hazel, Dan, Florence, Maurice, Lois and Irene.

Cap Maupin, a pioneer in many ventures, was at heart a farmer and stock breeder. Once he said, "I was as proud as a dog with five tails when I got my first pair of pure breed Chester White hogs."

In those days a "smoke house" filled with hams and bacon was a status symbol, and "hog killin'" to the early settlers was an annual occasion, occurring around November and December when the days were cold and frosty. In most cases the chore was carried out by the farmer and his family. When help was needed there was always an obliging neighbor who was willing to help; the prospect of getting fresh backbones and spareribs, with a heart or liver as a good measure, was considered adequate pay for his services.

In the fall of 1911, Cap staged a hog killing which set a record in Kellogg for all time; he butchered one hundred hogs, fifty on two separate occasions—one in November and the other in December. Butchering fifty hogs in one day with facilities geared to handle five or ten animals required a well-executed plan of action, for all stages of butchering were necessary for each animal dressed.

Weather being favorable, a date was set and a crew of ten men were engaged, mostly neighbors. On the day appointed the men arrived about daylight (7 a.m. in the wintertime) and were briefed as to each one's duty for the day. One man was assigned to keep the fires going under two fifty-gallon iron kettles to insure plenty of hot water for scalding. One man did the killing, and a second man bled the animals; a .22 caliber rifle was used for the execution. The carcass was then scalded and scraped by a crew of four. After the hair and thin outer skin had been removed and the carcass was rinsed in clean water, it was then hung on a beam in preparation for the removal of the offal. This operation was usually taken over by an experienced hand. The last and tenth crewman was a roustabout, lending a hand wherever needed.

The dressed carcasses were allowed to hang overnight to cool. Then came the cutting-up process, which took about three days for fifty hogs. Three experienced meat cutters were retained to divide the carcasses into "picnic hams" (shoulders), true hams, and bacon, and also to remove the backbones and spareribs. The scrap meat or trim was made into sausage and the fat rendered into lard.

Disposing of all these by-products from fifty hogs whose dressed weight averaged 210 pounds apiece was a major problem. The backbones and spareribs with the heads and a set of hamhocks, were hauled to Oakland and peddled out. (This was before Oakland adopted the "Green River" ordinance, which prohibits peddling within its city limits.)

However, this did not complete the hog-killing operation. After the hams and bacon had remained in the curing process the required time, about one week, they were hung in the smoke house for final curing, which usually took three to four weeks. The entire venture paid its way, but from the small margin of profit it was evident that the local market could not absorb so much home-cured meat in competition with packing-house products.

Cap Grows Hops and Prunes

Cap was among the first in Douglas County to plant hops. Around 1896 he set out ten acres and built a drier. The hops paid well until increased production brought the price down and two crop failures from hop mildew made him change to Italian prunes.

The same circumstances caused other hop growers in Douglas County to change to prunes. The *Roseburg Review*, in 1908, commented on the growing Italian prune industry in the lower Umpqua Valley: "Frank F. Wells has ten acres producing; A. B. Haines has eight from which he realized 13,000 pounds of dried fruit. Jim Stark of Elkton has ten acres, Eustace Schad has eight, and C. H. Maupin of Kellogg has ten acres of Italians."

When Cap's Italian prune orchard began to bear, he converted his hop drier into a prune evaporator. After the trees produced more fruit than the old drier could handle, he built a Kurtz tunnel drier, in 1916. Eventually the ten acres expanded to forty and became the main source of income for the Maupin family. When Eugene Fisher acquired ownership of the C. H. Maupin ranch, he bought a Miller-type evaporator from Alva Maupin at Yellow Creek and moved it to the Hudson claim in 1944.

Cap also set out five acres of Petite prunes. Because at that time, in the 1890s, the market for dried prunes was slow, especially for Petites, he tried another venture. As a license to distill alcoholic beverages was not hard to obtain then, he engaged a person who had a distiller's license to work up his Petite crop into brandy. Cap's hired hands, however, did their best to consume the output and were seldom able to do a day's work. The brandy project was abandoned. The distiller's vats were still around in 1900 on the Lyman Kellogg place, later owned by Roy Fisher.

Cap Builds a Sawmill

Around 1890, Cap, with Joe Roberts and John L. Smith, built the first sawmill in the Kellogg area on Wagner Creek, one-fourth mile from where it joins the Umpqua. Two attempts were made before a dam would hold. The first water wheel was an overshot and their headrig was a whipsaw. Ben Pilkenton of Oakland made the metal parts for the carriage in his blacksmith shop. The whipsaw gave much trouble and was finally discarded for a circular saw headrig with two saws, one above the other. The overshot wheel did not generate enough power, so a small turbine was obtained from W. B. Clark at Millwood and hauled to the mill site on the running gears of a farm wagon. Mechanical difficulties were overcome by Thomas Nicholson. Besides customers from the local market, settlers along the river from Elkton to Long Prairie placed orders with the Wagner Creek mill. The lower deliveries were made by rafting the lumber down the river, several orders in one raft.

In 1898, Cap sold the mill to Jack Howard and Tom Nicholson, who operated it until 1900, when Nicholson sold out to George and Edgar Madison. In 1904, the Madison brothers bought Howard's interest. Soon afterward George Madison acquired full control and operated it in conjunction with his ranch until his retirement.

The high water of the winter of 1904-5 destroyed the dam and mill framework and floated the carriage fifteen miles downstream, where it lodged on the Lou Rapp place. It was hauled home and reassembled on a new location about one mile farther up Wagner Creek. A steam threshing engine was used for power until a dam was built, and a larger turbine—from Ev Cooper's mill on Brush Creek—was installed with the smaller one. The two were arranged to operate in unison when needed.

When George Madison moved to the Robertson claim on the east side of the Umpqua River, the headrig and parts needed to operate the mill were set up on that place to saw lumber for his new house. The planer that Maupin brought from Millwood is stored on the Madison farm; some parts are scattered about on the last Wagner Creek mill site, and others are in an old shed nearby. The turbines are still in Wagner Creek, the only landmarks of a mill with a long pioneer history.

Captain Henley Maupin also did much for the improvement

of roads and schools, and he was repeatedly elected to the district school board. He died in 1934.

Charles McClellan Minter

Charles McClellan ("Clen") Minter, his wife, Mary Ann Powell Minter, and their one-year-old daughter, Anna Belle, immigrated to Oregon in the spring of 1884. Clen, as he was usually called, was born near Welchburg, Jackson County, Kentucky, on January 9, 1862. His wife was born near Cumberland Gap in Harlan County, Kentucky, on November 26, 1861.

They came west accompanied by Mrs. Minter's parents, Hiram S. Powell and Anna Dixon Powell; the latter's son, Cyrus Powell, and his wife, Amanda Minter Powell, and their small daughter, Lucy Belle. Anna Dixon Powell became ill and died on the railroad immigrant train near The Dalles in March 1884. The body was taken to Portland and then on to Elkton for burial.

Clen Minter spent sixteen years in Douglas County. The family lived in twenty different houses. During that period five boys and one girl were born within a radius of ten miles and no two in the same house.

Clen made several attempts to homestead but the allotted 160 acres then available could not be developed at the same time the homesteader worked for others. In spite of this handicap he gradually accumulated enough personal property and equipment to farm rented land.

Clen Minter was a strong advocate of public schools. School districts in 1891 were large, and schoolhouses were far apart. At that time the Minter family lived one mile up Yellow Creek, seven miles above the Crescent Ferry at Kellogg. There were fourteen children of school age living within two miles of the mouth of Yellow Creek, and the nearest schoolhouse was in Green Valley, six miles away. With the help of those living in the vicinity of Yellow Creek, Clen led in organizing the school district of Little Canyon in 1891-92. William Deardorff, a Mr. Spooner, and a Mr. Pichette (a French-Canadian Indian) were members of the first school board, and Minter was its clerk. Cora Fabrique of Wolf Valley taught the first term in an old cabin on the Thomas Delauney place at Yellow Creek. The next year a new schoolhouse was erected one-fourth mile from the mouth of Little Canyon.

In 1897, Minter moved his family to Kellogg, rented the Ziba Dimmick place, and operated the ferry for George Dimmick. Here he led a movement to vote a special tax for the purpose of building a new schoolhouse in that district; the old house could not accommodate the growing community. The tax carried, and a new building was erected in 1899. The carpentry work was done by Thomas Nicholson and Clen Minter. George Goble, with the help of his son, Walter, got out the foundation stones and laid up the brick chimney. The new school was located about a half mile along the Elkton road from the Crescent Ferry, on the northeast corner of what later became the land of Mrs. Mary Ann Minter.

The old schoolhouse was built in 1877, with W. W. Wells as the first teacher. W. F. Powell, who came to Oregon with his parents and attended school there in 1883, said that his teacher was Charles H. Fisher, later editor of the *Eugene Register-Guard*. Boyd Rader, whose family came to Oregon with the Ewing Powells in 1882, said that they spent their first winter in the old schoolhouse as no school sessions were held there in the winter months. Mary Dodge was his teacher the following summer. Other early teachers were Jesse Belle, Jenny Clarke, H. Andrus, T. J. Wilson, Alex Patterson, and Adilla Peters.

There were about thirty students enrolled in District No. 54 in 1897. All grades were taught by one teacher in one room approximately eighteen by twenty-four feet. Textbooks were Fish's *Arithmetic* Nos. 1 and 2; Mace's *History of the United States, Graded Lessons in Physiology and Geography,* and Reed's *Graded Lessons in English Grammar.* The primary grades were taught the vowels and consonants from a chart that served as an abridged reference for all grades. It touched on the fundamental principles of bookkeeping, general business methods, and handwriting. The Spencerian (slanting) System of writing was then standard; the Vertical System was adopted in 1900.

George W. Dimmick, who had a contract with Douglas County to operate the ferry known then as the Dimmick and Fryer Ferry, had been appointed county treasurer, and Clen Minter was hired as deputy to tend the ferry. In December 1899, there was an unusual rise in the river. A large tree floating downstream fouled and broke the ferry cable. After the flood subsided, the cable was in the process of being put back into service when Minter was drowned, January 19, 1900.

His death placed upon his wife the responsibility of providing for the family and keeping it together. Well-meaning friends urged her to farm out the three older boys and accept charity from the county for the three youngest children, which she refused.

Mrs. Minter was appointed to administer the estate of her husband. Clen's lease on the farm expired in the fall of 1900. She spent most of the summer settling her affairs, harvesting the crop, and finding a place to live. Wallace Fryer harvested the crop for one-third. Cap Maupin assisted her in finding a place to live by arranging with A. E. Ozauf of Scottsburg to grant her a loan of $150 to buy eighty-eight acres of unimproved land adjoining the Ziba Dimmick donation claim.

During the summer of 1900, the older boys cut and peeled logs for a barn, and the neighbors helped raise it. Boyd and Henry Rader put up a two-story rough-lumber house, sixteen by twenty-four feet, and a lean-to cover for a woodshed. A chicken house and a hog pen completed the ranch buildings.

By October all expendable property had been liquidated and the family moved in. A few farm tools, a team of horses, two cows, and a sow with six pigs were the extent of farm equipment and livestock; the household furniture consisted of the barest necessities. Chairs were hand-made with rawhide seats. Bedsteads were also hand-made, with slats for springs. Everything was of the plainest sort, but it was home, and home it remained for forty-five years.

Mary Ann Minter, almost single-handed and against great odds, kept the family together and gave them the advantage of a common-school education. Many a night the children were lulled to sleep by the hum of the old spinning wheel she had bought from Mrs. William Moore in 1885 — working up three fleeces of wool into yarn for payment.

Most pioneer women were trained to spin and weave from girlhood, but first they had to prepare the wool. The first step in preparing yarn was to take wool fresh from the sheep's back and remove all grease or lanolin. Burrs, pieces of straw, or any foreign matter had to be tediously removed by hand. The wool was then carded for spinning into rolls the size of one's finger. The next step was to spin the roll into a continuous thread, which had to be doubled and twisted into knittable yarn. The yarn was then washed thoroughly before being wound into balls for convenient handling. It could be dyed either before or after knitting. All of this required skill and hard work. Mary Ann Minter made her own yarn and sometimes sheared the sheep herself. She knitted the socks and mittens for five boys, and also managed to knit gloves and socks for others; for the latter she received from fifty cents to one dollar per pair.

Besides raising a family of her own, her greatest responsibility was to perform the duties of midwife for the community. She spent the last forty-five years of her life on the land she bought with the help of the Masonic Lodge, of which her husband had been a member. She died in October 1944, at the age of eighty-three and was buried beside her husband in the Kellogg Cemetery.

Early residents of Kellogg, even the second generation, are rapidly thinning as the years pass. The old schoolhouse that Clen Minter helped to build looks neglected and forgotten in its present setting. When the rural school districts consolidated with the Elkton High School district, the old schoolhouse—along with the grounds upon which it stands—was transferred to the American Sunday School Union by Douglas County to be used as a place of worship in the Kellogg Community. After nearly sixty years of serving the Kellogg community, the Sunday school disbanded in 1966. Eugene Holcomb and Mrs. Leona Madison were the last leaders. The old schoolhouse has fulfilled its mission.

A Note on the Oregon Volunteers

When word of the Indian uprising in the Rogue River country reached the Umpqua settlements in October 1855, S. D. Hadley was sent from Umpqua County with a request to Governor Curry asking permission to organize a company of volunteers to protect their homes. Permission was granted, with the understanding that members of the company were to furnish their own mounts, arms, ammunition, and clothing.

On November 8, 1855, Company 1, 2nd Regiment of Oregon Volunteer Riflemen, was mustered in at Roseburg with Captain W. W. Chapman in command, Ziba Dimmick 1st lieutenant; James Morrell, 2nd lieutenant; Lyman Kellogg, William Wells, Abijah Ives, Thomas Cozard, sergeants; William Allen, Abram Langdon, Johnson B. Goff, and Joseph Reed, corporals.

Privates of Company 1, 2nd Regiment of Oregon Volunteer Riflemen, were:

Simon H. Allensworth	James L. Garrett	William McKearns
George H. Burges	Edward Griffin	James McDonald
Wm. F. Bay	George Greenwald	James McGranery
Rufus Butler	Charles G. Henderer	John Nicholson
Edward Breen	William W. Haines	W. R. Patterson
Wm. Barr	William Golden	George Payne
Clayton F. Brambett	Francis Geiger	Benton P. Pyburn
Benjamin Brattian	Addison C. Gibbs	Samuel Rich
John Burrington	Calvin B. Green	William Robertson
C. A. Bartrutt	Ira Hanna	Thomas Stuttard
Henry Casey	A. T. Howard	George Snyder
Thomas Chapman	H. W. Howard	Andrew Sawyers
G. J. Chapman	John H. Hope	John J. Sawyers
	William Hubbard	James F. Savery

James T. Cooper

Daniel Craft

Alexander Canautt

William Canautt

William Davis

Russell Dimmick

Abel Pasco Fryer

Solomon Ensley

James Farmer

James Frain

J. Crosby Fitzgerald

David Frarey

Levi Gant

Clark Hudson

Shadrach Hudson

William Hilbert

William Hathaway

R. M. Hutchinson

Peter Johnson

Joe Kuntz

Levi Kent

James F. Levins

Thomas Levins

Ansel Langdon

James McKinney

John Marshall

S. R. Slayton

Jackson Swearengen

S. E. Smith

M. R. Sharp

Madison Scoby

Daniel Test

Daniel Thornton

D. C. Underwood

Ansel Weatherly

L. L. Williams

J. P. Wiggins

J. A. Zanders

The company never experienced actual combat; it was disbanded in January of 1856, and permanently discharged on May 8, 1856.

CHAPTER XIV

Hedden Bluff

The community of Hedden Bluff derived its name from a rim of rocks on the Philip Krumm donation claim now owned by the heirs of Cyrus Hedden. This sparsely settled area in the foothills of the Coast Range is about six miles west of Elkton. A spur ridge of the Coast Range extending to the Umpqua River at Elkton separates this precinct from the Walker School District on the north; the Umpqua bounds it on the east, and Mehl Canyon divides it from the Kellogg community on the south.

The first settlers in this area in the early 1850s were: Philip Krumm, John Marshall, Daniel Test, Dave and Daniel West (sons of Calvin B. West), Loren L. Williams, and a family named Dean. By 1880 these had left for other parts and a new group had moved in—the Smiths and the Suttons, who arrived in 1881, followed by the McClays, Rhineharts, Swaggarts, Carltons, Hamptons, Owens, and two brothers, Ples Rhodes and John Rhodes.

The Smith Clan

George Thomas Smith, Sr., head of the Smith clan, was born in Indiana in 1854. His parents separated when he was a year old, his mother retaining custody of him. She later married a man named McDonald, by whom she had two boys, Malcolm (Mack) and John. Both later took the surname of Smith, the same as that of their older brother.

George and his wife, the former Sarah Morris, with their one-year-old son, Irving; George's mother and her two younger boys; and two uncles of George, Oren and Byron Sutton, completed the group that came to the Hedden Bluff area in the fall of 1881. The record of the arrival of this group at Hedden Bluff was re-

206

counted by Mrs. Clara Powell Smith, in an article published in the *Roseburg Review* in the summer of 1952. Douglas County was observing its 100th anniversary as a county and the newspaper solicited articles of historical interest. Mrs. Malcolm Smith responded by sending her husband "Mack's" memoirs of his life at Hedden Bluff and on his homestead on Big Camp Creek. Because of its historic value the author feels that this unique and humorous piece of literature is worthy of being included. Mack's story follows:

"When four years old, Mother, John and I moved from Valparaiso, Indiana to Princeton, Missouri. When I was eight years old we moved to the Sacramento Valley in California where we lived for seven years, then we moved to Elkton, Oregon.

"We camped at Dodge Canyon for about three weeks or a little longer. Brother Johnie went fishing one day and a little wren lit on his fish pole. It was the first wren Johnie had ever seen. He said it was very tame and looked like a little hen. After that we called them 'little hen birds.'

"Brother George, Sarah, uncle Ore (Oren) and uncle By (Byron) Sutton came to Oregon the same time Ma, Johnie and I did and we all camped together. While we were camped at Dodge Canyon, George and uncle Ore started to walk to Loon Lake, they had a pack horse with them. They were going to look at the country to see if they could find a suitable place for a home. They stopped over night at Alf Walker's. Alf told them about some vacant land on Hedden Creek, so they decided to look at it before going to Loon Lake. It looked so good to George that he decided to homestead it, so never went to Loon Lake.

"They returned to Dodge Canyon to tell Ma and Sarah what they had found. Everyone was pleased with their description so George, uncle By, uncle Ore and I came back to Hedden Creek to build a house—16 by 24—out of logs. We thought it was the nicest house that ever was.

"George and uncle By went back to Dodge Canyon and uncle Ore and I stayed to take care of things at the new home. George had to make several trips to move everything down as the roads were muddy and bad. [They came over the military road through Mehl Canyon.] Ma and Sarah came on Christmas day 1881. They liked the new home.

"Johnie and I worked on the place most of the winter. Some time in February I went to work for Jake Sawyers. I worked for him until April. I also worked for Henry Beckley during haying and then bucked straw for the threshing machine. When threshing was over in the fall I sheared sheep for Barney Kellogg, then worked on George's place till January when Ples Rhodes came to get me to work for Frank Wells. I worked for him till the 27th of April.

"By this time Ma had decided to take up land joining George's place. That was in 1883, so Johnie and I began cutting brush on it. In June we built a nice peeled log house, size 16 x 16, but didn't get moved into it. The slashing was nice and dry so George set it afire and didn't stay to watch it. The slashing was so close to the house that it caught fire and burned down. Soon as the fire cooled down we had to build another house, but this one was built of black logs and looked awful compared to the first one. Ma papered the inside with newspapers which helped a lot. We made it 16 x 16 the same as the other one. We moved into it about the first of November.

"Johnie and I worked at home during the winter and for the neighbors during the summers. We lived in the log house until 1886-87, when we built a new lumber house. Ma thought it was the nicest house that ever was. I worked on the place and for the neighbors until 1890.

"When the new lumber house was finished I was nearly twenty-four years old so decided Ma and Johnie could take care of her place and I would get one of my own. I had already found a place that suited me on Camp Creek. I started to build my first house on Camp Creek the 7th day of March 1890. While building the first house I camped under a big tree that had burned down. It was about six foot through and burned underneath but not on top, so left a roof over my head. I slept under the log roof and built a bark shed for a kitchen. Later I split out boards to build a kitchen and flooring from the same log for the new house I was building.

"Uncle Etsel Sutton came to see me. He laid the flooring in the new house while I split it and carried it about one hundred yards to where the new house stood. All of my furniture was from split-out lumber, there wasn't a sawed board on the place. I made my washboard and washtub out of material at hand. The tub was a three foot block out of a log about two and a half feet through. The washboard was from a slab split out of a tree. I cut ridges on the board. My meat was salted down in a hollow I dug out in a log or a tree I had fallen for that purpose. I split out by hand, timber for a board fence around the orchard.

"I kept from six to twenty-five head of cattle, and from two to six hives of bees, a cat, a dog and a horse. I raised a good garden and the last ten years I lived there I had lots of fruit; apples, plums, and berries. I lived there fourteen years. I kept my bees overhead upstairs so the bears couldn't get at them. There was quite a lot of white clover on my place, and the bees made the finest honey from it.

"Johnie and I went to school in Cherry Valley, California a part of two terms, and part of one term at Capelle, California. Also part of a term after we came to Elkton. John went to Cherry Valley after I quit. I had to buck straw for the threshing machine.* I was fourteen and Ma needed me to work.

---

*Bucking straw meant keeping the threshed straw away from the tail end of a thresh-ing machine. This job was performed by a boy old enough to drive a horse hitched to a rail or pole with extended tugs fastened to each end. The horse would be driven between the machine and the pile of straw to be moved. The driver would then flip the outside tug over the pile and ride the rail through, serving as a binder to keep the straw from spilling over behind the rail. He merely quit riding the rail when he wanted to unload.

"I was out baiting bear traps on April 10th, 1890, carrying a deer on my shoulder. I was up a little creek east of Camp Creek on a deer trail when I saw a puma or a panther. It was different than any that I had ever killed before, coming like a streak down the hill towards me. He may have been after the deer ham on my shoulder, but I didn't wait to see, I shot him with my 45-60 Kennedy rifle.

"Another time when I was hunting deer there came up a real hard shower. I backed up under a leaning tree to keep dry. After the shower was over I went a little ways and saw fresh panther tracks that had been made since it had stopped raining. I put old Watch, my dog, after him and in just a few minutes he brought him back past me and it ran up a small hemlock tree. It was so small it bent over from the weight of the panther. I shot him with a 40-70 Sharps. In just a few minutes Watch treed another in a big cedar. I shot and killed it too. By this time it was getting dark and I went home. The next morning I went back to see if there were any more panthers and found a big old buck deer that the panthers had killed the evening before. They had just killed it before Watch treed them. They hadn't had time to eat any of it. If I had found it the same evening it was killed it would have been good to eat.

"I was going to Camp Creek from Johnie's one time. I was riding my horse and I saw a panther lying on an uprooted tree, when I tried to shoot it the horse kept jumping around so I got off. Standing on the ground, the brush was so high I could hardly see the panther, but I shot at it anyway but only crippled it. Old Watch chased it about one hundred yards and bayed it under a log. I crawled up close to shoot it in the head so it couldn't hurt the dog. When old Watch saw me getting close he thought he could kill it himself, so he ran up on it and they began to fight. They were so mixed up that I couldn't tell where the dog quit off and the panther began. The panther finally jumped on a pole out of the dog's reach and I shot him, skinned it and went home.

"When Forest McClay lived on the Marshall place above Johnie's, Forest's little girl (Josie) became sick. Forest was working in Loon Lake cutting brush for Henry Laird. Ma and Johnie wanted me to go out to the Lake to get him. I left Johnie's place about daylight and took my old cap and ball six-shooter with me. Just below the eight foot falls on big Camp Creek I found three panthers. I began to shoot at them and killed one and old Watch treed another one. I shot all the ammunition I had left into the one up the tree. It wasn't enough to kill him but made him awful sick. I didn't have any more bullets so I went over where I had killed the first one to see if I could cut a bullet out of him but I couldn't find any so I went back to where Watch had the other one treed. He got so sick he had to come down the tree. Watch then bayed it under a bank. I broke a pole and then took my suspenders and tied my hunting knife on the end of it. Then I crawled up over the bank and Watch seeing me so close thought he had help. He took hold right then. I saw that old Watch could almost handle him alone. I made a run at him with my stick with the knife on the end and the pole broke. I hit the panther over the head with the piece left in my hand. That stunned him, then I picked up the piece with my knife on it and killed him. I just took the scalps for there was three dollars bounty then at that time.

"I started on down the creek and when I came to where the third one had turned off, Watch wanted to go after it. He didn't want to leave any for seed. I didn't have any more bullets so I wouldn't let him go. Besides I didn't have any more time to spend on panthers. The reason I tied my knife on the pole I was too bashful to run in and knife him like they do in books.

"I went to Loon Lake then and found Forest McClay. He and I came back to Johnie's over the old Dickerson Trail.

We got to Johnie's about nine o'clock that night. (The little girl was very sick and lived only a few days.) After my experience with my old cap and ball six-shooter I decided right then to buy a new 38-40 Colts six-shooter, so as not to have so much trouble loading it. It most me $12.50.

"The second summer after taking the homestead, I stayed home and cut brush. Ma gave me a yellow kitten, I called him Sam. He grew to be a big cat, he wouldn't get on the table or snook anything. When he was about three years old I went to Gardiner to work in the logging camp and left Sam to run the ranch to suit himself.

"When I came back about New Year I found Sam at Ma's. He must have gotten lonesome so came about seven miles through the mountains. It was the first time he had been away from home since I had taken him to Camp Creek. I left him at Ma's and went back to my homestead. In about two weeks Sam came home and stayed with me five years then disappeared. I thought maybe a panther or a wild cat caught him for he never showed up again."

Epilogue to "Mack's" Story

Mack's account of his life at Hedden Bluff and the time spent on his homestead on Camp Creek is a valid description of incidents mentioned, attested by all who knew him; he was not given to telling tall tales for entertainment's sake, but he did have a keen sense of humor and a gift for satire. When Mack finally left his homestead around 1907, he sold his cattle. These cattle were used to him and he could move among them with ease, but if a stranger were present they would take to the brush like deer. When he delivered them to his brother Johnie's ranch at Hedden Bluff, after a cattle buyer had taken over, he had to fasten a blind over their eyes and drive each animal separately, with one man behind and another ahead, and with a rope tied to their horns. He and Johnie worked nearly two weeks delivering ten or a dozen head to his brother's place.

During January of 1906, this writer, then fourteen years old, spent a week visiting Mack at his homestead. While there he persuaded Mack to let him shoot the 38-40 Colts which Mack had bought with the bounty received from the panther scalps. But I had to promise to wheel a cord of firewood about one hundred yards to the woodshed for the privilege.

Mack had another varmint dog he called "Boomer," a large short-haired black and tan. His ancestry was anybody's guess but his loyalty and devotion to his master were never in doubt. When Mack left his homestead he gave the dog to Cap Maupin of Kellogg, but the dog would not stay with his new owner, returning to the homestead looking for Mack; and of course he found the place deserted. The writer finally persuaded the animal to stay at the Ora McClay place, where it had been fed on different occasions and was more or less familiar with the surroundings. When Mack visited his brother, who lived a quarter mile west of the McClay place, at Christmas time, the dog caught his master's scent and went frantic with joy. When Mack returned to work in a logging camp at Gardiner, he had to leave old Boomer behind; the poor dog grieved himself to death, for he died shortly after his master returned to Gardiner.

Mack's first cabin burned down around 1900; but he built another one after the design of the first, on the same site. The location was visited by the writer in June 1964, when all that remained to identify the site was a pile of stones from the original fireplace. The current owners of the homestead and the surrounding timber had burned the second house to discourage hunters from camping there and creating a fire hazard. A few aged fruit trees were all that indicated a fine orchard had once grown there. Fir trees, some two feet in diameter, were growing in the meadow, and a network of black-topped roads constructed by the Bureau of Land Management had invaded Mack's hunting grounds; one ran over the site of his old cattle barn.

George and Sarah Smith lived on their homestead for more than fifty years and reared a family of ten children. They were:

Irving Etsel, Letta, Ruth, George Thomas, Jr., Abbie, Harry J., Lawrence, Eliza Belle, and Maurice.

George, Sr., literally hewed a home out of the virgin forest. Most of his tillable land had to be cleared of stumps and logs. During the winter months he moved the stumps by pulling them with a home-made capstan when the ground was soft from the winter rains. He bought feeder cattle, keeping them through the winter and selling them the following fall. He planted an Italian prune orchard which eventually paid off.

By the first world war the boys had grown up and were on their own, and the four girls had married. Selling his ranch in the 1920s, he moved to Oakland, where he died in 1934.

Sarah Smith was a typical pioneer woman, doing her share in establishing a home and rearing a family. In spite of seemingly endless tasks she occasionally found time to take her youngest children for an all-day picnic along the Umpqua River near the mouth of Hedden Creek. The author well remembers these occasions as he was always included—George, Jr., and Harry were near his own age, ten to twelve years. For lunch there was a big basket of fried egg and ham sandwiches, with a goodly sprinkling of jelly or jam, *on home-made light bread.* The older boys were elected to carry the lunch and also the youngest boy, Maurice, then about two years old; it was a good long mile to the river from the Smith home. On the "out" trip everyone was fresh and didn't complain; it was the "in" trip that hurt. The little boy was tired and cross, and so were the big boys. Besides, they had sunburned backs from playing in the water and rolling in the warm sand all day. In spite of all these discomforts though, the annual occasion was looked forward to with great anticipation.

I particularly recall a Fourth of July picnic when I had the pleasure of being included. The year was 1905, and the Smith family had decided to spend the day on Paradise Creek at the foot of "Big Hill," seven miles below Elkton. With the exception of the four oldest children, the entire family, including Grandma Morris, Mrs. Smith's mother, all made the trip in the farm wagon.

Mrs. Morris was a large woman and well along in years and was unable to get aboard the wagon by climbing over the side in the conventional manner. Mr. Smith solved the problem by backing the vehicle up to the front door, laying a 2 by 12 inch plank to the rear end-gate, and walking Grandma to a chair that had been placed for her convenience. The plank was carried along and she alighted safe and sound at the picnic. The ritual of walking the plank was repeated on the return trip.

Sarah Smith outlived her husband by twenty-four years and died September 8, 1958, eighteen days short of her ninety-ninth birthday. Johnie Smith lived with his mother until she died. He was past middle age when he married Elva Traylor; they became the parents of three girls. Johnie died in the early 1920s.

Mack worked for the Gardiner Mill Company after leaving the homestead, operating steam logging equipment for a number of years. Upon retirement he married Clara Powell and settled down on a small place at Elkton. He passed away in 1939.

The Colwell Slide

Members of the McClay clan made their first appearance in the Hedden Bluff and Walker district in 1882. George A. Gould and his wife, the former Harriet McClay, with their five small children (Albert, Clarence, Frances, Grace, and Lucy), established themselves on a homestead back from the Umpqua on a bluff, above the John J. Sawyers farm at Hope's Elbow — later known as the Colwell Slide.

This area got its name from an incident which occurred in the winter of 1888-89, when the entire mountainside above the John Sawyers place narrowly missed sliding into the river. When Gould moved his family to Coos County in 1885, he relinquished his homestead right and the improvements to Uriah S. Colwell and his wife, the former Enna Burnette. They and their five small girls were living on the homestead when the near-tragedy occurred.

It had been raining continuously for ten days, and the river had inundated most of the lowlands. On the afternoon before the climax of the storm, there was a great roaring as of a high wind, though there was no air disturbance. The trees swayed and tossed as if by a tornado. Late that evening Colwell made a trip to his barn to check on the stock. While returning to the house he fell into a hole that had mysteriously appeared in the path. This alerted him to imminent danger. He made his way to the house, hurriedly gathered his brood together, and started for the home of his brother-in-law, Andy Hargan, one mile away. There the family spent the night.

By the next day the rain had stopped and a survey was taken of the damage done. The whole mountainside, which included most of the Colwell homestead, had moved several yards toward the river. The cabin had escaped serious damage but had been turned partly around. The barn had been divided in half and one part had moved some distance downhill. A mound of yellow clay encompassing about three fourths of an acre had been pushed up by the earth's disturbance; it remained in evidence for many years.

The family spent the remainder of the winter in a log cabin on the John Sawyers place. Neighbors helped them gather up their stock and get settled in their temporary home. One cow was missing for several days; she had fallen into a depression and was almost covered with brush and fir saplings. Old Bossie was helped out, and after a few good feeds she was back on the production line, furnishing milk for five little pioneer girls. Evidence of this slide is still discernible but nature has hidden the scars by a protective coating of second-growth timber.

David Byron McClay

The parents of Mrs. George Gould—David Byron McClay and his wife Melissa Jane — arrived at Elkton from San Jose, California, in 1884-85, accompanied by seven of their children: Forrest, William Byron, Oella, Elmer E., Alice, Olive, and Ora. They settled temporarily in the same log cabin on the John Sawyers place that later sheltered the Colwells. Mrs. Alice McClay Baker passed away in the fall of 1965, at a nursing home in Eugene, Oregon, having passed her ninety-sixth birthday.

When the Goulds moved to Coos County in 1885, Mr. and Mrs. McClay and four of their youngest children accompanied them. In the early 1890s, Ora McClay, the youngest of the Mc-Clay family, returned to Douglas County and took a 160-acre homestead on Little Camp Creek, one mile below Mack Smith's ranch. After receiving a patent for it from the government, he went into partnership with his brother Elmer; they bought the John Marshall donation claim where Elmer lived, and where his children, Marshall and Gladys, were born. (Gladys, now Mrs. Ole Bunch, lives in Sutherlin and Marshall is now a resident of Klamath Falls.) The Cyrus Hedden land was also rented and the two places were farmed together until Ora married the author's sister, Anna Belle Minter, in December 1903. They set up temporary housekeeping on the Hedden place until the spring of 1904, when Elmer vacated the house on the Marshall place. Upon Ora's marriage, the brothers dissolved partnership, Ora taking the Marshall claim and Elmer the homestead on Camp Creek. Elmer moved to the Hedden farm where he resided until moving to Klamath Falls in 1910.

Ora McClay rented his place at Hedden Bluff in the fall of 1907, moved to Coos County on land three miles above Allegany at the mouth of Hodges Creek (where it empties into the east branch of the North Fork of Coos River) and established a chicken ranch. He died in January 1908, and is interred in the McClay family plot in the Elkton cemetery. His wife (now Mrs. McCulloch) resides in the Patton Retirement Home at Portland, Oregon.

School Days at Hedden Bluff

This writer was ten years old in 1903, when he went to make his home with Ora McClay and his wife for five years. During this time he became acquainted with the families in the Hedden Bluff and Walker communities, and attended the Walker school during the three-month winter term when the Hedden Bluff school was closed. These neighborhoods, though divided into school districts, shared their social activities — Sunday school, school entertainments, box socials, country dances, Fourth of July celebrations, and Memorial Day programs.

Three buildings have housed the school at Hedden Bluff since District No. 86 was established in 1874. First to shelter the newly organized school was a log cabin appropriated by the district for its use until a schoolhouse could be erected. It was said that Anna Augusta West taught the first term there, but no written record as such has been examined for corroboration. A rough lumber one-room building about 18 by 24 feet was built around 1898-90. This building was hard to keep warm in winter because of the cracks and knotholes in the walls and floor. Wood for the stove was dumped behind the building, without protection from the weather; the teachers did the janitor work.

The third school building was erected in 1906. It stood one-half mile from the site of the two former ones. All three were built on the Cyrus Hedden land along the old military road through his property. George Smith, Sr., hauled the lumber for the new frame structure from William Stark's sawmill at Elkton. Jay Mulkey and Elwin Meacham did the carpenter work and painting. At this time the new school building, Ora McClay's house, and the ranch home of Henry Beckley were the only painted houses in the community.

The enrollment of school-age children in District No. 86, when the author attended classes there, was about twenty-three. The Walker school district enrollment was about the same. Some of the Hedden Bluff families, the Rineharts, Swaggerts, Carltons, and the Hamptons, had no children of school age in either district at that time. The Smith, McClay, Owens, Rhodes, Bunch, Cheever, and William Traylor families supplied the Hedden Bluff attendance. The Henry Traylors lived so far away from the school that their daughter Myrtle lived with their relatives, the Henderers, in order to attend the Walker school. The family farthest away was the Warren Cheevers at Mehl Creek. Vennie

Cheever Schad, then the only one in the Cheever family of school age, rode an old flea-bitten white horse called "Nig" the five miles between her home and the schoolhouse. Thus the old nag became the first school bus in the Hedden Bluff school district.

Six teachers taught in the old rough lumber schoolhouse at Hedden Bluff between 1904 and 1908; Ida Robison (later Mrs. R. O. Thomas), Roy Agee, Georgia Gould, Ella Dickerson, Giles Phelps, and Dora McAlister. In those days rural school districts boarded their teachers in the homes of children attending their classes. Some chose to pay board and stay in one place. Giles Phelps and Miss McAlister both had homesteads on the headwaters of Hedden Creek and boarded themselves. Later, School District No. 86 was consolidated with the Elkton Union High School District. Georgia Gould Richmond and Roy Agee are the only survivors of the six who taught school at Hedden Bluff from 1904 to 1908.

In May 1966, the author visited the site of the old school there, where he had attended classes sixty years before. The building was in an advanced state of deterioration and was being used to store bailed hay and shelter sheep. The doors had fallen off their hinges and planks had been nailed over the openings; the windows were boarded up and the foundations were giving way; it made one feel old just to look at it.

Georgia Gould

Although Georgia Gould, later Mrs. James Richmond, actually lived in Douglas County only two years of her life, her mother's family were pioneers of the lower Umpqua Valley. Her early life was spent in true pioneer manner. She was born in 1883, one of twins (her twin brother was George Gould, Jr.), on her father's homestead, later known as the "Colwell Slide." When she was two years old, the family moved to another homestead in Coos County.

The distance from the Hedden Bluff area to their new home was thirty-six miles over a mountain trail. The bare necessities for establishing a home were transported on pack animals. The twins were comfortably placed in two separate packing cases (about 14 by 20 by 18 inches), wooden boxes used commercially as containers for kerosene cans. The boxes were strapped to a pack saddle on either side of a gentle horse. Thus they made their journey to their "Elk Horn Ranch" home. The Goulds lived on this ranch for about twenty years and there reared their family of nine children.

Georgia prepared to teach school after the family moved to Allegany around 1900, but in 1905 she entered nurses' training at Mercy Hospital in North Bend, Coos County. After completing the course, she married Dr. James Richmond and they moved to Coquille, where the doctor established a practice. Dr. Richmond died in the 1940s; Mrs. Richmond, now past eighty, still resides in Coquille.

Roy Agee

Roy Agee was born near Wilbur in 1883, the tenth child in a family of twelve. His parents were John and Mary E. Agee. Roy took advanced courses in business administration by attending the San Francisco Business College and began teaching at the age of seventeen.

In 1908, he married Grace Brown, granddaughter of Henry G. Brown, an early pioneer of the Elkton area. That same year he went to work in the Douglas County Clerk's office in Roseburg under E. H. Lenox, where he remained until the fall of 1913.

Between 1921 and 1924, Roy Agee was deputy clerk for Coos County; and in 1928 he was elected county clerk for Douglas County, assuming the duties of that office in January 1929. He was re-elected five times, making a total of twenty-four years as county clerk. He retired in 1953 at the age of sixty-nine. When interviewed in 1960, he remarked, "I wanted a little time to myself. I enjoyed serving the public and am also enjoying my retirement." Roy and his wife reside on the Henry G. Brown homestead four miles northwest of Elkton.

Social Activities

Social life at Hedden Bluff in the early 1900s centered around Christmas programs, Fourth of July celebrations, neighborhood dances and "play parties." There were also the annual school entertainments, Sunday school, and periodical church services; usually all were well attended. A Reverend Mr. Dayhuff, a Methodist minister from Elkton, held services once a month when the weather permitted.

There were two factions in the community, one for and one against dancing. The "against" people also liked to dance, but they called their gatherings "play parties" and held them in the schoolhouse. (Then they prohibited dancing in a public school building.) The dance crowd had to hold their frolics in private homes for even they drew the line on public dance halls. The only difference between the two groups was that the dance people had music to hop around by, while the play-party folks had to jump around to the vocal rendering of *Skip to My Lou My Darling.* One game was called *"The Drunken Sailor,"* and it was played much the same as the Virginia Reel was danced. The participants chanted a ditty, "What shall we do with the drunken sailor/Put him in a long boat and sail him over/The fall of the year comes in October."

The dance crowd occasionally had Charlie Clements to furnish music. He had a mandolin upon which he was a real artist; he carried the instrument to and from dances in a muslin "poke." Rollie Letsom bought the old "bug" from Charlie for $5.00 and still has the historic instrument.

The Hargan Family

The Andy Hargan family from the Walker district was popular at the neighborhood dances because Andy was a good square-dance caller. Mrs. Hargan made fine wild blackberry pies, and their three lovely daughters were charming dancing partners.

In 1909, the Hargans sold their home place in the Walker community and moved to a small ranch three miles northwest of Elkton, where Hargan died in 1924. This place was then sold and Mrs. Hargain, with their youngest son, Delbert, moved to the Grubbe ranch (S. F. Chadwick donation claim), eight miles below Elkton, where they lived for two years. When Mrs. Hargan broke up housekeeping she lived alternately with her children. In June 1960, the following news item appeared in the *Oregon Journal*:

"Golden wedding anniversaries are becoming more numerous (probably due to the increased longevity) but there's a 50th anniversary that's really unusual. Guests of honor at the festivities will include the husband's mother, who, the day before the occasion, will celebrate her 96th birthday. 'Youthful' guests of honor are Mr. and Mrs. Charles Hargan (the former Addie Hurd) of Drain, who were married on June 5, 1910.

" 'Vivacious' and interesting will be Mrs. Andy Hargan, who was born at Sawyers Bar, California (Frankie Burnett, daughter of James M. Burnett and the former Clara B. Millington) on June 4, 1864. She came to Oregon as a child and her six children are still living. They include: Charles Hargan of Drain, Minnie Hargan Ware of Portland, Lillie Hargan Boak and Mabel Hargan Traylor of Veneta, William Hargan and Delbert Hargan of Eugene. She also has fourteen grandchildren, twenty-seven great-grandchildren, and thirteen great-great-grandchildren."

Mrs. Hargain died in January 1962, at the age of ninety-eight. None of the families of the 1880-1900s is now represented in the Hedden Bluff area except Eliza Belle Smith Cutlip, who lives just below the "Colwell Slide" area on a portion of the John J. Sawyers donation claim.

Traces of the old military road along which the three schoolhouses at Hedden Bluff were built may still be seen; other landmarks of former days, especially the familiar dwellings, have disappeared. There is no district school in session in the old schoolhouse — only memories of the play parties, the country dances, box socials, and Christmas programs that were once the way of life as it was lived at Hedden Bluff in the early 1900s.

CHAPTER XV

Coles and Wolf Valleys

During the early stages of the settlement of present Coles Valley, the area was identified under several names: Big Bottom, Garden Bottom, and Garden Valley. This area was one of the first to be settled in the upper Umpqua Valley. When Douglas County was created in 1852, that portion of Coles Valley lying northwest of Calapooia Creek remained in old Umpqua County; however, the entire area presents a natural unit both historically and geographically, as does Wolf Valley, now Tyee, sixteen miles northwest.

Hal J. Cole, son of Dr. James Cole (born in Coles Valley), in a letter in the *Oregon Journal* dated August 17, 1889, stated that his father, for whom the valley was named, was among the first settlers. Dr. Cole registered his claim in 1851. It is reported that the first claim he selected was down near the river, but he later moved back next to the foothills and registered a larger tract of 640 acres.

According to his son, the doctor was born in Kentucky in 1809. He married Louisa Leeper of Tennessee County, Missouri, in 1843. They crossed the plains in 1851, beginning their journey with three small children. One, whose name was Martha, died along the trail and was buried beside the Platte River. After they settled on their claim in the Umpqua Valley other children were born to them. Hal mentioned his brothers, Sidney and Will, and his sisters, Mary and Virginia. Sidney was the first white boy born in the valley.

Dr. Cole took an active part in the organization of old Umpqua County. As well as pursuing his professional obligations and civic activities, he was interested in establishing a herd of cattle, which was the purpose in taking a larger claim. As the only physician and surgeon in that part of the old Umpqua County, Dr. Cole rode many of the trails of the valley and mountains to bring relief to the ill and injured.

By 1852, most of the choice land in the valley had been claimed. George Shambrook and William Churchill filed on their claims in October of that year, and John Emmitt filed in November. Ferdinand Fortin came about the same time. Shambrook was a naturalized citizen from Cambridgeshire, England; Churchill was from Kentucky, and Emmitt was from Northumberland County, Pennsylvania. Calvin B. West selected a claim in April 1854; his stay in the valley was short but his family proved up on the land.

The West estate is reported to be the first to be probated in Douglas County. Proof of West's intentions was established through affidavits of H. C. Stanton and C. M. Reed, who testified they were acquainted with West and knew about his trip to the states and his death on the return voyage to Oregon, July 1855. Their testimony was corroborated by B. J. Grubbe, John Hatson, and John Fitzhugh. The date of West's death and the circumstances which caused it were established through the testimony given by members of his family. (Mr. and Mrs. Gerald Bacon are the current owners of the property.)

The French settlement just west of Coles Valley was established by Francois Archambeau, Joseph Champagne, David Gernot, a man named Gouler, Narcisse LaRaut, Ferdinand La Brie, and Charles La Point. LaRaut settled in Garden Bottom, the early name for the eastern portion of Coles Valley. All were natives of Canada except Gernot, who was born in France.

Some interesting details are revealed in the records of donation claims taken around Bunton's Gap, the settlement adjacent to Garden Bottom. Benjamin Jackson Grubbe, who helped organize the first school in Coles Valley, lost the certificate of title to his claim. In 1862 he made application to the U. S. Land Office for a duplicate copy. He was required to sign an oath of allegiance to the Union before it was granted. Thomas Nelson Grubbe, George Shambrook, and Jonathan W. Woodruff signed the indenture. T. N. Grubbe, who settled on his claim in 1852, was also required to sign an oath of allegiance; his affidavit was signed by his brother, B. J. Grubbe, and George Shambrook and Jonathan W. Woodruff, on November 17, 1863.

The Clayton Clan

Mrs. Lucille F. Clark, granddaughter of Ashford Clayton, has contributed all the following information concerning her own and her grandfather's family. The Claytons are of English descent. The family line can definitely be traced to Robert, a soldier who came to England with William the Conqueror in 1066. Robert was given an estate called "Clayton Manor" and from then on he was referred to as "Clayton of the Manor." A San Francisco collector of old documents acquired the record of the sale of this manor centuries after it was given to Robert. William Elmer Clayton, grandson of Ashford, bought the old document from the collector and placed it in a safe deposit vault in a San Francisco bank.

Ashford Clayton settled on his claim in Coles Valley in the fall of 1852. He and his wife, the former Jemima Harper, both natives of Ohio, started to the Oregon territory with their two small children in the summer of 1851. They had joined a group of immigrants at Independence, Missouri, but their caravan was delayed three weeks at the South Platte River crossing. Here the travelers were obliged to bridge the stream because quicksand in the river bed made fording dangerous. Ashford wanted to break camp the evening the bridge was finished, but the men were tired and wanted to wait until morning. During the night a rainstorm caused the river to rise and carry the bridge away. It was too late in the season to rebuild, so they returned to Independence and spent the winter there.

The journey was resumed in the spring of 1852. Mrs. Clayton and the two children—George and Harriet—were stricken with cholera. The children died along the trail, but their mother survived. Other children of the Ashford Claytons were Mary Ellen,

Jasper, Albert E., Clara May, Orie A., Mortimer, America Jane, Jessie, Grant E., Lorena B., and Alice E.

When the caravan reached American Falls on the Snake River, south of Fort Hall where the road turned off to California, they met scouts returning from escorting a party to the gold fields. The latter told such fantastic tales of gold strikes in the Sacramento River Valley that the whole train, with the exception of Clayton, left the Oregon Trail and went to California.

Clayton traveled alone for three days, then joined another caravan. This train had two wagons with rawhide-covered boxes to be used as boats where the rivers were too deep to ford. Their goods, women, and children were ferried across, but the stock had to swim. One of Clayton's oxen died along the trail, and his milk cow was used as a replacement. Descendants of this cow were owned by members of his family for the next forty-five years.

Immigrants crossing the plains always carried a jar of sourdough as a starter for their bread. A necessary ingredient for making this bread was soda, of which the caravan that Clayton had joined was running low. One day, as they stopped for the noon rest near a dry lake bed covered with about six inches of white dust, Clayton tasted the dust, decided it was soda, and gathered a bag full. He was ridiculed, but before the company reached Oregon they were all using Clayton's "dust."

When the caravan arrived at Oregon City, Clayton left his wife with some settlers for her to recuperate from the attack of cholera. He went on to the Umpqua country and took a claim on the west side of Coles Valley. A good rough-lumber house was built that fall; none of Clayton's buildings were of logs because he was able to get lumber from the W. P. Powers sawmill in the English settlement east of Oakland. Clayton had observed debris high in the trees along the river, which to him indicated that there had been a flood not too long ago, so he built back toward the hills. He reasoned that what the Umpqua had done once it might do again; and it did, in 1861 and in 1964.

The church house built by Dr. James H. Wilbur, in 1854, is still in excellent repair and is used regularly for Sunday school and church services by the Methodist Episcopal denomination in the present town of Wilbur.

The parsonage built by Dr. Wilbur with the help of the early settlers in 1854. It is still used as a residence by Mr. and Mrs. William A. Persons, who contributed these photos.

Ferry at Scottsburg between 1917 and 1929. Alex Sawyers operated this ferry by hired deputy until the concrete and steel bridge was completed at that site.

Robert Minte

Private ferry, 1913-14. Robert Minter, ferryman, has just crossed two fares over the river at the Jack Howard ranch in the Kellogg community. They were his sisters-in-law, Mrs. Nellie Whipple McElhaney and Mrs. Marjorie Whipple Dixon.

Early in 1853, Clayton returned to Oregon City for his wife, who had fully regained her health. On their return to the Umpqua Valley they established their home by making a garden and planting an orchard. In October 1853, their daughter Mary Ellen was born, the first white girl born in Coles Valley. Sidney Cole, son of Dr. James Cole, was the first white boy, born six months earlier.

The early settlers found natural food resources abundant. Wild berries of many varieties were plentiful; these were dried until the settlers could obtain jars for canning. Deer and elk supplied meat, and there were salmon for the taking. Clayton said that when he first came to the valley the grass was so high that all one could see of an elk was his antlers. The elk did not adjust to the presence of the settlers as well as the deer and soon retreated into the higher mountains.

Usually the weather in the Umpqua basin was mild, but Sam Evans—an early settler in Coles Valley writing about unusual weather conditions—related that in January 1888, the temperature fell to six degrees below zero, and the cold killed a grove of myrtle trees along the river bank. Clayton drove a team of horses across the Umpqua River on the ice.

Coles Valley was normally a peaceful community, but it also had its share of excitement. Well remembered is the dance-floor fight at the home of Joseph Champagne in the French Settlement in 1867, when Mary Ellen Clayton (then fourteen years old) was taken to a "Republican" country dance by her father. Trouble started when uninvited "Democrats" appeared; tension was still that high after the end of the Civil War. In the melee Ashford Clayton was shot twice, but survived. His assailant was stabbed in the neck with a pocketknife by a fourteen-year-old boy. Mary Ellen, narrowly missed by the shots fired at her father, jumped from the landing of an outside staircase to the ground without injury.

Clayton was unofficial physician in the community, setting broken bones, pulling teeth, and administering home remedies until a trained physician could be found. After a dentist opened an office in Oakland, Clayton refused to pull teeth, but some still insisted on his services, probably because the dentist charged a fee and Clayton did not. He pulled his own teeth by fashioning special forceps for the job.

In a recent letter, Mrs. L. F. Clark recalled an anecdote in which her grandfather was involved. Ashford had called on his old neighbors, the Joe Churchills, one summer evening and left his old saddle horse, "Jim," ground-hitched in front of the house. It was early twilight before he started home. Meanwhile, Mr. Churchill's son Frank and Horace Chicane, a neighbor boy, had slipped out, turned Ashford's saddle around, tied the bridle reins to the saddle horn and turned old Jim with his rump toward the hitch-rail. They had then hid in the bushes to see what would happen. When Clayton came out he mounted Jim and took up the reins, but the horse started off in reverse gear. Just then Clayton got a glimpse of the boys and he knew what was up, so he dismounted and chased them under the barn.

In the morning when Mrs. Churchill looked out she saw him sitting by the opening to the barn. She exclaimed, "Why, Mr. Clayton, what in the world are you doing?" He replied, "I'm waiting for those damn boys to come out, then I'm going to kill 'em." When Horace Chicane later recalled the incident he said he almost did. Hogs had been sleeping under the barn and the area was alive with fleas. A recent issue of the *Sun-Tribune*, Sutherlin's weekly newspaper, noted that Horace Chicane, an early resident of Coles Valley, had passed away in Lewiston, Idaho, at the age of ninety-four years.

Indian Trouble

In 1855-56, Southwestern Oregon was harassed by Indians. Nick Day of Coles Valley, sub-agent for the Umpqua tribes, reported that the Rogue River Indians were causing trouble by raiding the farms south of Roseburg. After each raid they retreated to the hills where it was impossible for the military units assigned to that territory to control them.

There was a fairly large encampment of Umpqua Indians at "Basket Point," later a part of the farm of Jesse Clayton (brother of Ashford Clayton). The settlers in Coles Valley were concerned lest these Indians join the raiding Rogue River Indians. An envoy, sent to persuade the Umpquas not to go to war, found that they had two or three old Hudson's Bay flint-lock muskets, which they were unable to fire—yet from this observation the messenger reported back that the Umpquas were on the warpath.

A few days later Jesse Clayton met about forty armed and mounted white men who told him they were on their way to kill off a few Umpquas. He tried to convince them that the Umpquas were a peaceful tribe but the men were adamant in their purpose. He hurriedly contacted Nick Day (John Bacon is current owner of the Nick Day place) and Ashford Clayton, and by a shortcut succeeded in heading off the self-styled Indian fighters. Day told them that if they wanted to fight Indians to go after the Rogues but leave the unarmed and peaceful Umpqua tribe alone. Day later confessed that he was not sure if it was his eloquence or the Kentucky rifles in the hands of the Clayton boys that persuaded them to return home and talk things over. Jesse Clayton had the reputation of being the best shot in that part of the Umpqua Valley. He was only allowed one shot at shooting matches. It has been said that he handled a pistol like a man throwing a rock; he was so fast he didn't seem to take aim, but could shoot the head from a grouse in a tall fir tree with his old Kentucky rifle.

Wolf Valley

Wolf Valley, situated fifteen miles northwest of Coles Valley, still retains much of its primeval grandeur. It was the last section of Umpqua County open to settlement. Encircled by the picturesque Umpqua River as it winds its way through a secondary chain in the Coast Range, its area is approximately twenty-five square miles.

The first white men known to have visited this section of the

Umpqua basin made up the exploring party sent out by the Hudson's Bay Company, led by Alexander Roderick McLeod, assisted by Michelle La Framboise and Thomas McKay, in 1831. The first white man actually to settle there was Jesse Clayton.

Jesse Clayton was born in Perry County, Ohio, in 1826 and first came to the Oregon Territory in 1847. Soon after he arrived in Oregon, the Cayuse Indians went on the warpath, and he volunteered his services. When the uprising was put down in 1849, he went to the California gold fields, but returned to the territory in 1850 and took a donation land claim west of what is now Wilbur. He sold this claim to Flemming R. Hill in 1853 but remained in Coles Valley until 1859, when he bought 146 acres in Wolf Valley from George Shambrook for $325.

Jesse developed the property to some extent, but he erected the buildings too close to the river and the 1860-61 flood washed them away. A new log house was built on higher ground, which was still standing in June 1962; but it was then rapidly falling into decay. Sheep had been using it for a shelter, the dooryard was overgrown with briers, and large oak and cedar trees had grown up around it, almost hiding it from view.

In 1868, Jesse made a trip back to his old home in Ohio, and there married Lydia Heckathorn on August 10, 1869. They came to the Umpqua Valley that same year and spent five years in and around Garden Bottom before they moved to his ranch in Wolf Valley, living their until their deaths; Jesse in 1900, Lydia several years later.

William Alexander Fabrique

William Alexander Fabrique, a veteran of the war between the states, came to Coles Valley in 1868. He was born at Corydon, Indiana, on October 17, 1845. At the beginning of the war, when he was sixteen, he and his two brothers, Dudley and Andrew, enlisted in Company B, 53rd Regiment, Indiana Infantry. These three young men went through the war together, serving with Sherman on his historic march through Georgia.

Fabrique had been studying medicine before enlisting, and at the close of the war continued the course. After two more years of study and one year of work under an older doctor he moved to Nevada, and then to California, where he attempted to homestead. When it was learned that the land upon which he had built his cabin was on an old Spanish land grant, he pulled up stakes and made his way to the Umpqua Valley.

Pioneering in Wolf Valley

Three years later on October 26, 1871, William Fabrique married Mary Ellen Clayton. When her Uncle Jesse moved to Wolf Valley in 1874, he persuaded the young couple to come with him. There the Fabriques took a homestead ten miles below Umpqua Ferry in the upper end of Wolf Valley. Fabrique and Clayton packed all their supplies in until a road was blasted out of the bluff at Tyee Point. A wagon was kept at the Cranfield ranch on the north side of the river below the Umpqua Ferry, which they used to haul supplies from Oakland to the William Lawrence place at the mouth of Hubbard Creek.

Whip-sawed lumber was used for Fabrique's house, and enough more was sawed for a lean-to and flooring for Clayton's cabin. Then they fashioned furniture from materials at hand; bedsteads and springs were wooden frames over which strips of rawhide were woven. Mattresses were made from straw or shredded corn husks, with a top pad of carded wool. The result was a far better bed than the saggy springs manufactured in those days.

For light, coal-oil lamps were used, and considered a luxury; candles were less expensive because they were home-made from beeswax and tallow. A candle mold was standard equipment in every home. Similarly, soap was home-made. Lye was obtained by using an "ash hopper" in which the hardwood ashes from the fireplaces and stoves were dumped. An old-time ash hopper was a V-shaped receptacle; when full of ashes, water was poured over them until it leached through and was caught in an iron kettle; this was lye. Soap was obtained by cooking fats (such as tallow or hog fat after the lard had been rendered out) with the lye-water. The result was a soft jelly-like mass which made a good detergent and was "stronger than dirt."

One winter the trail around Tyee was closed for several weeks by high water and the settlers ran out of flour. The Fabriques ground wheat in their wall coffee mill for each day's supply of graham flour, with which the sourdough biscuits were made. Most pioneer women made delicious hot bread three times a day, baked in a Dutch oven before the open fireplace.

The McGees and McKays

Enzie McGee and his wife Alice were the Fabriques' nearest neighbors. They lived on the mountainside one and a half miles below them on what is now called the Kearney Emmitt place; Enzie used to hunt with Fabrique. Later Charlie McGee (Enzie's brother) and his wife (the former Fannie Rice) took over the place. They later sold it to Kearney Emmitt and bought another farm on the Calapooia. There they raised two orphaned nephews, Robert and George Wilcox; at this writing, George is still residing on the Calapooia farm and Robert lives in Portland.

Antonie McKay, another neighbor of the Fabriques, was a three-quarter blood Indian who lived about three miles above them and was reported to have been a son of Thomas McKay. Antonie was held in high regard by the Fabriques as he could speak French fluently.

The McKays raised two orphans: their own grandson, Thomas McKay; and Eva Pecard, a half-breed French girl. She was sent to the Chemawa Indian School two miles north of Salem, but died early in life.

"Winter of the Big Snow"

Settlers in Wolf Valley, as in most communities in the Umpqua Valley, depended on their stock for a cash income. Clayton and Fabrique ran sheep on the bald hillsides along rugged mountain ridges near their claims, and their flocks had to "rustle" their own provender the year round. Occasionally the weather was not very cooperative.

Settlers called the late winter of 1892-93 the "winter of the big snow." It began snowing on the first of February and snowed every day or night, until the first of March. There was an average of twenty-six inches of snow on the level. That winter Clayton and Fabrique lost nearly all of their sheep. When the storm began, some of the sheep took to the top of the ridges and found shelter under the big fir trees growing close to the open places. When the animals took refuge under them, the continuous snow piled up so deep it bent the limbs down and smothered them. There would be as many as fifty head under one tree. The only survivors were those that had taken refuge under the cliffs along the bald hills; these were fed oats and corn while the snow lasted. Predatory animals such as coyotes, panthers, and bears, also took their toll. Nearly every settler kept a pack of hounds with which they systematically patrolled their ranges, often joining with neighbors to pool their dogs in a chase.

James Otey

James Otey and his wife, the former Mary Jane Woodruff, with their small daughter Mollie, were friends of the Fabriques, though they lived near Bunton's Gap. James was a son of Elwin W. Otey, who had taken a donation claim along the military road between Hardin Davis hill and the Gap. He was also a hunting partner of Fabrique, who employed a half-breed Indian named Johnson to hunt for him full time. It was said that "old Johnson" could track a bear after the hounds had lost the trail. Otey was a frequent guest hunter at the Fabrique homestead. He was a natural cartoonist and entertained his host's family after a day's hunt by drawing caricatures.

Jim had a hound he called "Old Blue" who used to visit the Fabrique home occasionally on his own. He would come to the door and scratch for admittance, then when the door was opened, would enter and offer his paw to all who might be present. After a good nap before the fireplace he would get up and go to his home near Wilbur, almost fifteen miles distant.

Another canine caller at the Fabrique home was "Old Soundwell." This dog belonged to George B. Yale of Coles Valley, and used to accompany "Old Blue" on the trail. He was part bloodhound, with the sad expression and abundant skin typical of his antecedents. Late one evening he appeared at the homestead and scratched on the door for admittance. Upon opening the door the family beheld a pitiful sight; evidently the hound had been fighting with a panther, for his lip was torn clear back to his ear. He was taken in, and with the help of her son, Harve, Mrs. Fabrique sewed the lip together. The courageous old dog barely whimpered when the needle passed through the skin. Old Soundwell recovered and lifted his voice on many another hunt.

Neighbors Come to Wolf Valley

Jesse Clayton's ranch was about five miles below the Fabriques, and his nearest neighbor was R. M. Hutchinson, whose land lay to the west and across the river. In 1881, Redding Threlkeld moved his family to Wolf Valley and settled on eighty acres of land adjoining Clayton on the south.

Threlkeld, a native of Indiana, crossed the plains to California with an immigrant wagon train in 1850. When he arrived in California he bought property at a place called Two Rocks, about thirty miles north of San Francisco. He returned east in 1860, married Lucinda Davidson, a native of Illinois, then went on with his bride to New York, where they took passage on a sailing vessel to Panama on their way to California. They crossed the Isthmus and continued on to San Francisco, then to Two Rocks. During the absence of Threlkeld, the town of Petaluma had sprung up on his property; he sold out and headed for Oregon. He arrived in the Umpqua Valley in 1874 and took a homestead on Deer Creek, adjoining the place of a man named Phil Dammotta. It was here, that same year, that Threlkeld's only son, Walter, was born.

Threlkeld sold his homestead in 1877 and moved to the Charles LaPoint place in the French settlement, where his daughter May was born. Several more moves were made—to Coles Valley, to Wilbur, to Oakland, and finally to Wolf Valley, in 1881.

A School Is Established

In 1882, a school district was formed in Wolf Valley and a one-room schoolhouse was erected about one-half mile south of the Threlkeld homestead. The Clayton and Threlkeld families supplied most of the pupils. There were five children in the Jesse Clayton home, but only three were of school age: Elizabeth (Lizzie), Frank, and Jesse Rea. Susan and Maude attended later. There were three from the Threlkeld family; Walter, Eva, and May. George B. Yale was their first teacher, followed by R. M. Hutchinson and Lou Clinkenbeard.

In 1887, a new schoolhouse was built at Rock Creek, located up the river toward Umpqua Ferry, nearer the center of the settlement. The Fabrique children consisted of Emma L., Cora J. (who later taught the school), Henry L., Harve H., Nannie A., Dudley A., and Lucille A. Mrs. Anna Powell Fabrique, widow of Dudley, is living in a retirement home in Portland, Oregon, at the present time. Lou Clinkenbeard taught the first term in this building. Jennie Clarke Norman, Mary Germond, and Tilla Rader were among the teachers following.

A humorous incident occurred while Cora Fabrique was teaching at this school. Kearney Emmitt was driving about twenty range cattle past the schoolhouse one day. Cora, being familiar with the spooky habits of half-wild range cattle, called the children inside to wait for the cattle to pass. Some vacationers from Roseburg were camped on the river below the schoolhouse; the men folk had all gone hunting and the ladies were fishing. One of the ladies caught an eel and mistook it for a snake and started to scream. About that time, others saw the cattle and bedlam broke loose—women and cattle running in all directions. Some of the women managed to climb convenient trees. Some of the cattle swam the river and were never reported as being found.

In 1895, the lower part of Wolf Valley organized a new school district, which when divided, embraced the area a mile or so above Hubbard Creek on the north side of the Umpqua, to the Kearney Emmitt place below the Rock Creek school. The lower district took all the territory below the Emmitt place to Lost Creek, which was two miles below the Powell homestead, and also that area known as the Basin. Their schoolhouse was erected approximately a half mile below Porter Creek, about the middle of the lower settlement. The lumber for the new structure was rafted down the Umpqua from the W. B. Clarke sawmill at Millwood; the late Hiram S. Powell was one of the hands who brought the raft down. Henry Rader taught the first term of school.

In 1907 a new frame building took the place of the one erected in 1887. Kearney Emmitt and his wife, the former Tilla Rader, donated the lumber for this building. The Emmitt children who attended were: Chester, Crystal, Ruby, Forest, and Floyd. Other pupils were Phillip Durham, Marion and Florence Mortensen, and Alma Moser. Marie Rasmussen was their first teacher. When the school was consolidated with the Oakland district, the school building was dismantled and returned to Kearney Emmitt.

Ewing Dixon Powell

Ewing Dixon Powell came to Wolf Valley in 1893. He was born in Harlan County, Kentucky, in 1845. His parents, Hiram Sargent Powell and the former Anna Dixon, in 1865, moved to near Welchburg, Kentucky, ten miles southeast of McKee, the county seat of Jackson County.

Ewing Powell married Abby Edwards in May 1868. Two sons were born to them, William F. and James; James died in infancy. Mrs. Powell died in July 1871, and Powell married Dina Jane Roach in October of that year. They were parents of five children. Four were born in Kentucky (Greene C., Drucilla, Martha, and Hiram S.), and one (Anna) after they immigrated to Oregon.

Powell brought his family to Oregon by way of railroad emigrant train to San Francisco. He was accompanied by his elder brother Clayton Powell, William Rader, and their families. Rader's wife was the former Arminta Powell, sister to Ewing and Clayton. The Rader children numbered five at that time: Henry, Mellisa, Tilla, J. Boyd, and Charles B. Four more were born in Oregon: Oscar, Rose, Emma, and Ray. The clan came to San Francisco by immigrant railroad train, where they took passage to Portland aboard the steamer *Oregon*. From there they came to Roseburg, Douglas, County, over the newly constructed Oregon and California Railroad, in April 1882.

Choice homestead land in Douglas County had already been settled. Like the majority of immigrants who came west shortly after the Civil War, Powell spent most of his cash for traveling expenses and worked by the day to support his family. For the first four years in Oregon he lived a nomadic life, moving from place to place wherever his work led him.

In 1886, he homesteaded forty acres east of William Rader's house on the headwaters of McGee Creek. During his seven years on this place he worked for ranchers around Kellogg, shearing sheep at five cents a head and splitting fence rails at one cent each. Since he had learned to be a shoemaker in Kentucky, he opened a shoe shop in Elkton around 1898, but the demand for handmade shoes was not enough to keep him busy, so he did not stay in business.

Powell moved his family to the lower end of Wolf Valley in 1893, and took ninety-six more acres that his homestead right allowed him. Members of the Powell family lived on the old homestead for sixty-seven years. Ewing Dixon Powell died in 1936, Dina Jane Powell in 1926.

Hiram S. Powell

Hiram S. Powell was eleven years old when his father moved to Wolf Valley. In 1911 he married Agnes Van Arburg. During his residence in Wolf Valley, now called Tyee, Hiram worked to

bring progress to that area by way of roads, schools, mail service, telephones, and electricity. He added more than three hundred acres of land to the original ninety-six of the Powell holdings; he died in 1952. His wife managed the farm until its sale
in 1960. She then moved to Roseburg, living there until her death
in 1964.

Lorenzo Van Arburg (father of Mrs. Hiram Powell) was a
veteran of the 1855-56 Indian wars and a member of the Volunteer Rifle Regiment under Captain Noland in the Lane County
Company. He had a donation claim in the vicinity of Eugene
which he sold before he came to the Umpqua Valley in 1856.
In 1882, Van Arburg married Jane Patterson, a widow with two
children (Grace and William Hamilton Patterson.) He made his
wife's homestead his home until his death in 1911. His widow
survived him by a number of years; she died in June 1928.

More Neighbors

When Ewing Powell moved to Wolf Valley, his nearest neighbor was George Crenshaw, a Civil War veteran. Crenshaw's farm
joined Powell's on the west. Later Hiram and Greene C. Powell
owned this property, but when Hiram Powell was married in
1911 it was divided and Greene took the upriver half. This part
is still owned by his son, Harold G. Powell.

Jules Pichette, a French-Canadian, and his family of four,
lived across the river and about one mile northwest of Greene
Powell, just above the mouth of what is now called Cougar
Creek.

A man named Bohanan (given name not learned), with his
family of seven, moved to the Cougar Creek area across the
Umpqua River opposite the lower end of Wolf Valley in the
early 1890s. Cougar Creek comes tumbling down from a small
Lorna Doone-like valley called the "Basin"; here Bohanan established a home. He spent most of time traveling, promoting what
he called a "Cancer Cure." Greene Powell traveled with him as
his understudy for about a year.

Cora Fabrique was engaged by Mrs. Bohanan to tutor the Bohanan children in the summer of 1894. As such she was up to receive her board and fifteen dollars per month. In settling up with Bohanan, *he* charged her board, claiming that his wife had no right to make such an agreement. Cora's father consulted a lawyer but was advised that she had no recourse.

Charles M. Minter moved his family to the Basin in 1895, when Bohanan left. Two years later the Minters left and Boyd Rader took over.

Mail Service Established

Mail service in Coles Valley was much the same as in most of the other earlier settlements before a regular routine was established. It underwent many interruptions and changes of postmasters. The first postoffice in Coles Valley was established on December 28, 1860, with F. M. Good as postmaster. It was discontinued in December of 1862 and re-established in 1874 with George Shambrook as postmaster; this time the office was listed as Umpqua Ferry. Postmasters after Shambrook were W. C. Clarke, John C. Shambrook, William K. Caldwell, Jonathan D. Baker, George Shambrook (Umpqua Ferry), Joseph Churchill, Maud C. Shambrook, L. S. Fortin, George B. Yale, and James R. Wilson.

Millwood, six miles below Umpqua on the opposite side of the river, had a postoffice established on July 10, 1890, with W. B. Clarke as postmaster. Succeeding him were his son, Rush R. Clarke, and his daughter, Mrs. Jennie L. Norman, who was the incumbent when the office was permanently discontinued on July 23, 1931.

Between the time the Coles Valley office was closed and the Umpqua Ferry office established, the settlers in Coles Valley and below got their mail at Oakland. The Oakland postmaster kept a box in which he stored all mail for the area and whoever chanced to come to the postoffice picked it up and distributed it along the way home—or relayed it to the nearest family, and so on, until the box reached the last family.

After the Millwood postoffice was established, the Wolf Valley mail was sent there. The same order of delivery below that office was practiced; whoever came along from that neighborhood acted as mail carrier.

In 1903, a postoffice was established in the lower end of Wolf Valley. Before the Postal Department would set up an office in that vicinity, the citizens affected had to agree to furnish carriers for the mail route for one year free of charge. Subsequently a route was instituted between Umpqua and Ewing Powell's residence in the new postal community. The office was housed in Powell's home, and officially called Tyee, with Powell named as its first postmaster. The new sixteen-mile route passed through private property all the way from Umpqua. A. B. Leonard, one of the later carriers, said that there were twenty-seven gates to be opened and closed twice during a round trip (three trips: Tuesdays, Thursdays, and Saturdays).

During the life of the postoffice there was one postmaster and three postmistresses: Ewing D. Powell, Mrs. Martha Clayton, Mrs. May Powell, and Mrs. Bessie Leonard. Mrs. Leonard served seventeen years and was the incumbent when the office was discontinued in 1931. Carriers during that period were James Bartram, Frank Minter, G. C. Powell, Robert Powell, Oscar Rader, Mrs. Martha Clayton, William F. Powell, and A. B. Leonard. Will Powell, the only one of the carriers living at this writing, carried the mail longer than anyone else—on horseback through the winter and in a one-horse buggy during the summer. When the county opened a road from Umpqua to the Ewing Powell ranch, Will used a model-T Ford touring car, and he finished with a model-A Ford pick-up.

The Tyee community is now served by a daily mail circuit from Oakland via Umpqua to the mouth of Little Canyon; here the carrier doubles back to Oakland over the Elkton-Oakland route, six days a week.

Finally . . . Roads

Because of its geographical isolation, Tyee progressed slowly. The community had a mail route, postoffice, and telephone before a public road was established through its neighborhood. This sparsely settled community could not build and maintain the miles of roads necessary to connect its people with outside marketing facilities.

In the 1880s, a wagon road was blasted around the foot of Mount Tyee, and a road of sorts wound its way along the river from the Ewing Powell homestead to Umpqua Ferry, sixteen and a half miles. The nearest market was Oakland, twelve miles farther on. It took two whole days to make the round trip. In the middle 1890s, Jesse Clayton circulated a petition for an open road from Umpqua Ferry to his south gate, but got no support.

In 1906, Henry Rader, Greene Powell, and his brother, Hiram Powell, with the support of most of the citizens of Tyee, promoted a six-mile road down the river below the Ewing Powell ranch to connect with the Elkton-Oakland county road. A horse trail had been in existence for about four miles to the Jake Reuter place, about one mile below Lost Creek. From there to the mouth of Little Canyon the trail kept up on the hillside to avoid the bluffs which had been the main barrier. A surveyor was engaged to run a preliminary grade. His pay was guaranteed by Henry Rader and the Powell brothers, if the county should turn down their petition. George McElroy and Frank and Robert Minter helped with the chain and did the swamping (cutting of brush). The county court accepted the preliminary survey. It was thus made official by the county surveyor, Oscar Edwards, and work began in earnest in the winter of 1907-8.

In 1909 the road was opened for travel. A Fourth of July picnic and dance were held in a natural wayside park one mile below Lost Creek to celebrate the occasion. However, earth slides and windfall trees kept the road closed during most of the first two winters. There is now a well-improved road on both sides of the river from Little Canyon to Wolf Creek.

In 1919, a county road from the Umpqua postoffice to the Ewing Powell ranch was surveyed by Oscar Edwards. This section of road, particularly around the base of Mount Tyee, has been widened to the Threlkeld homestead, about fourteen miles below Umpqua Ferry. A concrete bridge was put across the river at this point in 1961-62, to connect with an access road which opens that section of Douglas County to the Loon Lake and Reedsport-Scottsburg road. There is now a black-top highway over this section.

"Hold the Phone"

In 1907, the Oakland-Kellogg Telephone Company was organized. J. Boyd Rader was president, George McElroy, secretary and treasurer, Greene Powell, Louis P. Rapp, and Fred Bullock, directors. The company was financed by selling shares for ten dollars. Each share gave the holder the right to connect one telephone instrument, furnished by himself, to the circuit and build his own lines from his residence to the county road. Maintenance costs were met, when necessary, by annual dues of nine dollars and special assessments. A franchise was obtained and a metal circuit was constructed along the county road from Kellogg to Oakland. Some subscribers had from three to five miles of private line to construct and maintain.

When the line was first installed, trees were used for poles when convenient. Telephone instruments in those days operated on dry batteries. Considering the line construction, they rendered fair service. It just about kept one man busy full time to keep the line open, removing debris that wind and storm deposited on the wire during the winter months.

Two years before the installment of the Oakland-Kellogg line, Sam Jones of Drain put in a telephone service from Elkton to Kellogg and charged rental for his phones. His line was a ground circuit and paralleled the Kellogg line from the Smith Ferry to the Hutchinson ranch, a distance of about five miles. There was about an equal number of subscribers on each line through this territory. Sometimes they became tangled during a storm and often remained crossed for several days before the trouble was found. During these periods the patrons on both lines had a field day visiting and it did not take long before the local pranksters created the same situation on purpose.

There were several amateur musicians along the line, mostly fiddlers, and it was not hard to persuade them to give impromptu concerts. This was accomplished by leaving the receiver off the hook in the home where the program originated—the music was then broadcast as by radio. A lot of good entertainment was thus enjoyed on long winter evenings.

Electricity Installed

The installation of telephones was the first evidence of a shrinking world to come to the Tyee community. To be able to converse with friends, whom it formerly took a half to a full day's travel to reach, was indeed progress. Sometimes much relaying was needed to get a message through, but there were always listeners ready to help. Around 1936-37, the Rural Electric Administration put a power line through the lower Umpqua Valley. Now Tyee, along with the neighboring communities, enjoys every electrical appliance found in any town in the Umpqua Valley.

The Passing of Rural Schools

With the advent of the automobile, telephone, improved roads, and electricity, Tyee adopted a new way of life. One of the oldest institutions to give way to progress was the district school. The old Rock Creek schoolhouse was replaced by a new building.

The Porter Creek district also replaced its first building with one similar to the Rock Creek school. When both districts were taken into the Oakland Union High School District, the local schools were closed and the children transported to Oakland by bus. Henry Baird was the first driver. Different migrant families used the Porter Creek building as a residence from time to time; eventually it succumbed to natural deterioration.

A Semi-Private School

In 1943, a co-operative sawmill was built on Wolf Creek. In the same year a semi-private school was established in Tyee, situated near the mouth of the creek on the west side of the Umpqua. Philip and Oscar Hult of Triangle Lake in Lane County, with others of the corporation, promoted a community school system. Cabins were built for the employees and school facilities were provided. After they sold their holdings to Meyers and Sons, construction contractors from Burlingame, California, Meyers continued the community system and added about twenty five-room plywood houses and a new schoolhouse, which had all the facilities found in other modern public school buildings in Douglas County. The community was called Tyee Camp, and mail was sent to that address. Accessories from the old Porter Creek school were moved to the new community building.

Mill employees were allowed to have their own schoolboard and arrange the school year to suit themselves. All supplies were furnished by the county through the Oakland district. There were about thirty-five families in Tyee Camp and about thirty children of school age. A man named Spivendel taught the school until 1948, when he died from a heart attack.

Mrs. Thora Powell began teaching the Tyee Camp school that same year. One attempt was made to send the eighth grade pupils to Oakland but the roads were too bad. Her task was lightened one year by a high school girl who supervised the playground. Mrs. Powell was allowed twenty dollars a month for the janitor work; she taught for eight years.

In 1951, the mill burned down and an unsuccessful attempt to carry on was made by the Roseburg Lumber Company, who had purchased the Meyers holdings. But people started moving away, attendance dropped to five, and the school was closed. The equipment was moved to Oakland, and the Tyee Camp became a ghost town. The buildings were sold to Robert Minter, who salvaged the usable materials.

Many changes have taken place in Wolf Valley since Jesse Clayton built his log cabin. His old farm has been divided, and ownership of most of it has passed into other hands. The name of Wolf Valley has been officially changed to "Tyee," Indian for "Great among Its Fellows," which is appropriate as Mount Tyee stands guard at its south entrance.

Of the settlers who came to Wolf Valley before 1885, only two remain, Mr. and Mrs. William Powell. Mrs. Powell arrived there with her parents in 1881 at the age of five. William Powell arrived in the same general area in 1882, at the age of fourteen. In 1891 he married May Threlkeld; the wedding ceremony was performed in the log cabin her father had built in 1881-82. Reverend J. A. Huddleston officiated. Their seventieth wedding anniversary was celebrated in December 1962. At this writing, Mr. and Mrs. Powell are both in a rest home at Roseburg, in Douglas County.

Part Five

PARSONS AND OTHER PIONEERS

CHAPTER XVI

Circuit Riders and Churches

Dr. James H. Wilbur

The circuit riders (visiting preachers) came with the first wave of immigration and traveled the mountain trails long before roads were opened and mail routes established. They were welcomed by the pioneers, who were eager to hear the preached word and listen to news from friends who had shared the hardships of the journey across the plains.

When a circuit rider appeared in a settlement, word was spread of his arrival, and soon an old-time revival meeting was in progress. The visiting preacher found the latch string on the outside and platters of fried chicken on the inside. A stall in every barn was reserved for his horse. Most of the riders were able ministers and a few were qualified educators. Dr. James H. Wilbur could qualify as both.

In September 1846, Dr. Wilbur and his wife, the former Lucretia Ann Stearns, left New York aboard the bark *Whitton*, bound for the Columbia River by way of Cape Horn; they arrived at Oregon City on June 23, 1847. When the Oregon and California Methodist Conference met in 1849, Dr. Wilbur was made its secretary. The conference territory included western and southern Oregon and northern California. There were only six men to care for this vast area, two of them appointed to serve

California, and the remaining four to serve Oregon; Dr. Wilbur was assigned to Oregon City.

In March of 1853, he was appointed superintendent of the Umpqua mission field. He arrived at Bunton's Gap in September and settled on a donation claim of 563 acres in the immediate vicinity of what is now Wilbur. He advocated the founding of academies at certain points in the Territory so that educational facilities could be offered to children of the pioneers.

Dr. Wilbur began his campaign for the founding of a school by donating 58 acres of land east of his residence for this purpose. He solicited funds to build a two-story structure which was to be called the Umpqua Academy. It is told that when he once approached a sea captain at Scottsburg and asked for a donation, the captain refused, saying: "Why should I help build your school! I never expect to pass this way again!" Dr. Wilbur answered: "Then leave your mark and let it be know that you have passed this way." The captain took a gold coin, called a "slug," valued at about fifty dollars, and gave it to the doctor. Thus the stranger made his mark by helping to build the Umpqua Academy.

Dr. Wilbur did not confine his activities to the organization of a school. He moved freely among the settlers and was respected by all. The church built by him is still in use, and a thriving Sunday School is conducted there. The Baptists cooperated, both in the organization of his school and in helping build his church.

The school building was completed in 1854; the first principal was James H. B. Royal, who served two years. He was succeeded by Addison R. Flint when the Territorial Legislature recognized the school as an institution of higher learning in 1857. Some of the first persons enrolled were James Otey, P. P. Palmer, Calvin Burnside West, Anna A., and J. West; also Mary Kellogg (Mrs. John Fryer) and Harriet Kellogg (Mrs. J. B. Goff), who listed their home address as "Fort Kellogg."

The first building that housed the classrooms of the old Academy burned down in 1873. The school was moved to a new location one-half mile west on land donated by James L. Clinkenbeard in 1874, and new buildings erected. The land donated by Dr. Wilbur and the old dormitory were sold to James T. Cooper in 1877 for $400. Cooper sold the old building to D. R. B. Winiford and F. R. Hill for $300. Hill used part of the lumber to enlarge his hotel, "The Wilbur House." This historic building is still used as a residence—it is located on old Highway 99 where it intersects the Coles Valley Road at Wilbur.

In 1900, the Umpqua Academy was discontinued as a school of higher learning, and a county-supported school took its place. The property was sold to Douglas County in October of that year. G. W. Grubbe and E. E. La Brie were members of the board of trustees of Umpqua Academy that authorized the sale.

The impetus Dr. Wilbur gave to the spiritual and educational life in southern Oregon was unequaled by any clergyman or educator of his day. Many of the leading citizens of Douglas County, both business men and educators, received their training at old Umpqua Academy.

Calvin Brookings West

Calvin B. West came to the Umpqua Valley as an itinerant Baptist lay preacher in the fall of 1853. He remained in Douglas County less than a year, but left his mark. He had operated a small farm near Defiance, Ohio, struggling to support a wife, the former Elizabeth Hudson, and a family of five children aged one to nine. Early in the spring of 1853, West decided to immigrate to Oregon, where his wife's brother, John Hudson, had settled on a claim east of Scottsburg in 1850. Since he did not have sufficient funds to take his family, he decided to make the trip alone, confident that upon reaching Oregon he could obtain aid from his brother-in-law to bring his family later. Leaving Defiance on April 10, he traveled by canal boat to the Ohio River, where he joined three companions, a lawyer, a doctor, and a schoolteacher, who were bound for Oregon. West agreed to act as camp cook for the privilege of traveling with them, but was to furnish his share of the food.

West and his companions secured oxen and wagons at Independence, Missouri, where they joined a wagon train bound for Oregon. The Grand Ronde Valley was reached on July 24, where they met some men who knew the Hudsons and gave a good report of them. At The Dalles the caravan left the Oregon Trail and traveled the Barlow Road past Mount Hood to Salem, where it arrived on August 4. From here West traveled south until he struck the Territorial Road on the north side of Elk Mountain.

The first settler he met after crossing the divide was Warren Goodell, a Baptist minister, whose claim was situated where the town of Drain is located. Thomas Stillwell had a claim on the left bank of Elk Creek, one mile west of Goodell. After resting a few days and enjoying the hospitality of his new friends, West resumed his journey to Scottsburg, accompanied by Stillwell and a man called Crusen. They followed the old pack trail to Elkton, where they met Dr. Daniel Wells, who directed them to John Hudson's place. They arrived there on a Saturday and spent Sunday with him. West approached his brother-in-law for a loan to bring his family to Oregon, but the loan was deferred to a later date.

On the following Monday, West traveled back up the Umpqua, stopping overnight with his nephew, Shadrach Hudson, at Kellogg. Next day he proceeded to Bunton's Gap, where he met Benjamin J. Grubbe and Jonathan W. Woodruff, with whom he formed a close friendship. He also met Dr. Wilbur and J. O. Raynor, who helped him organize a camp meeting. A large tent was pitched beneath an oak tree near the site where the Umpqua Academy was to be built. West was later licensed to preach by a Baptist congregation, organized by Ezra Fisher in the home of William F. Perry at Deer Creek, in July of that year. Their pastor, the Reverend Thomas Stephens, officiated.

West was fascinated by the new country and, writing to his wife, described it in glowing terms. His letters gave an insight on the cost of living at that time. Flour was from $10 to $15 per hundredweight, beef 15¢ to 20¢ a pound, and butter 50¢ to $1 per pound. Oxen were $200 per yoke, cows $100 per head, and good American horses and mares $200 each; wages were from $2 to $3 per day, enough to buy a pair of pants. West also commented on the opportunities for Christian work and deplored the absence of schools and churches.

While at Bunton's Gap, he spent several weeks holding prayer meetings in homes while keeping an eye out for a place to settle and build a house for his family. About the middle of September, Grubbe and Woodruff helped him lay out a claim on the west side of the Umpqua in what is now Garden Valley, or Coles Valley. (Mr. and Mrs. Gerald Bacon are current owners of the land.) After locating the claim he was approached by Solomon Fitzhugh, who spoke for the Garden Valley and Bunton's Gap residents, offering him $800 a year plus board and washing, to teach a subscription school in what he called Garden Bottom.

West accepted the offer. Before working out the details of a contract, he helped get out and prepare the logs for a schoolhouse. The building, erected in the southwest corner of Garden Bottom, was completed on September 26, 1853.

A contract was signed with the trustees, Thomas Nelson Grubbe, Benjamin J. Grubbe, and Jonathan W. Woodruff, to teach their school for one year. Mrs. L. F. Clark of Santa Monica, California, wrote that her grandfather, Ashford Clayton, sold a cow to pay tuition for her mother, Mary Ellen Fabrique. School started on Monday, October 3, 1853, with nine students in attendance. The building was so cold that school was dismissed on Thursday to build a fireplace.

West made an urgent appeal to the American Baptist Home Mission Society for financial assistance. He asked for $300 for himself and $500 to be sent to his wife for traveling expenses to the Umpqua Valley, emphasizing the opportunity for Baptist work in the new territory — but the mission board declined to make the appropriation.

By April 11, he had completed his own house, of which he wrote: ". . . (it) has a good frame, sound timbers well got out and well put together. A very little more expense would make the middle part two stories high and give double bedrooms; this I think can be done hereafter when needed." While clearing ground for his house he prepared additional space and laid a cornerstone for a Baptist school to operate along the same principles as the Umpqua Academy. His diary confirms that $2,500 had been pledged toward its estimated cost of $10,000; this had been subscribed by Dr. James Cole, Willoughby Churchill, Hoy B. Flournoy, B. J. Grubbe, Dr. C. C. Reed, Aaron Rose, the Reverend Thomas Stephens, Thomas Thrasher, and John Wright.

During the winter of 1853-54, West received substantial money contributions from friends to help bring his family to Oregon. At the end of April 1854, he made the trip back to Ohio overland, reaching Defiance on September 27, 1854.

On May 25, 1855, the West family took passage on the S. S. *Northern Light* from New York, bound for the Oregon Territory. They were obliged to travel steerage, but the captain allowed them cabins early in the voyage.

After they arrived at the Isthmus of Panama, transfer was made to a small steamer going up the San Juan River to the Nicaragua Lakes and to the seaport on Virginia Bay. Here they boarded the *Sierra Nevada* bound for San Francisco. It was on this ship that the dreaded cholera broke out, and forty passengers died before they reached their destination. West helped care for the sick, but on the third day was himself stricken with the disease and died. He was given a burial at sea.

Mrs. West and the children continued their journey to Oregon. Upon reaching their intended home, they found the clearing around the house overgrown with weeds, stacks of building materials lying about, and no work done since West departed. The stones placed to mark the site of the proposed academy were hidden beneath a tangle of overgrowth. Mrs. West, realizing that she could not create a home there, bought a lot near the Umpqua Academy, and erected a small house where she boarded students attending the school. Among the descendants of Calvin B. West are lawyers, judges, teachers, research scientists, writers and builders.

The Reverend Allen Jefferson Huddleston

Allen Jefferson Huddleston was an ordained elder of the Christian Church, born in Indiana in 1834. He served as a sergeant in the Union Army under General Sherman throughout the Civil War and was with him on his historic march through Georgia. He was married to Sleigh Smith, daughter of the Reverend Charles W. H. Smith, a minister serving the Disciples of Christ Church, in Indiana. Huddleston was a member of the Methodist Church until after his marriage, when he joined the Christian Church and was ordained as an elder.

The Smiths and Huddlestons came to the Elkton area in 1872, and took homesteads on Bell Mountain, three miles east of town. After coming to Oregon, Huddleston served the church of his choice for nearly fifty years. During his circuit-riding days, he officiated at weddings and funerals and preached up and down the Umpqua Valley from Scottsburg to Umpqua Ferry.

After more than forty years of service in the lower Umpqua Valley, he died at his home in Willamina, Oregon, on October 8, 1920.

Mark C. Munson

Around the turn of the century the American Sunday School Union was represented in Douglas County by Mark C. Munson, the eldest son of a widow who made her home at Edenbower, a small community between Roseburg and Winchester. Mark was about twenty-five years old at the time of his connection with the Union.

Munson might be called a bicycle-riding circuit rider. He organized Sunday schools in remote sections of the Umpqua Valley. During the dry season, which was roughly three months out of the year, he rode and pushed his bicycle over the mountain trails, carrying his load of Sunday School literature; when it rained, he walked.

In 1901, he married Florence Adams from Kellogg. The Reverend Clapp, a Baptist minister, performed the ceremony at a Fourth of July picnic, which was held in a fir grove on the Siren Madison place near the schoolhouse in the Kentucky Settlement. This settlement got its name because of the predominance among its first settlers of those who came from Kentucky. It was always a part of the Kellogg community but by its geography was set apart from Kellogg's Prairie, Pleasant Plain, or Center Bend. After his marriage, Munson was moved to another area needing the services of the Sunday School Union.

John H. Mulkey

The Reverend Mulkey did his circuit riding in a farm wagon, as his wife usually accompanied him on his itinerary to Kellogg. In 1900, he was principal of the Elkton public school, and in connection with his school duties supplied the pulpit for the Christian Church congregation.

Mulkey frequently held services through the summer months in the surrounding communities; Kellogg was number one on his list. He used to arrive on Saturday evening and spend the night at the home of Mrs. Mary Ann Minter, whose house was about two hundred yards west of the schoolhouse where services were held. Two services were held on Sunday and a basket dinner was served at noon under the large maple trees nearby—their shade providing protective seating space for his large audience.

Mabel Madison Rader

This lady could qualify as a circuit rider, for she rode over the mountain trails for a number of years to keep a Sunday school active in her home community in the Kentucky Settlement.

Mabel Madison was born near Hastings, Nebraska, on Christmas Day, 1879, and crossed the plains in a horse-drawn vehicle with her parents in the summer of 1892. Her father was Siren

Madison, a native of Denmark, who had come to the United States at the age of seventeen; her mother was the former Isabelle Dalton of Illinois.

The Madison family came to Kellogg and the Kentucky Settlement in the fall of 1898 and bought the Cyrus Powell homestead. Mabel was then nineteen years old. She immediately became active in the community Sunday school, organized by a Mrs. Norman, in 1885. This interest she continued after her marriage to Boyd Rader in 1901, when they moved to their mountain home known as the "Basin." Her original Christmas programs are still remembered.

After they sold their Basin home in the 1920s and moved to Kellogg, Mrs. Rader continued active service in Sunday school work. Three generations of young people in both communities have benefited from it. Her husband, Boyd, died in September 1962. Mabel has recorded her Christian experiences and life story in a book entitled *The Lure of the West Lands: With Songs of the Prairie and Other Verses*, published in 1962 by the Swordsman Publishing Company of Los Angeles, California.

Organized Churches

The circuit riders, the lay preachers, and other dedicated persons had paved the way for the organization of church congregations. Church organization did not gain momentum until ten years after the settlement began in the Territory, and the Baptists and Methodists led in the field. The first Baptist church in Douglas County was organized by Ezra Fisher of the American Baptist Home Mission Society in the home of W. F. Perry at Deer Creek, on July 24, 1853, with the Reverend Thomas Stephens as pastor.

At that time there were only 484 church-connected Baptists in the Oregon Territory, ten ordained ministers, and thirteen churches. The Umpqua Association in Douglas County, from 1863 to 1876, had five ordained ministers: J. C. Richardson, W. Jeter, S. E. Stearns, J. Ritter, and J. A. Solver.

The second Baptist congregation in Douglas County was organized by the Reverend Thomas Stephens at Riddle on November 23, 1862; and the third was started by J. C. Richardson on October 6, 1865, on the east side of the Calapooia, where the former road from Sutherlin to Umpqua crossed the river. The Reverend G. S. Martin organized a congregation at Yoncalla on May 22, 1870. The Reverend Ezra Fisher stated in his memoirs that Jesse Applegate pledged $500 toward a meeting house. Fisher, a graduate of Amherst College, was a missionary sent to Oregon in 1846 by the American Baptist Home Mission Society.

In 1874, Joseph Ritter started a church at Roberts Creek in southern Douglas County. In May 1877, the Reverend S. S. Martin, brother of G. S. Martin, organized a church at Fair Oaks, east of Oakland. The old church building is still being used for Sunday school and church services. In 1881, the Oakland Baptist Church was organized by J. C. Richardson. The Reverend Thomas S. Dulin, who recently passed away at the age of 104 years, was pastor there in 1894.

The organization of the Gardiner church by C. P. Bailey was discussed in Chapter VIII. On April 19, 1885, George W. Black established the Mount Zion Baptist Church at Elkton. Few residents of the Elkton-Kellogg-Kentucky Settlement areas are aware that a Baptist church was officially organized at Center Bend (Kellogg) on that date. The movement toward organization began with a series of meetings held by the Reverend Black at Elkton, beginning on April 12, 1885. He was preaching at the Center Bend schoolhouse on April 19 when organization took place there. The charter members were: Mr. and Mrs. W. H. Larkins; Mr. and Mrs. E. D. Powell; Mr. and Mrs. C. M. Minter, and William and Esther Moore, all of Center Bend. The church was called the Mount Zion Baptist Church of Elkton, as it was to serve the Kentucky Settlement, Center Bend, and Elkton communities.

On Sunday, April 26, a business meeting was held at Elkton and a Sunday school organized with a man named Kilpatrick as superintendent. At the same business meeting, five more members were received: Mrs. Emmaline F. Henderer, Mrs. Elizabeth Conroy, Mrs. Charles Franklin, Miss Sarah Wilburn, and Mrs. Jane Bunch. W. H. Larkins, C. M. Minter, and William Moore were selected deacons; and E. D. Powell, Charles G. Henderer, and George W. Benedict were elected trustees. E. D. Powell acted as clerk. Henry Beckley presented the church with a secretary's book.

The American Baptist Home Mission Society made the new congregation a $100 loan to build a meeting house; this was erected on property just north of the later Elkton Mercantile Store site. At this point there is a lapse of seven years in the Baptist church records—which is explained in a notation following the last entry in 1885: "May 21st, 1892. For want of care and interest, many months and even years have passed since the last recorded meeting date."

When the Home Mission Society asked for payment, the trustees sold the lot and building to the First Christian Church of Elkton to pay off the loan. Their action caused considerable dissatisfaction among the members of the congregation who had not given their consent. On May 21, 1892, the old board of trustees were relieved of their offices and a new board selected. E. D. Powell was reinstated and C. M. Minter and William Moore were elected. They were instructed by the membership to return the money paid by the Christian Church, request a release of the property, and also have the organization incorporated; this was accomplished on August 11, 1892. A. E. McFarland, notary public at Elkton, drew up the articles of incorporation and they were signed by E. D. Powell, C. M. Minter, and William Moore. Because Moore could not write, he made his mark, witnessed by Henry Beckley and John Haney.*

On September 7, 1895, the trustees were ordered to transfer their property to the First Christian Church of Elkton. C. M. Minter, clerk pro-tem, recorded the last official action of the Mount Zion Baptist Church of Elkton. When the church sold its

---

*Records of the Mount Zion Baptist Church of Elkton are in the historical library of the Conservative Baptist Theological Seminary at Portland, Oregon.

property, some of its members united with the Christian Church. Mrs. Mary Ann Minter, one of the charter members, recalled that lack of activity by the congregation was responsible for the transfer of the property to the Christian Church members; she later united with this church body.

First Christian Church at Elkton

This church has carried on through the intervening years and is still active. Among its outstanding churchmen were evangelists Cain, Woodly, Ross, and Teddy Leavit. The congregation sponsored annual evangelistic services. During the summer months, divinity students from the Northwest Christian College at Eugene often spent their vacations working on farms around Kellogg and Elkton, and serving the pulpit on Sundays.

Methodists Organize

The only available written record of the founding of a Methodist congregation at Elkton is contained in a correspondence between Aubrey Mecham Conrad and Miss Mary Wells, who related her personal knowledge of the details of the occasion. The first activity of the denomination in the Elkton area, as in other sections of old Umpqua County, began with the circuit riders. The first church services held in the vicinity were in private homes.

The Elkton Methodist Church had its beginning in the home of Ira Wells in 1853; the preacher was Dr. James H. Wilbur. Wells was raised as a Methodist and his wife as a Lutheran, but they worked together in the sparsely settled communities. Mrs. Wells had brought her Bible, a leather-bound copy, from Germany in 1837; Ira had brought his Bible from Vermont in 1828.

The circuit rider would usually arrive on Friday and rest all day Saturday in order to be fresh for his battle with Satan on Sunday. Not all names of the early riders are remembered but a few of the first were Matthew Eldridge, I. D. Driver, the Reverend Aldrich, and R. A. Booth, Methodists; and Ezra Fisher, a

Baptist. Their visits to the remote settlements of Elkton were limited to about three times during the summer months. Miss Mary Wells, daughter of Ira and Anna Chandler Wells, recalled that people came from far and near—the Henderers, the Walkers, the Browns, the Fryers, the Stearns boys, the Levins boys, the Maupins, the Dimmicks, the Abe Langdons, and many others. They would bring well-filled baskets for a picnic dinner between the sermons, one at 11 a.m. and the other at 2 p.m.

As soon as the schoolhouse was built in District No. 66, church services were held there. The first organized Methodist work at Elkton was promoted in the early 1890s by T. B. Ford, assisted by the Reverend Campbell, a United Brethren clergyman. A class, or group, of professed Methodists was organized with T. B. Ford as superintendent. Soon others joined the movement, among them the Godfrey Rapp family from Kellogg.

Members of the first class of 1890 were Mrs. Eliza Jordan Dimmick, Mrs. Rachel Jordan, Mrs. Jane Schad, and Mr. and Mrs. Andrew Griffith. Members of the second class of 1903 were Miss Effa Levins, Miss Mary Wells, Mrs. Ida Rydell, Mrs. Mabel Binder, Miss Mary Binder, Mr. and Mrs. Jim Lyons, Mr. Russell Dimmick, Mrs. Ruth Blanton, Mrs. Kitty Kent, Mrs. Ella Finley, Mr. and Mrs. Frank Wells, and others.

Mrs. Anna Haines, acting for the first group, wrote to the Reverend Taylor, who was pastor of the Drain parish, and asked him for his temporary services. When the Reverend Stratford took over the Drain charge, he continued the practice of temporary services, initiated by the Reverend Taylor.

Around 1901, the Elkton congregation was put under the Gardiner charge, with the Reverend Edmondson as minister. Under his leadership, a church building was erected; it was dedicated in October 1903, by the Reverend Given, their first resident pastor. The building has served the congregation for sixty-one years. At this writing (1967) a Baptist Congregation, under the leadership of the Reverend Morris Willgus, has staged a comeback for their denomination in the Elkton area. They have pur-

ris Hacker's logging operation across the Umpqua River from Scottsburg, in 1886. Those
were the days when only "he" men wore beards.

he Cyrus Powell homestead house in the Kentucky settlement, built from hewn logs in 1885-86.
was later shingled on the exterior. Powell sold his land to Siren Madison in 1898. His son,
dgar J. Madison, present owner of the property, built another log house near the site of the
old one, which has long since fallen into decay.

Rice Valley Sunday School in 1905. Left to right, back row: Irvin Rice, Ada McCord, Irvy McCord, (teacher's name not learned), Addie Ellison, William Castor, T. C. Jones, Fred Rice, Fred McCord, Lizzy Dunaway, Charlie Jones, Sam Whittaker, Ikie Rice. Front row, standing: Flora Rice, Lollie Jones, Emma Dunaway, Mary McCord, Ruby Brown, May Dunaway, May Brown. Seated: Arthur Whittaker, Dunaway girl, Jim Jones, Annie Rice, Winnie Whittaker, Minnie Rice.

Rice Valley District School in 1905. Left to right, back row: Myrtle Lamb, teacher; Lester Melvin, Clinton Dunaway, Eugene Capps, Grace Whittaker, Jess Crawford (by the window), Helen Thiele, Lizzie Dunaway, Junie Crawford. Second row: Myrtle Crawford, Lou Thiele, Emma Dunaway, Maggie Stevens, Arthur Whittaker, Lonnie Crawford. Front row: May Dunaway, Angie Crawford, Winnie Whittaker, May Dunaway, Herman Stevens, Charlie Dunaway, May Stevens, and Herman Stokes.

chased the Methodist property and are giving a good account of themselves after eighty-two years of inactivity.

The Methodist church building at Elkton and the schoolhouse at Kellogg are the only remaining landmarks in their area reminiscent of pioneer efforts to provide church training for the young. The first schoolhouse, where Mount Zion Baptist congregation was organized, was replaced in 1899 by the present school building (unused but still standing). The old schoolhouse served as a woodshed until it was torn apart; the pieces were used to start fires in the stove of the new building. The church edifice which the Mount Zion congregation erected at Elkton was destroyed by fire in 1915. The Christian congregation built a new meeting house at Elkton in 1925.

Among the early spiritual leaders in the Umpqua Valley, many merit remembrance, particularly Mrs. Harriet Dimmick Cooper, Mrs. Elizabeth Peters, and Mrs. J. P. Anderson, all of the Kellogg community; Mrs. Sarah Smith and "Aunt Betty" Owens of Hedden Bluff; Mrs. Rufus Butler of Long Prairie; and the Misses Flora and Mary Wells of Elkton. All these served quietly and effectively in their respective communities.

CHAPTER XVII

Along the Military Road

The Sawyers clan in the lower valley contributed much to the development of the economy of old Umpqua County. The founder of the clan was John Jacob Sawyers, who was born in Tyrone County, Ireland, December 25, 1798. At the age of seventeen he enlisted in the British army as a fifer under Major-General Pakenham, and came to America as a British soldier in the War of 1812. When taken prisoner at the battle of New Orleans, January 8, 1815, he was returned to Ireland in an exchange of prisoners.

Sawyers returned to America in 1818 and settled in St. Johns, New Brunswick, Nova Scotia. His first wife died in 1822, shortly after their son Andrew was born. He then married Elizabeth Anderson and moved to Ohio in 1824. Here their four children were born: Mary, Margaret, James Earl, and Jacob Anderson Sawyers.

In the spring of 1854, Sawyers, with his family, came to Oregon by ox team over the Oregon Trail as far as The Dalles, where they took the Barlow route over the Cascades to Oregon City. They were met here by the oldest son, Andrew, who had come to Scottsburg in 1850; he piloted the family from Oregon City to Scottsburg.

Sawyers located on a donation claim five miles above that of his son and fourteen miles above Scottsburg. The military road ran diagonally through his land from west to east.

In 1864, Sawyers turned the home place over to his son, Jacob A., who at seventeen, was given the full responsibility of running the farm. Later, Jacob bought 320 acres northwest and adjoining the home place. After his brother James E. was discharged from the Union Army in 1865, the brothers formed a partnership and together purchased the Abe and John Fryer places; this gave them control over nearly 900 acres. When, in 1872, their father moved to Scottsburg, the boys divided the property.

The "fighting Irish" sobriquet easily applies to John Jacob Sawyers. He fought as a British soldier in the war of 1812; as an American in the war with Mexico during the years 1846-48; and, at the age of fifty-seven, he enlisted with his son Andrew in the Oregon Volunteer Regiment of Mounted Riflemen during the Rogue River Indian uprising in 1855. Sawyers died in 1878; Mrs. Sawyers survived him by fifteen years. John Jacob Sawyers deserves a memorial erected to his memory for the loyalty and patriotism he gave his adopted country.

Andrew Sawyers

Andrew Sawyers, the eldest son of John Jacob, was apprenticed to a Reuben Oliver to learn the carpentry trade. After finishing his service he went to New Orleans, where he met and married Fannie McDowell, December 25, 1844. He worked in New Orleans for five years. Then, in September 1849, he and his wife left for California by way of Cape Horn, aboard the bark *Mary Waterman*, which arrived in San Francisco in the summer of 1850. Carpentry work here was plentiful, at fourteen to sixteen dollars per day. In June of that year, Andrew purchased three shares in the Klamath Exploring Expedition, which later became the Umpqua Land Company. In October 1850, he and his wife came to Scottsburg on the *Kate Heath*, and in December of that year, their daughter, Anna Augusta, was the first white girl to be born in the lower valley.

Andrew took a claim on the upper end of what is now Long Prairie, twelve miles east of Scottsburg. From timber growing on his claim, he whip-sawed, sized, and dressed by hand all of the lumber he used to build his house. All the doors were put together with dowel pins; the only nails used in the building were for siding, flooring, and finishing work. (Mrs. Winifred Albro is the current owner of this 116-year-old historic landmark. She is proud of its history and keeps it and the surrounding grounds in excellent condition.)

When the old military road was located in 1854, it passed within a few yards of Andrew's house. In the journal kept by Mrs. Elizabeth Burchard, Andrew's half-sister, she recorded that a blockhouse was erected on his premises in 1855 when the Rogue River Indians went on the warpath. "Sawyers Rapids," now a famous fishing spot, is another landmark; but it was a formidable barrier in the attempt to navigate upriver in 1870. . . . Andrew Sawyers died on December 20, 1906.

James Earl Sawyers, Sr.

James Earl Sawyers, Sr., the second son of John Jacob Sawyers, farmed the recently purchased Allensworth and Fryer claims. He married Susan Gardiner, daughter of Isaac Gardiner of the "Tin Pot" area, (now Sunnydale) three miles west of Drain. They had three boys: James Earl, Jr., who was for many years treasurer of Douglas County; Jacob R. Sawyers, or "Little Jake," who farmed his father's land until he began driving the stage for the Coos Bay Stage Company around 1905; and Gard, the youngest, who was a natural-born trapper and hunter. Gard's skill as a hunter of predatory animals was phenomenal. . . . Now, all these boys are deceased.

James E. Sawyers, Sr., died quite young from a rattlesnake bite that he received while hunting his milk cows. The accident happened near his farm buildings. Because his shoe, near his great toe, was worn and the leather cracked, the fangs of the snake penetrated the foot through this weak place in the leather. He suffered for nearly two years and endured much pain before his death from the poison.

Later, Susan Sawyers, his widow, married Dick Dickerson, who was more a trapper than a farmer. Dickerson and his wife moved to Loon Lake, where Dickerson is given credit for opening the old trail from the Sawyers farm to the lake. The Dickersons had two children, a boy, Rollie, and a girl, Ella; both were teachers. This writer attended classes taught by Miss Dickerson at Kellogg and at Hedden Bluff in 1906—it is not known if either is still living.

Two years after the brothers dissolved their partnership in the ranches, Jacob moved to Scottsburg, where he continued his education in navigation on inland waterways.

In 1880 Jacob married Lucy Gardiner, a sister of Susan Gardiner (wife of James E., Sr.). Jacob and his wife moved back to the farm in 1881 and here their ten children were born: Elizabeth, John J., Mary E., Alex, Isaac, Thomas, Hilda, Margaret, Violet, and Jobie (who died while very young).

In 1908, Jacob A. left the farm in charge of his son Alex and moved the rest of his family still at home to Allegany in Coos County. He put a motor boat, the *Margaret*, in operation on Coos River between Allegany and Marshfield, and opened a hotel at Allegany.

While the Sawyers lived there a very sad accident occurred. Three of their younger daughters were members of a swimming and wading party which included their schoolteacher, who could not swim. While wading, the teacher went beyond her depth; two of the Sawyers girls, Margaret and Hilda, went to her assistance and all three were drowned.

Sawyers moved his family back to Scottsburg in 1906. He became an authority on the inland waterways of the Umpqua River and its tributaries, holding a captain's license to operate any boat on the lower river, one of the few to hold such a license in that area. Jacob Anderson Sawyers died in 1908; both he and Mrs. Sawyers are buried in the Scottsburg cemetery.

Old Military Road Recalled

Alex Sawyers was one of the ten children of Jacob A. Sawyers, all were born on the old homestead at Hope's Elbow, where Jacob grew up. On March 13, 1907, Alex married Myrtle Traylor, the same Myrtle who attended the Walker school, a daughter of

Henry Traylor. They moved onto the home place and later built
a new bungalow-type house on the northeast corner of the farm
near the county ferry crossing. The old military road survey
passed just south of the new house. (Here she celebrated her
eightieth birthday, November 13, 1966).

When interviewed in 1960, Alex recalled how the traffic that
passed along this road had fascinated him as a boy, and how his
father had related many incidents from his experience as a pack-
mule skinner along the trail from Scottsburg and as far south as
Grants Pass, in the 1860s.

As a very small boy he would accompany his father when
their wheat was taken to the Rochester Mill in Oakland over this
old trace, after it was opened by Colonel Joseph Hooker. Their
wheat would be made into flour at the gristmill. Generally two
or three parties would make the trip at the same time; if the
roads were bad they could double-team over the worst spots.
There were two routes from which to choose but Jacob preferred
the Mehl Canyon route because it eliminated two ferry crossings
of the Umpqua River; either route took two days each way. The
first night was spent at the Dimmick farm, or across the river at
the Fryer ranch. By either route, climbing the mile-long, acutely
steep Marvin Hill took half a day.

Upon arriving at the mill they were lucky if they didn't have
to wait a couple of days for their turn. Because sometimes there
were from three to six wagons ahead of them, camping equipment was always carried along. Now and then meals were taken
at the historic Deardorff Hotel which was near the mill.

A Small Boy's Dilemma

Alex also recalled that he hauled wheat to Scottsburg by himself when he was only thirteen or fourteen years old. One time,
when the roads were bad, his wagon—loaded with ten 120-pound
sacks of wheat—became mired down in a mud hole. As he was
too small to unload the sacks, all he could do was sit on the
wagon and wait for someone to come along and help him out of

his difficulty; fortunately James Bunch came along. Alex said Jim was laughing when he first saw him and was still chuckling after he had hitched his team ahead of Alex's and pulled the wagon out. Evidently the woebegone look on the small boy's face amused him. Alex, seventy-three years old when interviewed, still remembered the names of Mr. Bunch's horses, "Dave" and "Blue."

Another memory was of plowing when he was too young to lift the plow out of the furrow; when turning at the end of the row, he would tip the plow over on its side and let the horses drag it around on the shear.

John J. Sawyers the 2nd

John J. Sawyers (grandson of John Jacob Sawyers who came to Oregon in 1854) was the oldest son of Jacob A. Sawyers to be born and grow to adulthood on the home place at Hope's Elbow. He worked with his father for the Southern Pacific Railway Company when the line was being built into Reedsport in 1911-14. Jacob A. had his own boat, the *Comet*; John operated the company boats, one of which was the *Adak*. These boats were used to transport workers to and from the bridge construction and trestle work, from East Gardiner across the mouth of Smith River and the main Umpqua to the mainland at the mouth of Schofield Creek. They were also used to tow piling, or whatever else was needed to move material for the bridge construction over a broad expanse of water. Later, John Sawyers worked as a logger until a knee injury forced him to quit the woods.

John was a zealous fisherman and, when the steelhead and salmon began their run upriver, he could be found, with rod and line in hand, fishing from the steel bridge across the Umpqua at the mouth of Elk Creek. He was also expert in curing and smoking his catch.

John's latter years were spent at his home in Elkton. This writer spent profitable time with him reviewing the activities of the early settlers. His ability to recall names, places, and detailed incidents was phenomenal; and his personal contributions helped clarify many details concerning settlement of the lower Umpqua Valley. During these interviews the following tape recording was made of one memorable incident John recalled:

The Cougar Hunt

"My father, from a youngster growing up on the old donation claim, loved to hunt and by the 1870s had built up a reputation as a cougar hunter. One day he started to visit his brother Andrew who lived at what is now Sawyers Rapids, where the big fishing doings are held at the present time. At Paradise Creek, on his way down, he saw great cougar tracks in the dusty road. The animal evidently was packing something because there were scratches in the dust. A little farther along he saw evidence that a calf had been killed and dragged over a rail fence into a brush patch near a friend's residence. And a cow was bellowing wildly. (The friend's calf had been running with its mother until it was about a year and a half old and must have weighed at least four hundred pounds). Father went to the house of his friend [Mike] and told him that a calf had been killed—likely his and the cow was carrying on something terrible.

"They went back to take a look. Mike's little dog ran into the brush patch where the cougar had gone over the fence, but it came back almost scared to death. They went into the brush and found a bed by the side of the carcass of the calf where the cougar had lain after it had eaten its fill.

"My father knew where he could get some good dogs; Captain Hathaway had three and Henry [G.] Brown had one, a good varmint dog. If he could get them, he could go back and tree the cougar. Captain Hathaway and Brown let him have the dogs. On the way back along what was then known as the Hargan Grade, he met Bill [W. R.] Patterson's three dogs. I guess they were going on a visit on their own. These dogs knew Father and he had no trouble getting them to go along.

"He went back to where the carcass lay and the dogs took the cougar's track. The cougar treed in a short distance, but before my father could get to them, it jumped out and ran. It did this three times. It was ready to jump the fourth time when father decided he could kill it from where he was. It was a long shot for him, but he hit it through the lower jaw and the bullet broke both joints slick back to the throat. The cougar came out of that tree fast and the dogs were right on top of it.

"One of Patterson's dogs was hollering as thought it was being killed, so father ran down as close as he could and saw that the cougar had this dog's head in its mouth, and he thought the dog was being killed. Both the dog and the cougar were rolling around like a top and the other dogs were nipping the cougar on the outside to keep it going. Father thought he'd better finish the fight, so he shot the cougar in the head.

"My father didn't have any use for the carcass but he wanted to show folks what a monster he had killed. Among the many other cougars he had shot, this was the largest; it was a little over eleven feet from the tip of its tail to the tip of its nose. To show people that there really was such an animal, he cut its head off the way you would dress a hog and took it down the creek to Paradise bridge, so that when the stage came along the passengers could see the monster's head. He had started on toward his brother's place when he met the stage at what is now called Stoney Brook; stage drivers always watered their horses there. He told the driver that he had killed the biggest cougar he had ever seen. Father offered to bet that the head wouldn't go into the large wooden bucket with which they watered their horses.

"The driver thought this was out of all reason, so father got into the stage and took the bucket along. At Paradise Creek they tried to put the head into the bucket, which was twelve inches across, but it wouldn't go in. The driver didn't take time to view the body as he was convinced that father had won the bet.

"Cougars were so plentiful at that time (in the 1870s) that father had killed many on the old place and in the surrounding area; they were as common as deer are today. The neighbor's dogs would tree one every few days. Father would be working in the field when he heard the baying, but would wait till noon to go and see what they had treed. Sometimes it would be a wildcat; once it was a fisher (fishers were of the mink and martin family only larger and quite rare in Oregon), but mostly the treed animal would be a cougar. One week he killed seven cougars in and around the foothills and along the creek that came by the house—one a day for seven straight days."

William Spencer Sawyers

William Spencer Sawyers, born April 9, 1855, was the son of Andrew Sawyers. He inherited 200 acres of the home place and later bought 275 acres from his sister Fannie. In 1885 he married Belle Andrews (daughter of Asa and Mary Wentworth Andrews, who came to Oregon in 1878). William and Belle were the parents of five children: William Roy (who died in January 1967, at the age of eighty), Ralph A., and Oscar, who passed away some years ago. Two girls, Denabelle Sawyers Linville of Detroit, Michigan, and Miss Arizona Sawyers, of Portland, Oregon, are the only survivors at this writing.

Ralph Sawyers, Jr., grandson of William Spencer Sawyers, still resides on the ancestral acres. He recently built a new house, replacing the one his grandfather built. Ralph was awarded a certificate by the Oregon Historical Society in 1959, designating his place as a Century Farm. Ralph is the great-great-grandson of John Jacob Sawyers, the first of the clan to come to America.

A Seafaring Man Turns Farmer

Captain William Henry Hathaway was born in New Bedford,

Massachusetts in 1806, coming from a long line of seafaring men who were part owners of the boats under their command. The captain had long cherished a secret desire to quit the sea and try farming. Upon arriving in Oregon in 1850, he took a donation claim (No. 44), which contained 640 acres, and was located on the Umpqua River east of Hope's Elbow, north and adjoining the John J. Sawyers claim.

In 1837, before coming West, he had married Sarah Washburn and had fathered four children, but his wife refused to leave her comfortable home in Fair Haven, Massachusetts, for the precariousness of pioneer life, so she remained in the East.

Besides working his claim, Hathaway took an active part in the early development of Umpqua County by serving on road-viewing parties; he also built two bridges on the new county road. In 1855 he enlisted in the Umpqua County Regiment of Volunteer Riflemen, when the Rogue River Indians went on the warpath.

In 1864, he sold his claim to John A. Fryer, Sr., for $900, but was allowed to continue living in his cabin. In 1868, the captain's son, William Henry, Jr., came to the Elkton community with his wife and two small children and moved in with his father, but the following year he moved on to Gardiner, where he built an eight-room house (currently the property of Mrs. Minnie Graham).

On January 6, 1870, Captain Hathaway was robbed and murdered by an unknown assailant and his cabin set afire. Henry G. Brown, who lived two miles away, had seen the smoke rolling up from the neighborhood of the Hathaway cabin, but before help could arrive the cabin was consumed. The charred body of the captain and several of his hunting dogs were found in the debris. He had been shot through the head by either a pistol or rifle; only a six-months-old pup escaped.

It was while William, Jr., was living in Yreka a number of years later that the circumstances of Captain Hathaway's murder began to unfold. Miss Mabel Filer, a great-granddaughter of the captain, reported what she was told by her mother, Mrs. June Hathaway Filer:

"My mother thought that great-grandfather had some gold secreted in his mattress; it was so heavy that he never would let anyone make his bed. Years after my mother's grandfather was killed, Mother was sitting on the front porch of their home in Yreka, California, when a man walked down the street. Their old dog, the one rescued from the tragedy, was with her on the porch. As the man approached the house, the dog roused up and jumped over the fence; as the man fled, the dog grabbed him and took the seat from his trousers. They all felt that this man was the murderer of their great-grandfather.

"Time passed and the family moved to Colusa, California, sixty miles above Sacramento. On one occasion, Mother's oldest sister, Elizabeth, was visiting friends on their farm. Her hostess, pointing to a new-made grave under an oak tree, asked Elizabeth if she had relatives in Oregon and if one of them had been murdered. Of course she told them the story about her grandfather. They then said that a man had come that way very sick, and that on his deathbed he told how he had killed the great-grandfather and two other men; also how the dog had chased him in Yreka. . . . Alex Sawyers told us where the two other men had lived." (Miss Filer did not name the men.)

Mrs. June Hathaway Filer, Captain Hathaway's granddaughter and mother of Mabel Filer, had a life-long desire to visit her grandfather's grave. In 1960, at the age of eighty-eight, this longing was gratified. Through the courtesy of the *Drain Enterprise* and the cooperation of obliging residents of the Elkton area, the grave was located in the family burial plot on the Charles G. Henderer farm. A headstone was placed at the grave during a simple but impressive ceremony.

The Walker Story

Alpheus Walker, a native of Pennsylvania, crossed the plains in 1849, settling in Scotts Valley, east of Yoncalla. In 1864, he enlisted and served one year in the First Oregon Infantry, Company K. Three years later he married Jane Dougherty. They became the parents of four children: Melvina (Mrs. John Letson), Rosa (Mrs. Benjamin Butler), George, and Audrey (Mrs. Fred Riley).

The Walkers bought the Hathaway claim from John A. Fryer in 1874, moving to this location on the lower Umpqua in August of 1875, where the rest of their lives was spent. Mr. Walker died in August of 1909.

Though Mrs. Walker's eyesight was failing in her later years, she requested writing materials and recorded adventures experienced in crossing the plains in 1860, when she was twelve years old. Some of her lines overlapped, but with the help of her granddaughter, Mrs. Jannie Haines—who has the original copy— the manuscript was edited for publication:

"In 1859 we lived on a small farm near Des Moines, Iowa. Our family consisted of father, mother, and six children. Father, like a lot of other folks around us, got the gold fever. He sold our home of forty acres of good corn ground, and all of our stock—horses, cattle, and hogs. Early in the spring of 1860, he went to Council Bluffs for supplies. He bought a spanking new wagon, and with two other families we started our long journey across the plains. On May 1, a small girl who had a large wax doll was offered a pony by the Indians, and a trade was made. The Indian walked away with the doll as proud as if it were gold.

"At the Platte River we found several wagons waiting to cross. The next morning all passed over safely except one family. The strong current swept them down the stream, and their wagons overturned. Our men, with the help of their horses, rescued the people. One yoke of oxen was drowned; the others were rescued. Friends generously took the survivors in and helped them on their way.

"When we reached Fort Laramie, the government had soldiers stationed to protect the emigrants. We were allowed to proceed under the protection of the troops. The soldiers traveled with us until we had passed through hostile territory. One day when we were passing through a deep canyon, some Indians looked over the rocks and hollered, 'Is there any white soldier there?' Our men shouted back, 'Yes, hundreds of them!'

"We had chosen a man by the name of Carpenter as captain. He was a hard man and loved money more than life. He was bringing a drove of fine horses and stock and most of his drovers were hired help. Two men were along who refused to join our company; they always camped alone near us. One morning there was no movement in their camp. Our men went to investigate and found them dead and their stock driven off. The killing was supposed to have been committed by the Indians who had taken their cattle and what articles they wanted, and left. We stayed long enough to bury the unfortunate men. That night the Indians attacked us, but were driven off.

"Soon after this occasion one of our men broke the coupling pole of his wagon. The captain refused to stop, so father and two other families stayed with him. We were attacked by the Indians, who kept shooting into our camp trying to stampede the stock. They were finally driven off and we kept watch all night. The next morning our men found an Indian lying dead and it was noticed that he didn't look like an Indian. Upon washing his face he was found to be a white man.

"One day when we stopped for noon rest, some squaws and children came into camp. They had a little white girl, seven years old, whom they offered to sell for a number of horses, but the captain would not let the horses go. He said he needed horses, and children were plentiful. We heard later that the soldiers made a raid and captured prisoners, mostly children, so we hoped that the little girl was among the lot.

"When we traveled through the Utah Pass near Salt Lake City, we saw from a distance the remains of a wagon train where the Mountain Meadows Massacre occurred. We came to a place where the road separated near American Falls. The right-hand route was the Oregon Trail, which led to the Barlow route; the other was the Landers cut-off, leading into Honey Valley. We took the latter. I think the last day before we reached the settlement in Honey Valley was the hardest of all. We were short of provisions and had very little water, and father had portioned out our supply to the mules, as they were nearly exhausted from traveling over the desert.

"It was dark when we drove into the settlement. Our large yellow bulldog, who had had no water all day, ran ahead and drank so much that he died. Some Indians asked for him. The next day these same Indians brought some meat which they called wild goat, and we all had a feast for breakfast. It certainly tasted fine . . . but then they brought in our old dog Watch's hide to sell!

"My oldest sister was married on the way across the plains. She was fourteen and her husband was eighteen. We came to the Sacramento River where gold had been discovered, and there we found a number of disappointed people like ourselves. All the claims were taken and it was late October. We had been on the road twenty-three weeks. Father was lucky enough to find an empty cabin which he rented. . . . We came on to Oregon through the San Joaquin and Sacramento valleys in the spring of 1862 and settled east of Yoncalla."

Mehl's Mill

The Gottlieb H. Mehl donation land claim has long been

a landmark in the mid-Umpqua Valley. Gottlieb H. Mehl—whose debut into Umpqua County history in 1847 is without recorded family background—selected a claim of 324.29 acres in Township 23 South, Range 8 West, near the junction of the creek (which now bears his name), and the Umpqua River, about three and one-half miles west of the Kellogg community. This farm was then, and still is, a valuable piece of land with one and one-half miles of bottom ground fronting on the Umpqua River.

Mehl went to the California gold fields in 1849 to earn enough money to stock his farm, but became more interested in mining than farming and rented his place and stock. While he was away prospecting, his tenant absconded with the stock and burned the cabin. When the military road was opened through the farm in 1858, he returned and began to improve his claim. In the hope that the road through his property would bring him many customers, he built a combined gristmill and sawmill, in conjunction with a furniture factory. The development of more accessible areas drew away expected trade, so the claim was sold in 1864 and Mehl moved to Roseburg, where he, like many another early pioneer, just dropped out of recorded history.

The name, or names, of later owners of the Mehl place, from 1864 to 1883, have not been obtained, but the family of James and Flora Bunch, who moved to this location on the latter date, is highly esteemed by this writer because of his close association, since early boyhood, with members of this pioneer group.

Good Friends Come with Bunches

James Bunch was born in Missouri on September 24, 1853. He married Flora Bunch, whose family name was the same as that of her husband. She was born on June 14, 1852. When the Bunch family decided to leave Missouri in 1880, they came by train. The railroads had by then innovated what they called "Emigrant Trains"; the passengers were permitted to eat and sleep in the same coach throughout the journey. These trains furnished a safer and more convenient mode of travel than the long trek across the plains behind a pair of plodding oxen.

From San Francisco the journey was made to Portland by boat and again by train to Roseburg. They traveled on to Scottsburg, where they lived for a short time, soon returning to the upper river, when Bunch rented the Gottlieb H. Mehl donation claim. The identity of the owner at that time was not determined, but in 1891 John Hedden bought the property, which is still in the Hedden family.

During the years that Mr. Bunch farmed the Mehl place, he purchased additional land on Fitzpatrick Creek, adjacent to this property, which was always referred to by the family as the "home place."

Mrs. Jane Bunch passed away in the winter of 1884, while living with her daughter (Mrs. Flora Bunch) on the Mehl property. For the trip to the cemetery, winter condition of the military road made it necessary to remove the bed from a farm wagon and strap the casket to the running gears, enabling a four-horse team to convey the remains through Mehl Canyon to the Dimmick Cemetery at Kellogg.

Speaking of the terrible condition of the military road—on a trip from Oakland in a farm wagon loaded with supplies, the road was so rough that Mrs. Bunch lost her hold on her son William, then a babe-in-arms, and he fell out of the front end of the wagon between the horses; fortunately he was unhurt. Such was life along the military road!

Mr. Bunch farmed his land in conjunction with the Mehl property until his son-in-law, Warren Cheever, rented the Mehl property around 1895. Then he moved onto the Beckley ranch, and farmed this place until he returned to the homestead in 1912. After his retirement, around 1920, he moved to Oakland, living there until his death on October 19, 1924. Mrs. Bunch survived her husband by ten years; she died on October 12, 1934. Both are buried in the Dimmick Cemetery at Kellogg. James and Flora Bunch were the parents of six children: Mrs. W. B. McClay (Dora), Mrs. Warren Cheever (Sally), Mrs. E. E. McClay

(Maude), William, Mrs. Homer Haines (Jennie), and Mrs. Oliver Haines (Mary). The first two mentioned are deceased.

Farmer Finds Coins

Frequently discoveries are made reminiscent of pack-and-freight-train days along the old military road through the Umpqua Valley. On the farm formerly owned by Aubrey Cobbe (the donation claim of Robert A. Savery) is an area which was used for seventy years as a nooning place for pack trains and later by farmers hauling their produce to market. In the 1920s, while Cobbe was preparing a field for planting near this camp site, four rare old coins were uncovered—two Spanish and two American. The Spanish coins were dated 1744 and 1792; the American coins were a fifty-cent piece dated 1820 and a half-dime dated 1838.

Another Cobbe "find" was the evidence of a former dwelling. In 1854, Lieutenant Withers marked this location on his survey map as "Vanbipu's Station." (C. B. Vanbipu was a county commissioner of Umpqua County in 1858.) Here there is a spring, walled up with hand-hewn stones, in as perfect condition as in the year it was used by the early pioneers to protect their water supply. It is on the route of the military road between the top of Marvin Hill and the Jasper Shook ranch, and located at the foot of a steep decline leading off the ridge that the old trace followed. The present writer visited the area in May 1965. Still-distinct ruts—worn down by freight wagons—made it easy to follow the old road; some stretches were twenty-five per cent grade.

Near the spring is an area of about two acres below the road which is ideal for a building site. The spring itself is about ten yards above the road, which suggests that water may have been piped for domestic use by pioneer plumbing. The sections were slim fir saplings with a "V" cut in one side.

Dodge's Canyon

Early settlements in Umpqua and Douglas counties were often isolated from each other by the topography of the Umpqua basin; Dodge Canyon was one of these. In 1855, James Rufus Dodge, a native of Laneboro, Massachusetts, for whom this canyon was named, took a donation claim at the south end of the defile.

At the age of nine, he had been apprenticed to a tailor for three years, later going to Troy, New York, and working on a farm for eleven dollars per month. He also drove a tow horse on the Erie Canal at a slight raise in salary — twelve dollars per month. Dodge finally took up the blacksmith trade, being employed by the Pennsylvania Railroad in most of its Mid-western shops until 1852. That year he crossed the plains with his wife (the former Helen Mary Allen) and their three children. One, named Mary, later taught the Kellogg school, in 1883. The Dodges arrived in Linn County in November; three years later they moved to the Oakland vicinity and settled on a claim where he opened a blacksmith shop on the Elkton-Oakland road.

The next to settle in the Dodge Canyon area was John Goodman, whose father, Hugh Goodman, had settled in Yamhill County. On February 12, 1865, John married Polly Brinegar, daughter of his father's traveling companion while crossing the plains. A return trip to their native state of Missouri was undertaken after their first child, Ida, was born in 1866; the oldest son, William, was born there. Upon returning to Oregon in 1869, the Goodmans settled near present Lookingglass, eight miles west of Roseburg, where their daughter, Lena (Mrs. Joe Cole), was born. From here John moved to the Dodge ranch in 1883, where their son, Elmer, was born, December 3, 1884. Two more children, Minnie and Everett, were born on the Goodman homestead, one mile up the canyon from the Dodge ranch (later known as the Jim Leatherwood place).

The first neighbor above Goodman was the Ferber family; their land was later owned by George McHugill, Sr., who operated a sawmill on a small stream meandering out of the hills past the Shook and Stone homes.

Last of the Mountain Men

"Dad" Stone, one of the last of the redoubtable mountain men, is said to have come to the Douglas County area in the immigration of 1847. Standing well over six feet without socks, which he refused to wear, he weighed around 255 pounds, with not an ounce of excess fat. He was married and had three sons, all as robust as himself: Vernon, John, and Alexander. In the winter he ran a trapline and in the summer tended his hillside ranch. "Dad" Stone was well advanced in years when, in 1910, he trapped along the tributaries of the Umpqua, between the mouth of Little Canyon and Smith's Ferry. "Dad" Stone had an abundance of grey hair and a flowing white beard. His usual frontier garb was a black felt hat—well ventilated—a pair of old faded-blue denim overalls, and a jacket of the same material and age; in a burlap sack were carried traps and a few "possibles." He was a familiar sight as he trudged along the small streams leading back from the river, on his rounds tending his trapline.

Early Mail Carriers

Abe Cole lived about a mile above the McHughill place. He carried the mail between Elkton and Oakland from 1895 to 1898, and also had a contract with the county in 1889 to operate the Trenton Ferry when it was made a free crossing. His brother, Leander Cole, lived about a mile above Abe; Andy Grose lived up on the mountain east of Leander.

A man named Wright, who lived on a small squirrel ranch back in a fold of the canyon, eked out an existence by cutting stove wood and hauling it in a specially built rack on a farm wagon, drawn by a yoke of oxen (yes, oxen! in 1898) eight miles to Oakland, where he found a ready sale.

Tom Willan operated a sawmill about a mile from the top of Marvin Hill in 1895. Dave McCollum, son of John McCollum who had come to the Kellogg area in 1872, bought the mill from him and in the early 1900s moved to Hinkle Creek east of Sutherlin, where he operated another sawmill. (Ole Bunch of Sutherlin is a grandson of Dave McCollum.)

Sam Kraft, son of John Kraft, an early pioneer in Dodge Canyon, is probably the only one of his generation to still live in the vicinity in which he grew to manhood. Sam was born on March 9, 1890; his mother died when he was five days old. On March 16, Sam's father returned home after her funeral to find their house burned to the ground. Sam, who has a remarkable ability to recall early events, lives alone at his home near Oakland and is a familiar figure around town.

The present appearance of Dodge Canyon does not indicate that, from the 1870s to the 1920s, it had its own school district and was a self-sustained community. State Highway No. 125 takes up practically all the tillable ground on which the settlers raised their gardens and a little hay for a few cows and horses.

Ephraim H. Burchard

Ephraim H. Burchard was born in Steubenville, Ohio, June 24, 1829. His wife, Mary G. Sawyers, was a daughter of John Jacob Sawyers, born in Philadelphia, November 3, 1835. Ephraim and Mary were married at Hardscrabble, Virginia, November 24, 1852. Twins, David and Elizabeth, were born to them while they were still in the East; David died in infancy.

The young couple started to Oregon early in June 1854, accompanied by the John Jacob Sawyers family. They traveled by boat from Steubenville to Independence Missouri, where they obtained four oxen, two wagons, four cows, and one pony. Eight months were spent on the trail. It has been said that Mrs. Burchard rode the pony most of the way while carrying her six-months-old baby.

The Burchards took a donation claim of 180 acres, five miles east of Scottsburg on Long Prairie. Mr. Burchard was a printer by trade and followed that occupation for a short while before opening a general store in Gardiner and one in Scottsburg. The operation of the farm was turned over to "Uncle Job" Hatfield, who had known the Sawyers in Nova Scotia; Hatfield's claim joined that of Burchard on the west.

Ephraim served as justice of the peace in the Scottsburg precinct and was county assessor of Umpqua County in 1859 and 1860. Ephraim and Mary Burchard were the parents of six children: David; Margaret and John J., who died quite young; Elizabeth, who married Captain Henry Wade; William James; and Mary Jane, who married Fred Weatherly.

William James Burchard

William James Burchard was born on March 27, 1859, in a log cabin built by his father on Long Prairie. When he was four years of age, the Burchard family moved into Job Hatfield's new house, reported to have been the first frame house to be built in the lower valley. As Job had never married, they were welcomed into his home, where William "Bill" Burchard lived the rest of his life. This house is still in prime condition and is currently used as a residence by Gard Burchard, son of William J. Just after the flood of 1860-61, this 108-year-old landmark was moved by mule team to its present location — about 200 feet from the road on the north side of Highway 38, three miles east of Scottsburg. The house was not damaged by the high water but it was deemed prudent to move it to higher ground.

Bill Burchard married Mamie Davis in November 1884. Mamie, the daughter of James Davis, came to Oregon in 1877, when she was seven years old. William brought his bride to live in the Hatfield house, where they raised seven children. He was a prosperous farmer, an expert horseman, and a fair blacksmith. It has been said that he was exceptionally good at shoeing his own horses as well as those of his neighbors.

In the early 1900s, the farmers on Long Prairie organized a horse company consisting of eleven shareholders; Bill held two shares. On November 3, 1908, the company bought a German Coach stallion named "Brigant," nicknamed "Brigham," for which the sum of $2,750 was paid. Bill later purchased all of the shares. Brigham became a legend among the farmers in the lower valley. A colt sired by him would bring a much better price than one sired by other stallions in the country. When the animal died of old age in 1923, there was general mourning among the farmers who knew its record.

William and Mamie Burchard were typical of the pioneers in the Umpqua Valley who, by their example, passed on to their descendants the principles of responsible citizenship and a sincere respect for the rights of their neighbors. Mr. Burchard died on March 14, 1939; Mrs. Burchard on July 6, 1940.

Hiram Weatherly

Hiram Weatherly came to Oregon from Illinois, but was born in Genesee County, New York, on July 31, 1838. In 1860 he married Almira Lamphere, whose birth date was July 26, 1840. Hiram enlisted in Company B, 96th Illinois Volunteers in 1862, serving in the Union Army for three years and rising to the rank of major. He participated in many engagements – Shiloh, Fort Donaldson, Shelbyville, and Chickamauga.

While still living in Illinois, Hiram and his wife adopted a son whom they named Frederick. Fred, as he was usually called, had been born on January 6, 1865. When the boy was fourteen, Hiram brought his family to Long Prairie and bought the old John Hudson donation claim from W. R. Patterson, who had purchased it from Hudson. The creek passing through this place is currently called Weatherly Creek. It was first designated as as "Hudson Creek," then "Patterson Creek"; should the claim pass to other owners, the creek will no doubt get a new name.

Upon his retirement in 1894, Hiram turned the management of the farm over to his son. He died on April 9, 1915; his wife, Almira, on March 8, 1917.

Frederick Weatherly

Fred Weatherly married Mary Jane Burchard. They were the parents of seven children: Frederica, currently a teacher in Eugene; Mary Almira, wife of the late Charles G. Henderer of Elkton; Norman B., first married to Mabel Henderer who died in an accident, later to Irene McMichle; Van Worden, a twin of Norman's who died in infancy; Henry Wade, who died at the age of nineteen; Howard (deceased, 1952), who married Dorothy Canzler; and Floyd H., who married Edith B. Gross of Owotonna, Minnesota. Fred Weatherly lived on the home place until his death on June 27, 1935.

      ✿   ✿   ✿

The writer has a reverence for the past of which all these pioneers were a part. His purpose has been to give honor to their memory and influence, and to preserve for posterity a record of their settlement and way of life in old Umpqua and Douglas counties, where their descendants are privileged to live . . . Now, the story is told and the typewriter is covered.

THE END

Sources and Acknowledgments

Though the major part of the book is based on personal knowledge of the material, interviews with the persons involved, or, in some cases, a tape recording—acknowledgment is also due the following sources:

Books: A. G. Walling's *History of Southwestern Oregon;* Charles H. Carey's *History of Oregon;* Hubert Howe Bancroft's *History of Oregon,* Volumes 1 and 2; Mary Wells' *Passing of District 66;* Anne Applegate Kruse's *Yoncalla, Home of the Eagles and Halo Trail;* Maude Cole's *Away Back When;* Welcome Martindale Combs and Sharan Ross's *God Made a Valley;* Philip H. Parrish's *Before the Covered Wagon;* Lewis A. McArthur's *Oregon Geographic Names;* Reginald Ray Stuart and Jean Dell Stuart's *Calvin B. West of the Umpqua,* and the Douglas County Historical Society's *Umpqua Trapper.*

Newspapers and Periodicals: *Roseburg Plaindealer, Roseburg Review, Drain Enterprise, Oregon Journal, Oregonian, Drain Echo, Oakland Advance,* Frank Leslie's *Illustrated News* (New York, April 24, 1858), *Reedsport Courier,* and the *Oregon Historical Quarterly.*

Documents, Letters, and Diaries: Private letters and diaries from the Oregon Historical Library; Donation Land Claims records; Umpqua County records; National Archives on post-offices and postmasters, and the Military Road; Memoirs of James T. Cooper, passenger aboard the *Kate Heath,* 1850; Journal of Captain A. Lyman, Master of the *Samuel Roberts,* "A Journey to the Umpqua, 1850"; Dr. John McLoughlin's private letters. John Work's Journal; David Douglas's Journal; private correspondence between members of pioneer families;

Memoirs of the late Floyd C. Frear, retired Roadmaster and Surveyor of Douglas County; also family Bibles, some dating back to 1801.

Valued assistance in the compilation of this work has been received from many individuals, yet particular thanks are due the library staff of the Oregon Historical Society, for their prolonged cooperation beyond the requirements of their positions. The generous professional advice of the publishers in the preparation of the manuscript is also greatly appreciated.

My daughter, Mrs. Myrtle Christensen, typed the finished manuscript and performed many other helpful chores. My son, W. John Minter, assisted substantially throughout the entire project. My wife, Louise, edited the raw material, ironed out the rough spots, and gave advice and encouragement when the going got rough . . . To all, I am lastingly grateful.

H. A. M.

Index

Abdill, George B., 77, 78, 99
Abernethy, George, Provisional
Governor of Oregon, 137
Agee, Roy, 220
Aguilar, Martin, 13
Aiken, John, operated toll ferry,
Winchester, 126
Albro, Mrs. Winifred, 261
Allen, Wesley, 132
Allensworth, Simeon H., D.L.C., 262
Alvord, Maj. Benjamin, 42
Anderson, Mrs. J. P., 259
Andrus, H., 201
Applegate, Charles, 33, 36
Applegate, Jesse, South Road Com-
pany, 39; Donation Land Claim,
52, 53; attitude toward McLough-
lin, 37; winters in old mission
1843-44, surveys in Salem and
Oregon City, 38; sends provisions
to stranded immigrants, 47
Applegate, Lindsay, 32
Archambeau, Francois, 224
Ashley, William H., 23
Aspinwall, William, P. M. S. S.
Co., 55
Augur, Capt. C. C., 20

Bates, William, 28
Bell, J. N. R., 96
Belle, Jesse, 201
Binder, Anthony, 116, 117
Black, Arthur, 24
Bohanan, 238
Booth, Sarah and Anna, 120
Bridger, Jim, 23
Bridges, 162-166; 1st bridge at Elk-
ton, 162; last wood bridge across
Elk Creek, 163, 164; Kellogg
bridge, 164; Esther Wells Smith
bridge, 164; steel bridges at Elk-
ton, 165, 166; Scottsburg bridge,
166-168
Boyd, G. D. R., editor *Umpqua
Weekly Gazette*, 90
Brown, Alonzo, founder of New
Oakland, 132
Brown, George M., 63
Brown, Henry G., 113
Brown, Loyal P., 85
Brown, O. C., 128

Buchanan, Lt.-Col. Robert, 19
Bully Washington, 64, 67
Bunch, James, biography, 274; helps
friend, 265; life on Mehl place,
275
Burch, Benjamin, 41
Burchard, Ephriam H., 76
Burnett, Peter, 33, 35
Burns, Barkeley J., 65
Butler, Rufus, biography, 60

Cabin Creek, 48
Campbell, James, 48
Campoiga, Francois, 27
Cannady, John, Rice Valley (1851),
132
Canby, General E. R. S.,
assassinated, 110
Cardwell, T. W., 194
Cartwright, Darius B., 120
Cartwright, Kitty, 120
Chadwick, William Fowler, 85
Champagne, Joseph, 227
Chapman, John I., 149
Chapman, Thomas, 109
Chapman, W. W., bought H. B. Co.
property, 108
Chicane, Horace, 228
Chism, Gardiner, 75
"Chinnagouche," 62
Churchill, Joseph, 228
Churchill, William A., 224
Churchill, Willoughby, 251
Clark, Captain George Rogers, 32
Clark, Mrs. L. F., 225
Clark, or Clarke, William B., 98, 239
Clarke, Jenny (Norman), 239
Clarke, Rush R., 239
Clayton clan, 225-232
Clayton, Ashford, biography, 225;
life in Coles Valley, 227; fun with
fleas, 228
Clayton, Jesse, biography, 229
Clemments, Charlie, 221
Clinkenbeard, James L., 248
Clough, Huron W., 152
Coast guard established, consolidated
with Light Service in 1939, 72
Cobbe or Kobbe, finds coins, 276;
locates old spring, 276
Coffin, Rufus, 75

285